JANE AUSTEN
IN THE CLASSROOM

PETER LANG
New York • Washington, D.C./Baltimore • Bern
Frankfurt am Main • Berlin • Brussels • Vienna • Oxford

Louise Flavin

JANE AUSTEN
IN THE CLASSROOM

Viewing the Novel/Reading the Film

PETER LANG
New York • Washington, D.C./Baltimore • Bern
Frankfurt am Main • Berlin • Brussels • Vienna • Oxford

Library of Congress Cataloging-in-Publication Data

Flavin, Louise.
Jane Austen in the classroom: viewing the novel/reading the film / Louise Flavin.
p. cm.
Includes bibliographical references (p.) and index.
1. Austen, Jane, 1775–1817—Film and video adaptations.
2. Austen, Jane, 1775–1817—Study and teaching. 3. England—In motion pictures.
4. Women in motion pictures. 5. Film adaptations. I. Title.
PR4038.F55F58   791.43'6—dc21   2003006832
ISBN 0-8204-6811-8

Bibliographic information published by **Die Deutsche Bibliothek**.
Die Deutsche Bibliothek lists this publication in the "Deutsche
Nationalbibliografie"; detailed bibliographic data is available
on the Internet at http://dnb.ddb.de/.

Cover design by Lisa Barfield

© 2004 Peter Lang Publishing, Inc., New York
275 Seventh Avenue, 28th Floor, New York, NY 10001
www.peterlangusa.com

All rights reserved.
Reprint or reproduction, even partially, in all forms such as microfilm,
xerography, microfiche, microcard, and offset strictly prohibited.

Table of Contents

Acknowledgments | ix

1 | Introduction | 1

2 | *Northanger Abbey* | 17

3 | *Sense and Sensibility* | 35

4 | *Pride and Prejudice* | 55

5 | *Mansfield Park* | 97

6 | *Emma* | 123

7 | *Persuasion* | 157

Works Cited | 181

Index | 187

Acknowledgments

I wish to thank the University of Cincinnati for providing me with a sabbatical leave which afforded me research and writing time to complete this work. I am also grateful to the university for a Faculty Development Grant that gave me the opportunity to visit sites important in the life of Jane Austen and to study the film adaptations of her works. I would like to thank the British Library for permission to reproduce a facsimile page of Jane Austen's manuscript of the "canceled chapters" from *Persuasion* on the cover (Egerton f.5/MS Facs 2051). My editor, Phyllis Korper, is deserving of gratitude for her support and assistance in preparing this book. I want to thank most especially Jim Flavin for his contributions: his insights, his judgment, and most of all, his patience made the writing of this book a pleasant experience.

Introduction

I love Jane Austen. How or when my "love affair" first began, I don't recall. But, in 1983, as I was exploring ideas for a dissertation, I decided to write on the novelist I knew and loved best. Why do I love Jane Austen? Her wit, the depth and complexity of her characters, the love story, her language and style, the values and ethic that pervade her work, the comedy, Elizabeth Bennet and Mr. Darcy. Perhaps no other novelist has created such appealing characters whose presence lingers in our minds long after the book is closed. Elizabeth and Darcy become real through the language and style of Jane Austen's creation. Devotees of Austen lament she wrote only six novels.

But reading Jane Austen isn't the only pleasure. I also love to teach the novels. This is more problematic, of course, because students, especially young and inexperienced readers, often do not share the same joy in reading a Jane Austen novel. I have taught Austen in a variety of courses, either as an individual novel in an undergraduate "introductory literature" class, or several novels in a Jane Austen as "Major British Writers" selection, or as an Honors Topic in a seminar on Jane Austen and the Film Adaptations. My success in teaching the novels has varied from great fun to dismal disaster, from "I've learned so much about couples and marriage" to "It's all stupid and who lives that way anyway?" The outcome I wish to share with readers of this text and their students is that they, too, will learn, if they haven't already, to love Jane Austen.

I believe I've found a workable approach to teaching Jane Austen. It begins with how to "view the novel," that is, how to take a complex work of fiction and isolate the central issues that are manageable and relevant to contemporary readers. Jane Austen, like her creation Elizabeth Bennet, was a "studier of character." Approaching Austen primarily from the point of view of character—the wise, ridiculous, vain, stupid, selfish, innocent, and lively cast—opens the closed mind to the possibilities of the study of human behavior.

While I never fail to find something new and intriguing in reading Austen and in teaching the novels in the classroom, the films have added a new dimension of my love affair with Austen. I would characterize the experience as varied, from obsessive fondness for some films to anger and disappointment with others. The value of the films in the classroom, though, is immeasurable. As a window into the cultural world of the late eighteenth century through the re-creation of the style of dress, conversation, and daily living, the films make teaching Austen in the contemporary world possible and inviting. "Reading the film" becomes a means of exploring the richness of texts in a new, comparative way.

In this book I document my approaches to teaching the novels and the film adaptations. The segment of each chapter called "Viewing the Novel" includes approaches I use when teaching Jane Austen's novels, focusing on the major issues, themes, and ideas that I have found appealing to students. This segment does not represent an exhaustive critical study but rather a guide in preparing to teach the novel. I also list analytical questions for discussion and writing that grow out of these major issues.

In the segment called "Reading the Film," I share approaches to analyzing the film adaptations that I've found successful in the classroom. My approach to film analysis is geared toward the film as "adaptation" or transference of the novel. Before viewing a film, I review with students the basic expectations of a transposition of text to film. I ask them to consider in their analysis of a film adaptation these four elements:

1. The limitations of film medium. Time constraints in film necessitate limiting scenes and characters from the novel.
2. The visual vs. literary mode. Films use visual and aural effects to express what is explicitly stated in writing.

3. Historical accuracy vs. contemporary taste. An eighteenth-century world cannot be reproduced exactly; contemporary tastes and values contribute to the appeal and popularity of film.
4. Issues of "fidelity." Films may represent the novel accurately in terms of plot and dialogue but may not always re-create the spirit of the novel or maintain the conceptual integrity.

I also provide students with specific questions to guide their viewing of each film. These questions form the basis for classroom discussion and for writing about the films.

The Popularity of Jane Austen

Many writers have explored the reasons for the popularity of the Austen film adaptations. A survey of the participants at the Jane Austen Society of North America Conferences will testify to the interest in costuming and re-creating aspects of Jane Austen's world. Beyond simply imagining the world of Elizabeth and Darcy or Emma and Knightley, contemporary readers desire the experience of walking through great homes that have the look and feel of Austen's era, viewing the landscape she looked on with a "picturesque" eye, dancing the country and line dances from the balls her characters attended, and feasting on the foods and wines spread on elegant dining room tables or well-manicured picnic lawns. While it is impossible to reenter Austen's world, the films invite readers into a pretty and often glamorized re-creation of that time and place. This "reactionary escapism" lets readers and viewers fantasize about a simpler world of wealth and leisure seemingly without obstacles and drudgery (Troost and Greenfield). The polite manners and decorum of the period are especially appealing in our contemporary world. In addition, the subject of romance, courtship, love, and marriage acted out in a wealthy and privileged environment attracts female audiences especially.

On a more complex level, the appeal of Austen's adaptations derives from the kinds of characters, lives, and situations Austen created in her fictional world. For Troost and Greenfield, such things as the nature of the characters Austen creates, "a perfect balance between recognizable types and idiosyncratic personalities" make them intriguing to modern viewers. Not only can we identify with individual characters, but we are also entertained by the bizarre and flawed personalities (3). Austen's comic fools, Mr. Collins, Mary Musgrove, Mrs. Elton, and others are thoroughly enjoyable for their uniqueness and variety. The more problematic issues of Austen's novels, of how pride begets prejudice, of how sense conflicts with sensibility, or of knowing the limits of one's rights and place in society, for instance, have always been subjected to critical analysis by readers of Austen's fiction. While many of the film adaptations tend to suppress thematic concerns in favor of the romance plot, enough is retained to satisfy the student of Austen's fiction who revels in its complexity.

Of all the great works of literature, we might ask why Jane Austen's novels are so often made into films and why the adaptations are so successful. George Bluestone, writing in 1957 (reprinted in 1971) on film adaptation, singles out Jane Austen's novels as particularly well suited for adaptation, especially *Pride and Prejudice*. The attributes of her style are especially conducive to adaptation: "a lack of particularity, an absence of metaphorical language, an omniscient point of view, a dependency on dialogue to reveal character, an insistence on absolute clarity" (118). In terms of subject matter Bluestone also notes the remarkable "modernity" of Austen's novels:

> Jane Austen's preoccupations are still very much with us. The world of *Pride and Prejudice* meets the requirements of Hollywood's stock conventions and, at the same time, allows a troubling grain of reality to enter by the side door. It depicts a love story which essentially follows the shopworn formula of boy meets girl; boy loses girl; boy gets girl. It presents rich people in elegant surroundings. It seems to allow for social mobility. . . . It offers an individual solution to general problems. . . . If wickedness is not punished, virtue at least is rewarded. Neither the upper-classes nor the middle-class worlds are all white or all black. . . . Above all the story has a happy ending. (Bluestone 144)

At the same time, Bluestone notes that Austen was aware of the economic and political problems of her time, including the realities of war. She was aware of the seriousness of the subject she so comically portrayed. Although Bluestone was writing in 1957 about the popularity of the 1940 film adaptation of *Pride and Prejudice*, the same can be said of the appeal of the Austen film adaptations today.

Approaches to Film Adaptation

Reading a novel is a very different experience from viewing a film. In an often-quoted statement, Joseph Conrad explains that his purpose in writing a novel is to make the reader "see": "My task which I am trying to achieve is, by the powers of the written word, to make you hear, to make you feel—it is, before all, to make to see" (qtd. in McFarlane 3). In other words, the author writes so that a reader can visualize the scene created by language. The filmmaker has the same goal. As D. W. Griffith says, "The task I am trying to achieve is above all to make you see" (qtd. in McFarlane 4). But just as films and novels have as their object making the unseen visible for a "viewing" public, a related purpose is to "make us read." To further our understanding and appreciation of the art of novels and films, we learn not only to visualize the scene, whether it be on the page or on the screen, but also to analyze the elements of film or literature that make visualization and the experience of the medium possible. We "read" into film values, ideas, attitudes, concepts, and arguments beyond what is visually displayed. In the same way we "see" in a novel the places, faces, figures, etc., that are linguistically presented. We read the film and view the novel.

In adapting a novel to film, by necessity much is lost. The film can never give us all the richness and complexity of the novel, all that a writer hopes to stimulate in the mind's eye, but it can give us more than character and event. And while we are trained to "read" literature for its subtle signs and literary elements that cue us into meaning and appreciation, we are often not so skilled at reading the subtext of the visual images on screen. Reading a film teaches us to understand the implications of choices made by the film adapter in compressing a many-houred reading experience into a two-hour viewing of a film. The purpose of this text is to provide some approaches to teaching the film adaptations of Jane Austen's novels through analysis of both "viewing" text and "reading" film.

When each new Austen film is released, I meet it with both enthusiasm and trepidation. My first response is to measure the adaptation against the Austen text. The question of fidelity, what has been left out, what added, what changed, is central to my viewing. Are the characters represented as I imagined them? Is the cultural milieu Austen's or a Hollywood version? Is the spirit of Austen, the ironic satiric stance and the moral judgment, true in the film? I have to confess my first response is usually one of disappointment, because, of course, the film can never replicate the complexity, style, and imagination that is Austen's, or for that matter, that of any writer from a culture and time so far removed from our own. The demands of appealing to a large and diverse contemporary audience and turning a profit at the box office mean that the film must be altered, condensed, and modernized.

The second response I have, and usually one that comes with repeated viewings, is how the film stands as an art form in its own right. I attempt to evaluate the degree of success of the adaptation, not judged in terms of authenticity and fidelity to the novel, but in terms of the performances, script writing, and vision of the director. Imelda Whelehan writes that for many film viewers, we have "an almost unconscious prioritizing of the fictional origin over the resulting film" (3). Our inability to appreciate the films as art originates in our tendency to see films as "inferior or shadowy copies of the originals" (Whelehan 3). Whelehan reminds us that the critical interpretations of the novels tend to add to the burden of film viewing and appreciation. As viewers of film adaptations who watch both for appreciation and with a critical eye, we must remove as an obstacle to judgment the sole criterion of fidelity.

To lessen the importance of primacy to fidelity in film criticism, many critics suggest using a range of possibilities for adaptation. Geoffrey Wagner's terms for assessing the degree of fidelity to the original are "transposition" or transference of novel to screen with minimal interference; "commentary," where the original is taken but modified; and "analogy," where changes in content make the original unidentifiable (Whelehan 8, McFarlane 10–11). These approaches invite readers and viewers to free themselves from issues of fidelity and instead approach the viewing of the films as a means to analyze and evaluate both literary text and film adaptation. George Bluestone, writing about the 1940 film adaptation of *Pride and Prejudice*, tells us that "the screen writers and director, by taking liberties with Jane Austen's text, by imagining what she has not told them, have managed to render her meanings, almost as if destroying the book were a precondition for its faithful resurrection" (140). Joseph Epstein agrees, arguing that it's not the fidelity to the text that makes a successful adaptation: "It's magic, baby, pure magic" (qtd. in Solender 105).

Another way to think about the film adaptations is as representations of our own contemporary cultural values. We know that novels were the register of culture in Jane Austen's time—historical and cultural artifacts that speak of "contemporary" mores and manners in late eighteenth-century England. Just so, films are one register of contemporary twentieth- and twenty-first century culture. While novels of one era can be made into successful films in another era, we must expect that for the film to be appealing, it should reflect to some extent the present cultural tastes and values. While documenting one culture, it must appeal to another. The study of film adaptation, then, becomes a critique of both the culture of the novel's era and of the contemporary culture that produced it.

Another rewarding approach to film analysis is to look at film as "a convergence among the arts," as Brian McFarlane suggests. *Intertextuality*, or how a novel is approached through adaptation, is an avenue of exploration that yields rich results (McFarlane 10). My approach in this text is to invite readers of Austen's novels and teachers of her works to approach the films as companions to the novels, equally worthy of study and interpretation. Comparative analysis reveals not only how each complements the other but also how criticism of one reveals truths about the other. McFarlane suggests that studies of film adaptations are most worthwhile when approached from two avenues: examining what is actually possible to transfer from the novel and noting what factors other than the novel influence the film (22). The chapters that follow examine the choices made by the filmmakers to adapt the novels and raise issues of historical and cultural contexts, of values and ideologies, of genre restraints and differences, and of artistic and creative imagination.

Using Film in the Classroom

While Austen's fiction lends itself well to film adaptation, re-creating Austen's world, either real or imagined, necessitates some obvious changes. Many of these changes make for popular films but at the same time undermine the values and cultural mores of Jane Austen's world and sacrifice the literary merits of the novels. An effective use of the films in the literature classroom is to focus on these changes. Not only does this analysis sharpen students' ability to "read the film," it also helps them to "view the novels" critically. As students visualize characters and settings and hear dialogue spoken, their readings of the novels become more critically astute. As additions and deletions, as well as more subtle changes, are noted, students can analyze why the changes were made and evaluate the effectiveness of the alterations on the film. The point of such comparison is not merely judging fidelity to the original or fidelity as the measure of success. Instead, studying the works "intertextually" is a means to understanding both the novel and the film. The essays in Troost and Greenfield's *Jane Austen in Hollywood* examine the most recent (1990s) film adaptations. The focus of the essays is on features of the film adaptations that reveal contemporary trends in alterations. This list (paraphrased from "Watching Ourselves Watching" 6–8) highlights the most common alterations in these recent films:

- The films are, by necessity, shortened versions of the novels, which heightens their appeal although at the expense of much of the complexity of the novels.
- The films are imagistically appealing rather than linguistically interesting. The films display beautiful clothing, homes, and attractive and sexy lead actors,

which "promote the equation of human physical beauty with worth" (Troost and Greenfield 6). This countermands Austen's theme of the difficulty of judging appearance and reality, manners vs. morals. Also, scenery intrudes into the films, endorsing rather than satirizing the Picturesque.

- The "delicate" Austen satire is lost or even subverted by the films. In varying degrees the popular films tend to promote the very values Austen was attacking.
- Passions in the stories suffer. The reticent, reserved manner of the male figures of the novels is made more emotional and romantic. Prudence and restraint give way to open and intense displays of feeling, especially with the male characters and around children.
- Austen's undercurrent of feminism is not made more obvious or prominent, despite our more liberal contemporary views on the rights and roles of women. (Troost and Greenfield 6–8)

In spite of these alterations, the films provide a window into the text, especially for reluctant readers in the literature classroom. The simplification of the novels on every score from language to conflict to romance to satire makes the text more accessible. The films serve as an introduction to the reading, stimulating interest in the characters and their fates. They help students to visualize costume, settings, and manners that are strange and unusual but also appealing, thus engaging interest. Most important, the adaptations make the "archaic" language and dialogue not only understandable but also more believable and lively. Although I do not offer the films as a substitute for reading the novel, they may invite the curious but reluctant student to find out more about this writer and her world.

Viewing the Novel/Reading the Film —Questions for Analysis and Discussion

I provide students with a series of questions to guide their viewing of the film. As students view the films, I ask them to record their responses and questions. After discussing the student responses and exploring the issues they raise from the films, we analyze the film with questions related to *Casting and Characterization, Changes from Novel to Film, Conceptual Integrity,* and *Cinematic Technique*. These topics also provide a basis for writing about the film adaptations. The questions below are ones that are general to Austen film adaptations and can be modified to suit particular novels and films. More specific questions are included in the chapters that follow.

1. Research the contemporary film reviews from popular magazines and newspapers for an individual film. Analyze the trends, such as the appeal of Jane Austen and the popularity of the film, the major themes or ideas that reviewers focus on, and the kind of adaptation. Present a summary of the reviews and write a response to the analysis. Do you agree or disagree with the reviewers?

2. Compare a scene from the novel with the screenplay to analyze what changes were made. A good example would be to choose a scene from the novel rendered as interior monologue or free indirect thought or other indirect rendering. Then compare how it is "dramatized" on the screen. Is dialogue invented? Is voice-over used to convey thought? How are abstractions and narrator comments rendered?

3. Choose a character, scene, plot event, or dialogue that represents a significant change from the novel. Analyze how this change affects the film. What does it contribute? What purpose does it have in the film? How does this change affect your reading of Austen's novel?

4. The six Austen works are essentially novels of courtship and romance. Analyze how a particular novel would appeal to late eighteenth-century taste and values. The films are popular and very successful with early twenty-first-century viewers. What changes in the theme of romance and courtship are made to accommodate the taste and values of contemporary audiences? What is the overall effect of such changes?

5. Because of restraints on time, the visual medium of film must eliminate much that is spoken or thought in the novel. While a novel allows for greater expansion of dialogue and interior consciousness, the film has the advantage of visual imagery and film iconography. Examine the visual language of the film and what it conveys. What feelings, thoughts, ideas, values, etc., are conveyed through visual elements? How are these scenes treated in the novel—through description and narration? Dialogue? Interior monologue? Omniscience?

6. Consider the determinants of class in Austen's novels and the late eighteenth century: wealth, property, rank, and ancestry. How are these conveyed through the contemporary medium of film? How does a contemporary audience distinguish the highest classes from the lower? Consider also what contemporary film audiences use as determiners of class—such as stock portfolios, grand houses, neighborhoods, clothes, cars, education, professions, vacations, "conspicuous consumption." What markers of class are changed from novel to film?

7. Examine the appeal of the Austen films in the early twenty-first century. Some have suggested their popularity reflects nostalgia for a simpler, more elegant, well-mannered time. Do Austen's novels glamorize her era? What is most

appealing about late eighteenth-century life for the gentry? Does Austen disclose the negative side of life for this class? Does she represent what life was like for the lower and working classes or for the poor? How realistic do you find her portrayal of all classes? Consider how the film portrays Austen's era. Does the filmmaker glamorize life from Austen's time? What makes the era "appear" attractive on film? Does the filmmaker make "visible" the classes not conspicuous in an Austen novel? What is the effect on the film of these additions?

8: Analyze the feminist implications of Austen's novel and the film adaptation. How did Austen depict the opportunities, limitations, identity, intelligence, and values of her female heroines? How does the film adaptation reinforce, enhance, or subvert Austen's feminine characters? Consider especially how contemporary audiences would perceive Austen's concept of an independent, intelligent, strong-minded heroine. Note the activities that Austen's heroines engage in, activities that suggest the accomplished woman of the time. How are the Austen heroines depicted in the contemporary films to suggest strength and intelligence? Note the physicality, athleticism, willingness to speak out, and daily activities of the film heroines.

9. How are Austen's male protagonists rendered in the novels to suggest their class, character, and "gentleman-like" qualities? How are their emotions and passions presented? If the eighteenth-century value of "restraint" means that a gentleman does not openly display feelings, how does Austen make us aware that the male protagonists are men of strong feeling and passions? How do the cinematic heroes satisfy contemporary interest in men who more openly express their feelings and passions?

10. How is literature used in the film? Examine how novels, plays, and poetry are incorporated into the film. What seems to be the purpose of the incorporation? How does it enhance character or action? Are these same literary elements in the novel? Why or why not?

11. Austen's novels are told from an omniscient point of view with limits on the degree of interior consciousness. For example, we know the heroine's thoughts in much detail throughout the novel but seldom have knowledge of what the hero or secondary characters are thinking except as expressed through their spoken words. How does the filmmaker handle this limited point of view? How does the film use the camera eye as a kind of limited omniscience? How does the filmmaker reveal interior consciousness? How is the omniscient narrator's commentary treated through visual or other means in the film?

12. How do the films use music? Consider how the score or soundtrack for the film complements the action on screen. Consider also how music—singing, piano

playing, and dancing—is used symbolically to reveal character or to further the plot. How faithful to the novels are the film adaptations in terms of their use of music?

13. Read the setting of the film. If scenes are set indoors, examine the details of furnishings, lighting, space, etc., to determine the filmmaker's intent. Compare the setting with specific details from the novel. Has the filmmaker included invented scenes out of doors or moved indoor scenes outside? What is the effect of these changes?

Anticipating Problems with Literature

Finally, in preparing a course devoted to novels and films, an instructor should anticipate the difficulties students are likely to experience in reading great literature, particularly Jane Austen's novels. Typical problems encountered by students reading Jane Austen's novels include the complexity of syntax; diction that is obsolete or uncommon; the leisurely pace and long descriptions or slow exposition; the sheer length of the text; allusions to classical literature, the Bible, or other works; historical references; and manners that seem foreign in our more casual and relaxed era. Once again, the films are helpful to transition students to the novels, because the language is modernized, long descriptive passages are replaced with visual images, and manners are contemporized. I also make use of the vocabulary list below to introduce students to the language of Austen's novels. I select a sample of words that have changed meaning from Austen's time and focus on how precise Austen was in choosing the correct word. This helps students become more conscious of language as they read. The selections below are useful to show how language changes over time.

Some Words from Jane Austen

affection A strong word for deep emotion built on a relationship of two amiable persons, an emotion of slower growth and more lasting than love. (Jane Austen to her niece Fanny Knight: "Anything is to be preferred or endured rather than marrying without Affection!" (18 November 1814)

amiable "The really amiable man . . . is the man who is strong in his actions because fine in his emotion, who habitually exerts himself to do his duty, because he has a delicacy for the feelings of others" (Tave 126).

candour	"now: frankness, bluntness. In JA nearly always, warm sympathy, freedom from malice" (Gillie 159).
elegance	"now: refined and tasteful, usually in outward appearance. In JA: rather more what we mean by 'distinguished,' and used about the mind or character as well as the appearance" (Gillie 159).
entail	"To convert an estate into a 'fee tail'; to settle land or an estate on a number of persons in succession so that it cannot be bequeathed at pleasure by any one possessor" (OED).
improve	"in JA often used in a semi-technical context to mean 'enhance the appearance (of an estate or garden) by the art of landscaping'" (Gillie 160).
"the living"	"A benefice" or spiritual livelihood, maintenance, or support; means of living (OED).
mean	inferior, poor, in ability or learning.
mortification	the hurting of pride and self-importance.
nice	"now: usually, 'pleasant,' 'agreeable.' In JA: usually 'exact' or 'precise'" (Gillie 160).
preferment	"An appointment or post which gives social or pecuniary advancement; chiefly, an ecclesiastical appointment" (OED).
quiz	"now: seldom used. In JA: as a noun, 'an amusing oddity,' 'absurdity.' As a verb, 'to tease,' 'to make fun of'" (Gillie 161).
repulsive	"now: very disgusting. In JA: generally, 'unforthcoming,' 'cold in manner'" (Gillie 161).
sensible	"now: reasonable, rational. In JA: often, 'conscious,' 'aware'" (Gillie 161).
stout	"now: inclined to fatness. In JA: in good health; firm in opinion" (Gillie 161).
tease	"now: to make fun of, usually playfully. In JA: to vex, annoy" (Gillie 161).
tolerable	"now: endurable. In JA: acceptable, as good as to be expected" (Gillie 161).
understanding	"in JA used much as we use 'mind' (qv); the rational faculty, intelligence" (Gillie 161).

The Jane Austen Adaptations

As of this writing, I have reviewed fourteen Jane Austen adaptations available on video that might be used in the classroom, including feature-length films and television mini-series. (Some other televised versions of the novels are also available on video.) Linda Troost and Sayre Greenfield's *Jane Austen in Hollywood* summarizes the making and release of the films. Between 1970 and 1986, British filmmakers produced seven feature-length films or television mini-series, and between 1995 and 1996 three films were made in Hollywood and three others with Hollywood influences (Troost and Greenfield 1). A feature film of *Mansfield Park* was produced in 1999. Although close analysis of the film adaptations might lead to disagreement as to the degree of faithfulness to the original novel, nearly all of these films fall into one of Wagner's categories of *transposition* (transference "with a minimum of apparent interference") or *commentary* ("where an original is taken and either purposely or inadvertently altered in some respect... when there has been a different intention on the part of the film-maker, rather than infidelity or outright violation") (qtd. in McFarlane 10–11). The obvious exception is *Clueless*, which is loosely based on Austen's *Emma* but has such dramatic alterations in characters and setting as to be almost unrecognizable as a version of the Austen novel and could therefore be considered an "analogy." Likewise, Whit Stillman's *Metropolitan* is often discussed as a contemporary analogy of *Mansfield Park* or even as a "compilation" of Austen's novels in general. As McFarlane iterates, the purpose of these categories is not to ascribe value to one as superior to another but rather to determine the intent of the filmmaker in terms of fidelity and then assess the film as to degree of success in achieving its intended purpose (22). What follows is the Troost/Greenfield compilation of "Austen Adaptations Available on Video" (*Jane Austen in Hollywood* 205–7). Asterisks mark the videos that I reference in this text—the ones I use in the classroom.

Emma

***1972 (BBC). Writer Denis Constanduros. Director John Glenister. Producer Martin Lisemore. With Doran Godwin (Emma Woodhouse), John Carson (Mr. Knightley), Donald Eccles (Mr. Woodhouse), Robert East (Frank Churchill). Mini-series.

***1996 (Miramax). Writer and director Douglas McGrath. Producer Patrick Cassavetti. With Gwyneth Paltrow (Emma Woodhouse), Jeremy Northam (Mr. Knightley), Toni Collette (Harriet Smith), Ewan McGregor (Frank Churchill). Feature film.

***1996 (Meridian [ITV] and A&E). Writer Andrew Davies. Director Diarmuid Lawrence. Producer Sue Birtwistle. With Kate Beckinsale

(Emma Woodhouse), Mark Strong (Mr. Knightley), Samantha Morton (Harriet Smith), Raymond Coulthard (Frank Churchill). Telefilm.

***[*Clueless.*] 1995 (Paramount). Writer and director Amy Heckerling. Producers Scott Rudin and Robert Lawrence. With Alicia Silverstone (Cher), Paul Rudd (Josh), Stacey Dash (Dionne), Brittany Murphy (Tai). Feature film.

Mansfield Park

1983 (BBC). Writer Ken Taylor. Director David Giles. Producer Betty Willingale. With Sylvestra Le Touzel (Fanny Price), Nicholas Farrell (Edmund Bertram), Anna Massey (Aunt Norris), Robert Burbage (Henry Crawford). Mini-series.

***1999 (Miramax and BBC Films). Writer and director Patricia Rozema. Producer Sarah Curtis. With Frances O'Connor (Fanny Price), Jonny Lee Miller (Edmund Bertram), Harold Pinter (Sir Thomas), Alessandro Nivola (Henry Crawford), Embeth Davidtz (Mary Crawford). Feature film.

Northanger Abbey

***1987 (BBC and A&E). Writer Maggie Wadey. Director Giles Foster. Producer Louis Marks. With Katharine Schlesinger (Catherine Morland), Peter Firth (Henry Tilney), Robert Hardy (General Tilney), Googie Withers (Mrs. Allen). Telefilm.

Persuasion

1971 (Granada [ITV]). Writer Julian Mitchell. Director and producer Howard Baker. With Ann Firbank (Anne Elliot), Bryan Marshall (Captain Wentworth), Basil Dignam (Sir Walter Elliot), Morag Hood (Mary Musgrove). Mini-series.

***1995 (BBC and WGBH). Writer Nick Dear. Director Roger Michell. Producers Rebecca Eaton, George Faber, Fiona Finlay. With Amanda Root (Anne Elliot), Ciaran Hinds (Captain Wentworth), Corin Redgrave (Sir Walter Elliot), Sophie Thompson (Mary Musgrove). Telefilm; released as a feature film from Sony Picture Classics.

Pride and Prejudice

***1940 (MGM). Writers Aldous Huxley and Jane Murfin. Director Robert Z. Leonard. Producer Hunt Stromberg. With Greer Garson (Elizabeth Bennet), Laurence Olivier (Mr. Darcy), Maureen O'Sullivan (Jane Bennet), Edmund Gwenn (Mr. Bennet), Edna May Oliver (Lady Catherine de Bourgh). Feature film.

***1979 (BBC). Writer Fay Weldon. Director Cyril Coke. Producer Jonathan Powell. With Elizabeth Garvie (Elizabeth Bennet), David Rintoul (Mr. Darcy), Sabina Franklyn (Jane Bennet), Moray Watson (Mr. Bennet), Judy Parfitt (Lady Catherine de Bourgh). Mini-series.

***1995 (BBC and A&E). Writer Andrew Davies. Director Simon Langton. Producer Sue Birtwistle. With Jennifer Ehle (Elizabeth Bennet), Colin Firth (Mr. Darcy), Susannah Harker (Jane Bennet), Benjamin Whitrow (Mr. Bennet), Barbara Leigh-Hunt (Lady Catherine de Bourgh). Mini-series.

Sense and Sensibility

1985 (BBC). Writer Alexander Baron. Director Rodney Bennett. Producer Barry Letts. With Irene Richard (Elinor Dashwood), Bosco Hogan (Edward Ferrars), Tracy Childs (Marianne Dashwood), Donald Douglas (Sir John Middleton), Peter Woodward (John Willoughby). Mini-series.

***1995 (Mirage/Columbia). Writer Emma Thompson. Director Ang Lee. Producer Lindsay Doran. With Emma Thompson (Elinor Dashwood), Hugh Grant (Edward Ferrars), Kate Winslet (Marianne Dashwood), Alan Rickman (Colonel Brandon), Greg Wise (John Willoughby). Feature film.

Northanger Abbey

Northanger Abbey was written in 1798 and 1799 and originally entitled *Susan*. It was sold to Crosby and Co. booksellers and intended for publication in 1803. In 1816 the manuscript and copyright were returned to Austen for the original purchase price. Later, it was revised and retitled *Catherine*, but after Austen's death in 1817, it was retitled once again by her brother Henry and published as *Northanger Abbey* along with the two-volume *Persuasion* in 1818 (Chapman, "Introductory Note to *Northanger Abbey* and *Persuasion*" xi-xiii).

Northanger Abbey was the earliest written of the published Austen novels although it was published posthumously with Austen's last composed novel *Persuasion*. I like to include it as the first novel in a Jane Austen course for many reasons. The heroine, Catherine Morland, is the youngest, the least educated, least worldly of Austen's heroines. The novel has elements of parody, mocking sentimental and Gothic fiction of the period. Subtly, Austen moves the novel from parody to romance as the young Catherine wins the love and attention of Henry Tilney, a clergyman from a wealthy family. Most interesting about *Northanger Abbey* is the presence of the narrator who comments on the composition of her novel, appraising her heroine's qualities as a heroine, mocking her adventures, and commenting on the process of novel writing and the value of novels to the education of her readers. This "meta-text" allows us to understand Austen's relationship to her fiction, for in *Northanger Abbey* her persona as the ironic narrator is foregrounded. Beginning a course with this novel assists students in understanding the satiric viewpoint of the later novels, where the narrator's presence is not so obvious. In the novels of Austen's mature Chawton period, the ironic narrator retreats into the background through increased incidences of free indirect discourse, making the satire much more subtle and effective.

Viewing the Novel
—Approaches to Teaching *Northanger Abbey*

I include here a general discussion of the main issues, themes, and ideas in *Northanger Abbey*. My "Approaches to Teaching *Northanger Abbey*" complement the analytical questions that follow this discussion.

Parody, Gothicism, and Sentimental Fiction. The cult of the Gothic novel originated in the late eighteenth century with Horace Walpole's *Castle of Otranto* (1764). The primary characteristic of Gothic fiction, according to the *Encyclopedia of Romanticism*, is its "concern for the workings of the mind manifest through the supernatural, which can be presented as real within the context of the fiction or as contrived by one or more characters." The genre features natural phenomena, an ominous or threatening atmosphere, and remote settings that incite fear and danger. The emphasis on the antique, ruins, and decay is in sharp contrast to the heroine, who is often a youthful ingénue threatened physically, especially sexually, by a clearly defined villain (McGuire 240). The novels are designed to create suspense and excite fear in readers through a conflict between innocence and evil. The settings are remote and isolated, such as castles or monasteries with hidden passages, ruinous staircases, and trapdoors. Fear is intensified by storms and darkness and the surprise appearance of supernatural beings and ghosts. Henry Tilney's tongue-in-cheek account of Northanger Abbey recited to Catherine on their approach sums up the formula. He begins by taunting Catherine, "are you prepared to encounter all the horrors that a building . . . may produce?" (*NA* 157). He goes on to describe "a hall dimly lighted," an "ancient housekeeper," "gloomy passages," "peals of thunder," "a secret subterraneous communication," and other trappings of the Gothic to whet Catherine's appetite for horrors (*NA* 158–9). Ann Radcliffe's *The Mysteries of Udolpho* (1794) epitomizes the form at its finest. The relationship of the young heroine Emily and the villainous Montoni is parodied by Austen in *Northanger*

Abbey, as Catherine Morland comes to think General Tilney a villain on the scale of a Montoni (*NA* 187). While visiting Northanger Abbey, Catherine is guided back to reason by her mentor/lover Henry Tilney, as she learns to distinguish the real from the fictional. Austen also parodies the sentimental fiction popular in the late eighteenth century. Catherine Morland meets in Bath a young woman, Isabella Thorpe, whose speech and manners suggest the sentimental novel in its excesses and falseness. While *Northanger Abbey* mocks the Gothic novel, it is not actually parodic in style and is decidedly unsentimental.

The Ingénue and Her Education. *Northanger Abbey* is primarily a novel of education. Catherine Morland is a youthful seventeen, the youngest of Austen's heroines. She is a typical ingenue, credulous and unschooled, on the verge of womanhood, about to leave home and enter the social world. As somewhat of a tomboy and an avid reader of Gothic and sentimental novels, Catherine is quite unprepared for the complex social world represented by the city of Bath. Here she experiences the beginning of her womanhood with an awakening sexuality. She has no female role models to instruct her in how to be a woman—much less in how to be a "heroine." Her own mother is too busy raising ten children to attend to her education. Her chaperone, Mrs. Allen, provides little guidance, although the narrator bestows ironic praise on her in the role of guardian: "she was admirably fitted to introduce a young lady into public, being as fond of going every where and seeing every thing herself as any young lady could be" (*NA* 20). However, this is her sole qualification to be a guide, for her judgment extends only to the effect an action might have on her newest gown. Catherine's new young friend Isabella Thorpe is very world-wise, but proves to be a conniving, deceptive, insincere fortune hunter, who plays at female submission and passivity to attract male admiration. Thus, Catherine Morland's education will entail learning the conventions of social intercourse while attempting to distinguish truth from fiction, both in literature and in life.

Henry Tilney is Catherine's mentor and eventual suitor. Although his knowledge and education far exceed Catherine's, he never resorts to lecturing or scolding, nor does he gloat or become pedantic. Catherine is charmed by his wit, "an archness and pleasantry in his manner which interested, though it was hardly understood by her" (*NA* 25). Henry Tilney is Austen's wittiest hero, and he teases, questions, exaggerates, and uses irony to charm Catherine into loving him. Most important, Henry teaches Catherine to think for herself, to judge and evaluate, to look for evidence, to be wary of authority, to compare, and to test knowledge against practice. He mocks the cliches of conversation and behavior at Bath, opening Catherine's eyes to various levels of language, meaning, and intent. His dissertation on the word *nice*, and his analogy of dancing with marriage are delightfully witty and entertaining even if Catherine misses the fun. Her wonderfully ironic comment, "I cannot speak well enough to be unintelligible" (*NA* 133), sums up the charm and artlessness that beguile Henry. The novel teaches us that students learn only when they are *willing* to learn; Catherine is very willing to please Henry and, in the process, learns to think independently and grows in self-confidence. While Catherine exclaims on her own education—"I have just learnt to love a hyacinth"—Henry continues, "the sentiment once raised, . . . you may in time come to love a rose" (*NA* 174). Catherine has learned to appreciate a simple flower, the hyacinth, an indication of her educability, while Henry foresees her enlightenment into the complexities of the rose, the symbol of love and sexuality. We witness Catherine's maturity when she makes a decision on marriage to Henry Tilney without parental knowledge or authority.

Self-conscious Narration. Northanger Abbey is a self-conscious novel in which the narrator, in the persona of the author, comments on her creation as she tells her story. The opening chapter introduces readers to not only the heroine but also the concept of "heroine" as created by a writer. Catherine is described as "born to be an heroine" (*NA* 13); "she was in training for a heroine" (*NA* 15); "something must and will happen to throw a hero in her way" (*NA* 17). Austen is intentionally obscuring the line between fiction and reality to call attention to the novel as a literary form and to separate her novels from the Gothic thrillers and sentimental writings of the period. Austen speaks directly to readers through the narrator to defend novels against reviewers and even self-deprecating novelists whose "performances . . . have only genius, wit, and taste to recommend them" (*NA* 37). Her famous defense of the novel appears in this same passage: "It is . . . only some work in which the greatest powers of the mind are displayed, in which the most thorough knowledge of human nature, the happiest delineation of its varieties, the liveliest effusions of wit and humour are conveyed to the world in the best chosen language" (*NA* 38). Within the text, Henry Tilney's comments on novels are consistent with Austen's narratorial voice, furthering the distinction between kinds of literature and emphasizing their value in understanding human nature. On the other end of the scale, John Thorpe disparages novels by proclaiming, "I never read novels" (*NA* 48); he then contradicts himself by naming some he has read, discrediting one he hasn't read, and in ignorance, confusing the author of one book with another. If we had any doubts before, we are assured of the ignorance of the loutish John Thorpe through his denigration of novels. Through her characterization of the unheroine-like Catherine, who finds a "hero" in the pleasant young clergyman Henry Tilney, Austen debunks the notion of Gothic horrors in "the country and the age" (*NA* 197) in which they live and makes a claim for novels that are realistic and true. Gradually, narratorial intrusions disappear, and the novel's heroine progresses to a mature and feeling young woman of sense and judgment.

Viewing the Novel
—Questions for Analysis and Discussion

The questions below address the larger issues of each volume and are designed to promote analytical thinking as the basis for discussion. These questions ask students to "see" into the text and complement the central issues of "reading the film" that follow.

Volume I

1. Examine the tone and voice of the narrator in the opening chapter. How is satire used to introduce the "heroine" of the novel?

2. Describe fully how you envision Catherine. In how many ways is she not "a heroine"? Do you find her a likeable character? Why or why not?

3. The first volume of the novel is set in Bath, although Jane Austen provides few descriptive details of the setting. What scenes in the novel provide images of Bath? Describe how you envision Bath from reading the first volume.

4. Catherine makes errors in judging people outside of her family and friends while in Bath. Examine her relationship with Isabella and John Thorpe, and analyze the nature of her mistakes in judgment. What character flaws in Isabella and John are visible to the reader?

5. Mr. and Mrs. Allen are entrusted with the care of Catherine in Bath. What are the positive and negative qualities of their guardianship? Compare their care and guidance of Catherine with that of Mrs. Thorpe for her children.

6. Henry Tilney's mentoring of Catherine could be viewed as a lesson in language and critical thinking. Examine how he teaches her to think in analogies; avoid

cliches, slang, and oversimplification; use language with precision; be more discerning; and recognize false and artificial language.

7. How does Catherine respond to Henry's mentoring? What is the broader consequence of these lessons?

8. What does Catherine Morland already know about morals and manners before setting off for Bath? What dialogue or scenes exemplify her maturity and moral character?

9. Why is Henry Tilney attracted to Catherine? What scenes suggest a chemistry or attraction on his part?

10. What examples of narratorial intrusions are evident in the first volume? What seems to be Austen's intent in her comments about novels and novel writing?

Volume II

1. The second volume of the novel is set in Northanger Abbey. The abbey is not as Catherine had imagined it to be. What descriptive details does Jane Austen provide of the abbey? How do these details contrast with Catherine's notions of what an abbey should be?

2. What happens at Northanger Abbey to change Henry's fondness for Catherine into love?

3. Catherine imagines terrible things about General Tilney. What is the source of her mistrust of him? Consider not only the influence of Gothic novels on her imagination but also the connection to the general's actual behavior and reports about him. Has the general made some of the same errors in judgment about Catherine?

4. When Catherine mistakenly assumes General Tilney was not "afflicted" by the death of his wife, Henry asks her, "What have you been judging from?" (*NA* 197). What *has* Catherine been judging from? Examine the sources of her misjudgments throughout the novel.

5. Does Catherine Morland have a positive female role model in the novel? Consider the parental "authority" figures—her mother, Mrs. Allen, and Mrs. Thorpe. What could she learn from them?

6. Consider also the influence of Catherine's peers—Isabella Thorpe and Eleanor Tilney. How well do they serve to tutor her in the appropriate manners and behavior of a young woman?

7. How does the visit to Woodston reveal Catherine's growth in maturity and judgment? Are there other examples when her maturity and sense are evident?

8. Evaluate Catherine's maturity at the end of the novel. Would you believe her sufficiently mature to marry? How is she a suitable wife for Henry?

9. What are the lessons this novel teaches readers about decision-making and judgment? How does this subject relate to the theme of young love and romance?

10. What is humorous or funny about this novel? Analyze the kinds of humor and "fun" that Austen has in this work. Does the humor mask a serious intent?

Reading the Film
—Approaches to Teaching the Film

Using Film in the Classroom

Currently (2004), only one film adaptation of *Northanger Abbey* exists although a film with script by Andrew Davies is in production. The critics of the 1987 Maggie Wadey film have not been enthusiastic in their reviews. Elsa Solender refers to it as a "rather curious *NA* . . . that re-Gothicized the plot that Austen 'deconstructed' in her satire." Solender refers to the film as "Austen *a la Bronte*" (107). Essentially, this goes to the core of the problem with the film: it creates a Gothic world at Northanger Abbey that Austen essentially debunks in her novel. Instead of the formulaic trappings of a medieval abbey, Austen's heroine discovers an "improved," modern, and very livable home. In the film the setting is an actual castle that confirms Catherine's vision of Northanger Abbey rather than debunking it. The film is a useful tool for pointing out this discrepancy between Austen's subversion of Gothic fiction and the adaptation's revival of Gothic elements. The film also tends to romanticize the relationship between Catherine and Henry. The value in reviewing the film is to compare it with Austen's more realistic love story, which has Catherine being mentored as well as wooed by Henry. However, there is much to like in the adaptation, which is credited as "From the Novel of Jane Austen." The Bath segment especially is a good representation of characters, events, and dialogue from the novel. The scenes at the Roman baths are helpful to understanding the social and cultural setting of the novel.

Jane Austen incorporated Ann Radcliffe's *The Mysteries of Udolpho* into her satirization of Gothic novels in *Northanger Abbey*. The Maggie Wadey script incorporates scenes and illustrations from the Radcliffe novel into the dreams and fantasies of young Catherine. An effective activity for students is to read

Radcliffe's *Udolpho* and examine how Jane Austen used her characters, scenes, and Gothic elements in *Northanger Abbey*. Then the Wadey film can be analyzed to discover how the illustrations, scenes, and characters are used in the adaptation.

My focus here is on four general issues of film analysis that may serve as the basis for analysis and discussion of the film adaptation: *Casting and Characterization, Changes from Novel to Film, Conceptual Integrity,* and *Cinematic Technique*. These approaches may also prompt ideas for writing about the novel and its film counterpart. My discussion is limited to the 1987 BBC/A&E production of *Northanger Abbey*, written by Maggie Wadey.

Casting and Characterization

Catherine Morland is a seventeen-year-old adolescent embarking on her first solo trip into the adult social scene at Bath. Austen does not overtly mention the adolescent sexual awakening that is likely a component of her "education" in Bath. The film makes this the dominant element in her adventures at Bath and Northanger Abbey. The opening scene of the film has Catherine reading in orgasmic pleasure, *The Mysteries of Udolpho*, while sensually eating a ripe plum; in the novel, she is introduced to the book in Bath. Her fantasies, daydreams, and nightmares, played out in the film, have as much an erotic nature as a fright factor. Other characters too, such as Isabella Thorpe, are made much more sexualized than in the novel. Katherine Schlesinger, as Catherine Morland, is appropriately gawky, wide-eyed, and awestruck as she visits the Gothicized Northanger Abbey. While not pretty, Schlesinger plays Catherine as a well-mannered and pleasant young woman in love for the first time.

Peter Firth plays Henry Tilney as a charming and flirtatious gallant, but he seems at times a bit rakish in his attentions to Catherine. No mention is made of his being a clergyman, although we learn he has a profession and is taken away "on business." His behavior is at times "odd," as he postures and plays games with Catherine. Some of the most enlightening scenes of the novel involve Henry's mentoring of Catherine in the ways of the complex social world of Bath, in how to express herself and to interpret what others say, to think critically, and to evaluate the actions and words of those around her for truth and reliability. The film makes Henry not a tutor but a lecturer and Catherine not a student who learns to think for herself but a follower who copies what she believes will please Henry. The novel shows the progressive education of Catherine in independent and rational thought, while the film features Catherine only as the victim of too much indulgence in Gothic horrors and an almost robotic devotee of Henry.

Robert Hardy is well cast as General Tilney. He has the appearance of authority that inspires fear in not only young Catherine but his own children as well. However, his character flaws are extended to include a lecherous interest in Catherine that haunts her dreams. In the novel General Tilney's fault is essentially a rigid militaristic control over his children. His tyranny extends to Catherine when he expels her from Northanger after learning he was misinformed about her fortune. He can be faulted for judging her on the rumor of her wealth and for failing to see her actions as motivated by "an innate principle of general integrity" (*NA* 219), thus making her a suitable partner for his clergyman son. In the film he is far more sinister. The attentions to Catherine's person become more diabolical when she is dressed in his dead wife's riding costume. Hardy seems a bit unsure of how to play the general, as he must not appear overly lecherous, yet the film seems to want viewers to think he is interested in Catherine for himself rather than his son. The film implies a rivalry between Henry and his father for the attentions of Catherine. Marilyn Roberts analyzes this feature as a playing out of the Oedipus complex as General Tilney becomes a sexualized father figure who must be defeated by the son (132–33). In one of Catherine's imagined scenes, Henry, riding a white horse, rescues her, clad only in a white sheet, from the general and John Thorpe. Her fantasy suggests the general's patriarchal authority is a subconscious sexual threat inspired by her reading of Gothic fiction. Her nightmare scenes in the film depict the general as an ominous figure, a Montoni, forcing young Catherine onto a bed and threatening her with a sword. An additional character flaw the film adds is General Tilney's gambling addiction. His debts prompt his obsession with marrying his children to fortunes. This motive is more probable for modern audiences since the novel doesn't provide a clear rationale for the general's cruelty to Catherine, given his own fortune and Henry's profession.

Cassie Stuart's Isabella Thorpe is appropriately giggly, sly, over-curled, and over-flounced. Her cloying sweetness conveys her excess of sensibility and her duplicity. Jonathan Coy plays John Thorpe as the loutish figure Austen created. He leers at Catherine, gazing up and down her figure. Eleanor Tilney, played by Ingrid Lacey, is less passive, more assertive, and "modernly spunky" (Roberts 137). She meets her lover secretly in the garden of the abbey and at one point is overheard telling her brother Henry that she doesn't know how much longer she can endure her life with her tyrannical father. In the novel Eleanor is a model of feminine modesty, passivity, duty, and obedience to her father. When "the man of her choice" accedes "to title and fortune" (*NA* 251), their marriage takes place. Wadey's film makes Eleanor appear more unhappy and "abused" by the heavy-handed control of the general, but she does argue for using "sense" in matrimony, just as the later Elinor Dashwood becomes representative of sense.

Changes from Novel to Film
(Significant Deletions, Additions, and Revisions)

Additional Characters. The Marchioness is an invented character not in Austen's novel. According to Marilyn Roberts, she is based on Lady Laurentini from *The Mysteries of Udolpho*, a figure who haunts Udolpho. In *The Mysteries of Udolpho*, Lady Laurentini is thought to be dead, and her ghost haunts the castle; in the film the Marchioness's ghostly white skin and emaciated body recall Lady Laurentini. The film's Marchioness is the widow of a guillotined French aristocrat, who encourages the general in his gambling and sets off the rumors about Catherine's wealth. She furthers a sense of the dissipation at Northanger Abbey by appearing to be the general's mistress. Related to the Marchioness's addition to the film is the scene in which her African page draws Catherine out of doors and turns a cartwheel on the lawn. This adds an exotic quality to the already curious world of the abbey, suggesting an unconventional way of life truly different from the norm of "Christian England" (*NA* 197) familiar to Catherine. The child takes Catherine by the hand as if he senses her own youthful innocence as she jealously watches Henry sing an Italian duet with a talented young woman. Watching the African child turn a cartwheel, she imagines herself being dragged away by two figures and then rescued by Henry Tilney on a white horse. Apparently, she associates the bondage of the black child with her own status at the abbey.

Invented Scenes. The most interesting, and controversial, additions are the imagined scenes taken from the plot of *The Mysteries of Udolpho*. Marilyn Roberts reads this addition as a psychoanalytical approach to portraying Catherine's character (130). The fantasies begin with the opening scene of the novel as Catherine is reading *The Mysteries of Udolpho* perched in a tree, eating plums. This is not incompatible with her character from the novel, since Austen describes her as a kind of teenaged tomboy who loves to read, albeit novels of sentiment. By having her read *The Mysteries of Udolpho* before being introduced to Gothic fiction by Isabella Thorpe in Bath, the film connects the Bath section more obviously to the second (Northanger Abbey) volume of the novel (Roberts 130). These scenes also provide viewers what the Austen novel does not supply for readers: a visual depiction of the essential nature of eighteenth-century Gothic novels. Austen would have assumed a reader's familiarity with both the sentimental novel (which is featured in the Bath segments, especially with Isabella Thorpe's gushing friendship) and the Gothic novel (which is featured in the second volume of the book with its mysterious rooms and furnishings). However, because most modern readers and viewers will not have this awareness of Gothic conventions, the film visualizes Catherine's imaginings.

More important, though, the fantasies are a revelation of Catherine's psychological state. As we see the figures in the daydreams take on the appearance of the people she meets in Bath—John Thorpe, General Tilney, the Marchioness, and Catherine herself—we understand young Catherine's fears and fantasies, which have an erotic quality. We can more easily, too, understand why Catherine, "*Udolpho*-obsessed" (Roberts 130), would nurture suspicions about General Tilney's role in the death of his wife. Fantasy and reality intermingle in the mind of a teenager, hungry for thrills, adventure, and romance, especially an ingénue with little experience and education. Even the final scene of the film can be read as consistent with the novel, for Catherine, recently evicted from Northanger Abbey, still daydreams of romance with Henry Tilney. Her dream is of a rescue by a romantic hero who will save her from the tyranny of the general and the boredom of life at Fullerton. In the film, through the fog of her imagination, Henry Tilney emerges in the flesh to profess his love. Catherine's costume changes as she moves from the swing on the lawn to the grove of trees where Henry awaits, blurring daydream and reality. Thus, the ending nicely unites the daydream of romance with the actual appearance of it.

The bathing scene at Bath is another of the interesting features of the film. The actual Roman baths are used as the setting for a social gathering of ladies in tall feathered hats eating lunch in the water. This is an invented scene: in the novel Catherine Morland never immerses herself in the waters of Bath. The warm spa waters were drawn into the Pump Room, a kind of salon during the period, and the water was taken medicinally. Catherine does drink the water, but she is not in Bath for health reasons, so bathing would have been unlikely. In addition, it's questionable whether the baths were used recreationally at all. Even more unlikely is the co-recreational bathing: the presence of John Thorpe in the water while the ladies are bathing violates propriety.

Deleted Scenes. A notable deletion in the film is the visit to Woodston, the parsonage of Henry Tilney. Austen uses the excursion to allow Catherine to see what might be her future home. More important, Catherine shows her maturity and good sense while at Woodston. The youthful Catherine has a tendency either to misunderstand conversation or to blurt out her reactions without reflecting. At Woodston she regulates her emotions and responses so as not to appear overconfident or too certain of the future. Eliminating this scene in the film loses one opportunity to show that Catherine has grown in the confidence and womanhood necessary for us to believe her readiness to marry.

Settings Changed. Jane Austen describes Catherine's first sight of Northanger Abbey, where she is hoping to see "massy walls of grey stone, rising amidst a grove of ancient oaks, with the last beams of the sun playing in beautiful splendour on its high Gothic windows" (*NA* 161), but instead "so low did the building stand, that she found herself passing through the great gates of the lodge . . . without having discerned even an antique chimney" (*NA* 161). Catherine's observations of the home continue to deflate her expectations of a Gothic enclave; instead, she is welcomed into an elegant, modern, tastefully decorated home. The film makes every effort to incorporate Gothic features, with screaming birds, darkened passages, and a mysterious note that directs her to the statue of the unknown woman. The abbey in the film is actually a moated castle, not an abbey at all, and hardly the modern apartments the novel describes. The novel debunks Catherine's Gothic imagination, but the film heightens its intensity and reality.

Conceptual Integrity (Themes, Ideas, Spirit of Austen's Novel)

Education of the Heroine. In the novel Catherine's "education" is begun half way into Volume I when she is disabused of faith in the artificial and insincerely sentimental offerings of friendship from Isabella Thorpe. She acts independently when she corrects John Thorpe's lying excuse to the Tilneys by saying, "If I could not be persuaded into doing what I thought wrong, I never will be tricked into it" (*NA* 101). And she questions Isabella's dancing with Captain Tilney while she is engaged to Catherine's brother. Likewise, in the film Isabella Thorpe disappears from her consciousness as she enters the world of Northanger Abbey until she receives John Morland's letter confirming her disloyalty. After reading Isabella's letter, she judges her a false and dangerous friend. However, the novel also has Catherine lose her belief in the Gothic horrors of the abbey when Henry reminds her that they live in the heart of England where such trespasses of law as the murder of one's wife would be investigated and punished. The film, though, courts these Gothic musings from beginning to end, even with the foggy romanticized appearance of Henry's rescue at Fullerton. It is not clear in the film if Catherine has learned anything, since the nightmarish, outlandish, strange world of General Tilney's establishment has never been proven to be a fabrication but rather seems a vision of reality. Thus, one theme of Austen's novel, the education of the heroine in separating the fictional world from reality, is never realized.

Gothicism. The film actually presents itself, in its prequel and through its fantasies of Catherine's novel reading, as a Gothic thriller. The appeal appears to be directed toward an adolescent viewer who would know this formula of sex and terror from contemporary movies. The problem for "readers" of Austen film adaptations is that the film becomes exactly what Austen was critiquing in her novel. Catherine nearly estranges herself from Henry Tilney by seeing the world through the lens of Gothic horror, an improbable and unflattering view of his family. She must disavow the authority of such reading and remove herself from its power to distort reality. This she does by burning her *Mysteries of Udolpho*. However, Austen is not against reading novels, even "horrid" Gothic fiction, for both Henry and Eleanor Tilney speak of reading *Udolpho* with pleasure. Austen's narrator makes a claim for the power of novels to move the maturing reader through their "genius, wit, and taste" (*NA* 37). The film invites viewers to share the Gothic experience but leaves the heroine disabused of novels entirely.

Henry Tilney. While Henry Tilney is the hero of the novel, one of the most charming and witty of Austen's heroes, in the film he is a rather priggish "teacher," who as Bruce Stovel writes, "tells the heroine what to think, rather than asking her to think for herself" (241). A conceptual change from the Austen novel is that the Catherine at the end of the film seems infatuated with Henry but hardly mature, without the self-awareness that would make her ready for marriage. In the novel we see her grow in confidence and judgment. In the film she remains a gawky teenager willing to be led wherever romance will take her.

Point of View. Austen's novels begin in omniscience and progress toward a limited omniscience that is restricted almost completely to the mind of the heroine. This film locates many scenes outside the heroine's mind and point of view. In some cases, scenes are invented; in other places, conversations Catherine overhears in the novel are filmed without her being present. The problem with this change in point of view is convincingly argued by Bruce Stovel: "Jane Austen uses her chosen vantage point to trace the growth of her heroine's ability to think for herself and make meaningful choices. The Catherine of the film adaptation does not really get the chance to think, let alone choose" (244).

Cinematic Technique: Reading the Visual Elements of the Film

Dream/Fantasy Sequences. The film's video depiction of the imagined horrors of the Gothic experience is an excellent device for showing how the mind creates what it reads on the page. Catherine "sees" what the language of *The Mysteries of Udolpho* suggests. The filmmakers have done an excellent job of showing the evolving complexity of Catherine's dreams and fantasies as the characters from the book merge with the people she meets in Bath. Likewise, the misty fog scene at the end of the film is a device to visualize the thin line between hope, fantasy, and reality.

Music and Sound. The music in the film has been described as a kind of choral chanting, suggestive of some cultist sacrifice. It also has similarities to 1980s "new wave" music, perhaps intended to modernize the film and appeal to contemporary audiences. Although not consistent with Austen's Regency world, the music is effective for the Gothic experience of the film.

Reading the Film
—Questions for Discussion and Writing

1. Analyze the character of Catherine Morland as depicted in the film. How consistent is her characterization as an ingénue? How does Katherine Schlesinger portray Catherine Morland? What character traits are retained in the film? Which are lost?

2. The film includes a much more sensational and sexualized interpretation of the novel. Although Austen does not explicitly write about Catherine's sexual awakening, how realistic do you find this film rendition of her growing into womanhood? How consistent with the undertext of Austen's novel is this interpretation? Consider also the influences of Catherine's readings in Gothic

and sentimental novels and her friend Isabella Thorpe's influence on Catherine's burgeoning adolescence. Read the film for details that suggest a sexual initiation as much as an education into reading and thinking.

3. In what other ways is the film "sexualized"? Consider the costuming, makeup, gestures, and demeanor of characters as well as action and dialogue that suggest sexual undertones.

4. Analyze the casting of Peter Firth as Henry Tilney. How well does his portrayal match your perception of Henry from the novel? In what ways is he changed? Does Henry mentor as well as woo Catherine in the film? Does Firth's Henry seem a likely match for Catherine?

5. Analyze the character of General Tilney as portrayed by Robert Hardy in the film. Are his character flaws invented, or is there a basis for them in the novel? Examine closely his relationship with Catherine. What are the reasons for his attentions to her? Are they consistent with the novel?

6. Austen's novel is about the education of an ingénue on many levels. What lessons does Catherine learn in the film? How does the film suggest her youth and naiveté? Examine scenes that suggest growth in maturity.

7. Is there evidence that Catherine is disabused of the influence of Gothic and sentimental novels in the film? What scenes visually depict moments of enlightenment?

8. The Marchioness is introduced in the film in Bath and later at Northanger Abbey. What purpose does she serve in the film? Consider Lady Laurentini's sources in *The Mysteries of Udolpho*. How do her dress, makeup, and demeanor suggest debauchery? How does her invention contribute to the character of General Tilney? How does she add to the special aura of Bath and, later, the exotic world of Northanger Abbey?

9. The Wadey/Foster production has been compared to a Fellini film. What particular scenes add to this sense of hedonistic or carnivalistic atmosphere? Why do you think the filmmakers created these "fantastic" scenes? Do they have sources in the novel?

10. This film production devotes many scenes to Catherine's "imagination"—her dreams and fantasies derived from reading Gothic novels. How do these invented scenes coincide with the reality of her experience? Do they have a sound psychological basis in her life as well as in her reading? Do they have counterparts in the novel?

11. How are the female characters portrayed in the film? Compare the three young women—Isabella Thorpe, Catherine Morland, and Eleanor Tilney. Is their

behavior typical of young women of this time and place, or are they caricatures or stereotypes? Consider how they compare to their novel counterparts. Examine how costuming and makeup choices contribute to the depiction of their characters in the film.

12. Does Catherine Morland grow into an independent, self-confident adult woman in the film? How suitable for the wife of Henry Tilney is she? Has the film developed her growth sufficiently to justify his proposal of marriage?

13. Austen's novel is comic in many ways, including the use of irony and characterization. Is comedy evident in the film as well? If so, what kinds of comedy can you identify?

14. The novel creates two worlds through separate volumes: the world of Bath and the world of Northanger Abbey. How does the film link the two worlds?

15. Northanger Abbey in the film is actually a moated castle. How does the setting function to advance the plot or characterization in the film? How is the setting inconsistent with Austen's novel? What point is the film making through the castle setting?

16. How are sound effects and music used in the film? Examine music within the film as well as the score.

17. What symbolism do you see in the birds that frighten and fascinate Catherine at the abbey?

Film Credits

Northanger Abbey

BBC/A&E 1987.
Screenplay by Maggie Wadey.
Directed by Giles Foster.
Produced by Louis Marks.

Cast

Catherine Morland	Katharine Schlesinger
Henry Tilney	Peter Firth
General Tilney	Robert Hardy
Mrs. Allen	Googie Withers
Mr. Allen	Geoffrey Chater

Isabella Thorpe	Cassie Stuart
John Thorpe	Jonathan Coy
Eleanor Tilney	Ingrid Lacey
Frederick Tilney	Greg Hicks
James Morland	Philip Bird
Mrs. Thorpe	Elvi Hale
Mrs. Morland	Helen Fraser
Mr. Morland	David Rolfe
Marchioness	Elaine Ives-Cameron
Alice	Angela Curran
Miss Digby	Tricia Morrish
Edward Morland	Oliver Hembrough
Thorpe sister	Anne-Marie Mullane
Thorpe sister	Michelle Arthur
Jenny	Sarah-Jane Holm
Page Boy	Raphael Alleyne

Sense and Sensibility

Jane Austen began writing *Sense and Sensibility* in 1797 under the title of *Elinor and Marianne*. It was believed to have been written as a novel of letters, but according to the author of the *Memoir*, the novel was composed "in its present form" after the completion of *First Impressions*. In April 1811 Austen was in London correcting the proofs, and the novel appeared in October, its authorship identified only as "By a Lady" (Chapman, "Introductory Note to *Sense and Sensibility*" xiii–xiv).

While I find much to admire in *Sense and Sensibility*, it has always been my least favorite of Austen's novels. I find Elinor Dashwood an unattractive heroine, lacking vivacity and wit. The character of the hero, Edward Ferrars, is largely unrealized, and what we do discover about him is dull and mundane. Equally flawed is the character of Marianne Dashwood, whose childlike obsession with sensibility dooms her to correction. The penance seems to come through marriage to Colonel Brandon, a good and decent man but one whose character is presented without charm or vitality. Marianne's acceptance of him comes over time and is unconvincing. The problem for me stems from its being a "concept" novel, in which the principles of "sense" and "sensibility" are acted out through characterization. My students, however, have responded favorably to the novel. Their identification with Marianne is strong: many have been wounded by a false and duplicitous lover. Lucy Steele, with her jealous attentions to her rival, makes a good foil to Elinor, whose restraint and decorum make her the model of sensible behavior.

Viewing the Novel
—Approaches to Teaching *Sense and Sensibility*

I include here a general discussion of the main issues, themes, and ideas in *Sense and Sensibility*. My "Approaches to Teaching *Sense and Sensibility*" complement the analytical questions that follow this discussion.

Sense, Sensibility, and Sentiment. Sentimental novels were popular in Europe in the mid- and late eighteenth century. One description of this genre from the *Encyclopedia of Romanticism* defines its qualities: "Sentimental novels were marked by stock characters (a chaste maiden under siege by an artful rake, avaricious parents, and faithful servants), histrionics, and unrealistic rhetoric to heighten human action and feeling. When fostering emotion, rather than instruction, became the true purpose of Sentimental fiction, many women, especially young girls, were warned to avoid reading novels. . . . Sentimental novels were attacked as amoral, anti-Christian, and overly sexual" (Goldstein 520–21). Austen's *Juvenilia* parodies the excesses of sentimental fiction, and her novel *Sense and Sensibility* furthers her attack on the popular novels of the period. *Sensibility* is a term that represents heightened feeling and a belief that a kind of natural wisdom results from indulgence in emotions. Sensibility at its extreme is characterized by a preoccupation with the natural world, an opposition to conventions and artifice, and a self-absorption that relies on feelings as a determiner of morality and a basis for judgment. Sensibility prompts a person to measure moral development by the degree of suffering and strong emotion experienced. *Sense* is a term used to refer to an individual who follows a rational approach to knowledge and judgment. The "truly sensible" individual is compassionate, has strong feeling (sensibility), is attuned to the natural world, and is sympathetic to the human condition, but is guided by morals and values in making judgments (sense). The truly sensible person unites sensibility and sense by balancing passion and reason and avoiding excesses that produce blindness, self-absorption, and cruelty.

In Marianne Dashwood, particularly, and also in her mother, her sister Margaret, and Willoughby, Austen fashions persons of sensibility. Elinor Dashwood is her representative of sense. While the novel shows the progressive deterioration that results from excess sensibility in Marianne, Elinor gradually discloses a character of true sensibility as she has both sense and finely moderated feelings: she "possessed a strength of understanding, and coolness of judgment, which qualified her . . . to be the counsellor of her mother. . . . She had an excellent heart;—her disposition was affectionate, and her feelings were strong; but she knew how to govern them" (*SS* 6). Neither character is pure caricature, though, for while Marianne's excesses of sensibility endanger her happiness, yet she is intelligent, and her judgment is capable of revision: "She was sensible and clever; but eager in everything; her sorrows, her joys, could have no moderation. She was generous, amiable, interesting: she was every thing but prudent" (*SS* 6). Each character has the capacity for sense and sensibility as Elinor's emotional pain and compassion are rendered fully, and Marianne learns to moderate her excesses.

The novel avoids the melodramatic endings characteristic of the novels of sentiment. The "villain" Willoughby is not banished from society, nor does he suffer severely for his ill-use of Marianne. Neither is Marianne left to suffer the pain of lost love: "Instead of falling a sacrifice to an irresistible passion, . . .—instead of remaining even for ever with her mother, and finding her only pleasures in retirement and study, . . .—she found herself . . . submitting to new attachments, entering on new duties, placed in a new home, a wife, the mistress of a family, and the patroness of a village" (*SS* 378–79). Included in the novel are the interpolated stories of the two Elizas, whose tragic fate was typical of the novels of sentiment. Austen's satire mocks the excesses of sensibility and the tales of romance by creating a story that ends realistically and sensibly.

Marriage and Money. Familiar to students of the Austen novels is the relationship of love, courtship, and marriage to money. The legal system gave preference to patriarchy, and inheritance laws ensured that the great homes and capital remained in the hands of the already well endowed, as represented by John and Fanny Dashwood. The plot of the novel places four women at the mercy of an economic system that denies them the wealth and social world they were born into. Left without inheritance upon the death of their father, the Dashwood sisters are expelled from the home and society that would have formed the basis of connections to the social elite and links to eligible young men of fortune. As Emma Thompson summarizes it in her *Diaries* of the making of the film, "*Sense and Sensibility* is about love and money. Perhaps its main question is, can love survive without money? A pithy question.

Romantic codes teach us that love conquers all. Elinor disagrees. You need a decent wage, a competence. Some people need more. Some people need more money than love. Most people would rather have love with a comfortable amount of money. It's a difficult thing to accept" (255). Every relationship in the novel has at its core the issue of money, including both Elinor Dashwood's and Lucy Steele's attachment to Edward Ferrars; Willoughby's relationship with Marianne, with Eliza, and with Miss Grey; and Colonel Brandon's relationship with the first Eliza and later with Marianne. Ironically, power resides in the coffers of two wealthy widows: Willoughby's benefactress, his cousin Mrs. Smith, and Mrs. Ferrars, who use money to manipulate their heirs. The central issue for Austen is how women, and men, are to live and love in a world where money is so predominant a concern and where proper values determine that marriage for money alone is mercenary and wrong.

Issues of Class and Society. Austen's primary subject is the middle-class gentry in England in the late eighteenth and early nineteenth centuries. She often represents the upper and aristocratic classes, but seldom do the lower classes figure into the plots of her novels in meaningful ways. Her overall attitude is a generous and egalitarian one. She mocks the hypocritical, the proud, the interfering, and the foolish. She laughs at pretension, follies, and obsessions across classes. Her democratic approach to virtue and vice means the wicked and good are found at all levels of society. Often her method is to match bad manners in one class with a representative example in another. Austen also separates manners from morals, removing class distinctions in human affairs. Often the difficulty for characters is making judgments fairly and accurately when good manners and amiability may mask weakness and even wickedness, as Marianne learns about Willoughby, while poor manners or lack of sociability may disguise goodness and generosity, as Edward Ferrars demonstrates.

Class is a prominent issue in *Sense and Sensibility* as the Dashwoods are removed from an upper-class world of fortune to a restricted middle-class environment, where money is hard to come by. The most-satirized characters are those like Fanny Dashwood who are snobbish, miserly, and mean. Sir John Middleton and Mrs. Jennings, while wealthy, are generous and welcoming. Lucy Steele and her sister Anne are uneducated and mercenary, the daughters of a poor clergyman. Money moves the plot, for had Willoughby his inheritance and Marianne hers, their love might have been realized in marriage. When tested by the option of delaying wealth and marrying for love, Willoughby chooses an engagement that guarantees him fortune, thus denying him the possibility of a marriage of affection. Had Colonel Brandon been allowed to marry his first love Eliza, he would have saved her and her daughter from future ruin. Edward Ferrars would not have been discouraged from courting Elinor and disinherited when his engagement to Lucy Steele became known. Underscoring these plots of marriage and class are the values displayed by characters of all classes. The ideal marriage results when some means to livelihood is combined with a true affection that grows out of compatibility and mutual esteem.

Issues of Judgment, Authority, and Manners. The courtship plot becomes a test of judgment, both in knowing others and knowing oneself. All of Austen's characters exhibit some degree of blindness, and the plots develop with increased or climactic awareness of values and abilities. Rarely does Austen invent a reliable authority, mentor, parental figure, or wise friend to teach the heroine the proper course of action. Her plots are ones of trial and error for the heroine, and she learns through experience. Related to the problem is the society in which they live, for conventions of the time dictated restraint, reticence, and a rather superficial surface that prevented full disclosure and the open expression of thoughts and feelings. Mrs. Dashwood is reluctant to ask her daughter Marianne about her relationship with Willoughby; Colonel Brandon does not reveal to the world the crimes Willoughby committed against Eliza; Lucy Steele's engagement is a secret that Elinor keeps even though it deters her from further intimacy with Edward; and Willoughby fails to disclose to Marianne his prior engagement to Miss Grey. The difficulty of knowing and the problem of communication, of too many secrets made and kept, complicate the young lives of the characters.

Viewing the Novel
—Questions for Analysis and Discussion

The questions below address the larger issues of each volume and are designed to promote analytical thinking as the basis for discussion. These questions ask students to "see" into the text and complement the central issues of "reading the film" that follow.

Volume I

1. Analyze Elinor Dashwood as the character of "sense." In what scenes is her sensible character most obvious? She is also a character of strong but unrevealed emotions. What are examples of moments in the novel when her pow-

erful feelings are made known to the reader? Are they also evident to other characters in the scene?

2. Analyze Marianne Dashwood as the character of "sensibility." What elements of the Novel of Sensibility heroine does she display? In what scenes is her sensibility most obvious? Is Marianne also a character of "sense"? What are examples of her sensible and intelligent character?

3. How does Marianne's "sensibility" find fault with Edward Ferrars?

4. What is Colonel Brandon's initial attraction to Marianne? What qualities does Colonel Brandon share with Marianne? Is he a character of sense or of sensibility?

5. How is Willoughby portrayed as the heroic figure of sentimental fiction? In what scenes is he represented as a figure of sensibility like Marianne?

6. Does Willoughby display behavior that should have forewarned the Dashwoods of his future actions? What efforts were made by them to learn his character? In what ways is the relationship between Willoughby and Marianne "improper"?

7. How does Marianne so egregiously mistake Willoughby's character? What in her character or in his causes her blindness?

8. Describe Mrs. Dashwood as a mother figure. How does she help or hurt her daughters' chances for happiness in life?

9. Why do you think the author began the novel with the confusing genealogy of the Dashwood family?

10. What role do the Middletons, especially Lady Middleton and her children, and John and Fanny Dashwood serve in the novel?

Volume II

1. How does the removal to London advance the plot?

2. How is Lucy Steele characterized? What scenes or details reveal her character? What is her most obvious flaw?

3. Evaluate Edward Ferrars's relationship with Elinor. How do you judge his loyalty to Lucy Steele when it is obvious he has stronger feelings for Elinor?

4. Does Mrs. Jennings compare or contrast with Mrs. Dashwood as an adult authority figure? Why does Marianne dislike her so much?

5. Is Mrs. Jennings an Austen comic fool, the object of satire, or a lovable character? Does she have sense? Sensibility? How would you evaluate her?

6. What parallels has Austen set up between Edward Ferrars and his engagement to Lucy Steele and Willoughby's engagement to Miss Grey? Which characters are most reprehensible? How are Edward and Willoughby alike in their backgrounds and upbringing?

7. How is Colonel Brandon's story of the first Eliza's ruin a parallel to Marianne's? How are they different?

8. How is Marianne's behavior changed in London? Consider her relationship with her sister Elinor as well as with others.

9. What kind of woman is Mrs. Ferrars? What motivates her behavior toward her sons?

10. Why do you think Fanny Dashwood favors Lucy Steele? How do Lucy's manners reflect her character?

Volume III

1. What failures of disclosure (secrets, lies, etc.) prevent characters from making sound judgments?

2. How is sensibility redefined when combined with sense? By which characters and in which scenes is "true sensibility" exhibited? Consider how Marianne has changed through her experience. Has Elinor also changed?

3. Evaluate the scene in which Willoughby visits Elinor. Should Willoughby be forgiven after his confession of his love for Marianne? Does he redeem himself through his confession?

4. How is Willoughby "punished" for his treatment of Marianne? Would you expect Austen to make his fate less fortunate? Why do you think Austen ended her story this way?

5. How would you evaluate Edward Ferrars's honoring of his commitment to marry Lucy Steele, a woman he does not love? Had he not been bailed out by Lucy's marriage to Robert, what would you project their chances for happiness in marriage to be? What point about Edward's character is made through his willingness to honor his commitment in spite of the fact that he loves Elinor?

6. Examine how Marianne comes to accept and love Colonel Brandon. Is Austen's treatment of their relationship satisfying and convincing? What events have established Brandon's character?

7. What problems with courtship and knowing one's suitor are presented in the novel?

8. How is Lucy Steele's experience representative of the dangers faced by young people in courtship?

9. What does this novel suggest are the essentials to a good marriage? What is appropriate behavior in courtship? Are these examples relevant today?
10. How does the novel avoid the melodramatic ending of the sentimental novel?

Reading the Film —Approaches to Teaching the Film

Using Film in the Classroom

The Emma Thompson *Sense and Sensibility* continues to be the most popular of the Austen film adaptations. It is also one of the most useful as a gateway into the Austen novels. The cast is attractive and endearing, and the costuming and settings give a flavor of English country life. Additionally, the romantic plot is appealing, especially to female audiences. One danger of the film is that it is too seductive. Thompson's film turns the sense and sensibility issue around, making the sensible but unemotional Emma the character in need of reform, while the strong-feeling Marianne is encouraged to transfer her sensibilities from one passionate lover to another. Critics have deemed the film "fairly 'faithful'" on one hand (Solender 104), and Jane Austen "harlequinized" on the other (Kaplan 178). I like to show the film in two segments after reading portions of the novel. Our analysis of the film focuses on the issue of fidelity to the text, especially how the characterization is altered, with attention to the issues of "sense" and "sensibility."

My focus here is on four general issues of film analysis that may serve as the basis for analysis and discussion of the film adaptation, and my discussion is limited to the 1995 Columbia Pictures *Sense and Sensibility*, screenplay by Emma Thompson.

Casting and Characterization

Emma Thompson's Elinor is a much more emotional and a much older Elinor than Austen's nineteen-year-old heroine. Emma Thompson gives a mature, sensible look to her performance and is also, as we expect of Elinor, compassionate and sympathetic. Marianne Dashwood, seventeen in the novel, is played by twenty-year-old Kate Winslet as an exuberant and energized young woman. She is an attractive character we come to admire more than her sober, restrained sister. One critic who finds fault with the Thompson film's presentation of Elinor and Marianne writes, "Elinor was all wrong. . . . Thompson's Elinor is mature, kind, intelligent, and perceptive;

she is our Elinor Dashwood, sensible and true. But in the film, Elinor is also repressed.... She is dutiful to the expectations of women in the nineteenth century" in that she controls her anguish and frustrations and hides her shock and despair. In the novel her "self-restraint is an achievement. But in the film, that self-restraint needs correction." In the film "it is Elinor who transforms and 'faces herself,' not immature and self-involved Marianne—the exact opposite of what Austen intended" (Dickson 50–51). To be consistent with the older cast of Dashwood sisters, Gemma Jones plays Mrs. Dashwood, a woman much older than the fortyish mother of the novel.

One reviewer referred to Austen's male heroes as "two sticks walking about in frock coats" (Alleva 15). While Austen's Edward is a decidedly unromantic "hero," he is loyal and honors his commitments even in defiance of his mother and her fortune. Casting Hugh Grant as Edward Ferrars and giving him more presence through invented scenes convert a dull but principled clergyman into a romantic hero. Hugh Grant's Edward is handsome, funny, and humane, kind, gentle, charming, and romantic, someone Elinor can more than "esteem." His characterization is more fully realized through invented scenes, such as the ones with Elinor at Norland where we see their growing attachment, Mrs. Dashwood's approval, and Fanny Dashwood's disfavor. Edward's kind attention to young Margaret garners Elinor's approval and love. Instead of restraint, cinematic Edward is shown making "a rich web of emotional bonds" through invented scenes with Elinor, and a paternal bond with Margaret that prefigures a future role as parent (Nixon 36). The scene in the stable, where he attempts to tell Elinor about his previous engagement, makes him appear more honorable than in the book, where he departs Norland without explanation.

Colonel Brandon, as played by Alan Rickman, is made sexier, more macho, and more youthful than his depiction in the novel. We first see him transformed by hearing Marianne play and sing, revealing his real appreciation of her music and his own sensibility. Brandon is given scenes at Cleveland in which he rescues Marianne in the storm, paralleling the heroic scene of rescue by Willoughby. His impassioned plea to Elinor to give him occupation, as Marianne lies in a fever at Cleveland, reveals the intensity of his feelings. His courtship of Marianne after her illness, reading to her and being gently attentive, matches Willoughby's courtship in the first half of the film, creating a stronger sense of his character and appeal. He is shown as gentle, kind, and impassioned, making Marianne's transfer of affection to him more romantic. However, the film suggests that Marianne's change of heart toward Brandon is the result of "sensibility," not "sense," a transfer of her passions from Willoughby to Brandon rather than a correction of excess sensibility.

Greg Wise is an excellent Willoughby. He is handsome in a rakish sort of way, a playboy who looks boldly into Marianne's face while "making love" to her whole family. Wise also plays Willoughby as youthful, clever, and fun, contrasting him with the older and more sedate Colonel Brandon. The film depicts Willoughby and Marianne in informal poses, sharing a degree of intimacy that should have warned the family of potential danger. The Allenham visit is replaced with a wild carriage ride that seems shocking even by modern standards. Wise's performance at the ball in London is exactly right—the expressionless gaze his Willoughby gives Marianne is chilling.

Margaret Dashwood is given a much larger role in the film. Played by Emilie Francois, she is a poised and spirited young girl. Margaret's expanded role becomes a means of exploring the "feminine" side of the male characters, Edward Ferrars and Colonel Brandon. They become brother/father figures to her. Her attachment to Edward and her friendship with Brandon are benchmarks of their acceptability as mates for her sisters. She is also a spokesperson for the world of feminine possibilities, the future of young women in the nineteenth century as she imagines herself traveling the world as a pirate or living in a treehouse, a "house of her own," unlike that of her mother and sisters. Almost a tomboy, she fences with Edward and speaks openly and frankly. "Margaret's recalcitrance ... voices a resentment that her mother and sisters clearly feel but will not allow themselves to express openly, and it is one of the ways in which she is constructed in the film as a figure, by virtue of her youth, for healthy nonconformity" (Samuelian 149).

Imogen Stubbs is a bold player as Lucy Steele. Her intense gaze and shifting, greedy eyes suggest both her dogged possessiveness of Edward and her degree of insecurity in holding him. She is costumed and made up in a slightly overdone way to suggest her lower class, and she obviously possesses more guile than beauty.

Changes from Novel to Film
(Significant Deletions, Additions, and Revisions)

Characters Deleted. The wife and family of Sir John Middleton are deleted. His companion in the film is his mother-in-law, Mrs. Jennings. This deletion removes the satire of family life and Lucy Steele's opportunity for showing herself to be considerate of children. It also heightens the comic potential: Sir John and Mrs. Jennings are portrayed in the film as two good-hearted and generous souls who love to tease but also willingly take the Dashwoods under their protective wing. Lucy's sister, Anne Steele, is deleted. Anne in the novel is silly, unattractive, uneducated, and penniless, almost another version of Lucy. She is a satirical figure who represents the difficulty, yet the necessity, of marriage for women with little fortune, charm, or beauty. Her desperation to find a husband helps us understand Lucy Steele's reluctance to give up on Edward Ferrars even when he is disinherited. Even a poor clergyman is better than spinsterhood, which is Anne Steele's fate. The Steele sisters parallel and contrast with the Dashwoods, who marry for love not money; Anne Steele's character is redundant.

Settings Changed. Locations are changed in the film to allow for changes in the characterization of Willoughby. Combe Magna is some thirty miles from Cleveland in the novel. By making it only five and a half miles in the film, Marianne can view his estate from the hill in the rain and catch the fever that nearly takes her life. Colonel Brandon's presence there allows him opportunity to rescue her as Willoughby had in the sprained ankle incident. Finally, the proximity of Combe Magna to Barton Cottage makes it possible for Willoughby to watch from the distant hilltop as Marianne is married to Brandon, capturing his sense of longing and regret.

Deleted Scenes. Even though Willoughby lives thirty miles from Cleveland (in Austen's novel), he rides this distance to tell Elinor of his feelings for Marianne. His story exonerates him to some degree, and it opens the way for Elinor's compassionate offer of forgiveness. Willoughby's admission of having loved Marianne makes him less a reprobate or villain. In the film, even though Willoughby is within six miles' distance, he does not make this journey. The probable reason for deleting the confession scene is that it would again put his strong and attractive masculine presence on the screen at a time when Alan Rickman's Colonel Brandon is about to replace Willoughby as Marianne's lover. It would be dangerous to make Willoughby's presence felt when Colonel Brandon is tortured with feeling for Marianne and seeking "occupation" to relieve his anxiety. As Cheryl Nixon observes, "the film will not allow Willoughby to do what its heroes cannot do: express his emotions verbally. If Austen's dramatic display of Willoughby were added to the film, his emotional power would again throw into relief the emotional weakness of Edward and Brandon" (42–43).

Conceptual Integrity (Themes, Ideas, Spirit of Austen's Novel)

"Sense" and "Sensibility." While Elinor is drawn primarily as a figure representing "sense" or reason in the novel, she is also a character of "sensibility." She represents the Austen ideal of a character of strong emotions who practices restraint, exertion, and self-control. In the film her failure to *express* strong emotion is faulted as a failure to feel, and Elinor is "redeemed" only when she violently displays her passions, as in the sickbed scene with Marianne and in the final meeting with Edward when she breaks down in tears after learning he is not married to Lucy. In the novel, Marianne's failure to control her passions, her selfish and narrow view of the world, her self-righteousness, and her defiance of conventions are faults that are in need of correction. In the film these qualities make her more appealing and are not seen as faults in her character. Austen's novels are a reaction against the Sentimental novels of the late eighteenth century, which were filled with bathos and trite emotion. The most admired and heroic characters in her fiction control (at least visibly) their emotions. While her male figures are men of strong feeling and passion, they show restraint as gentlemen of manners and class. Hugh Grant and Alan Rickman play their roles with much more feeling and intensity in keeping with the contemporary notion of the "man of feeling" in touch with his "feminine side."

Romance vs. Realism. While the novel is anti-romantic, the adaptation is ultimately a romantic film. The duel wedding at the end, as Colonel Brandon showers the congregation with gold coins, fails to address the issue of where Edward and Elinor will get the money to live. He will have only the small living from Colonel Brandon's parish, and, according to the novel, the inheritance from his mother will not be restored for some time. Continuing the sentimental or romantic ending, the film suggests that Willoughby is unhappy in his marriage to Miss Grey, for we see him (a lone figure on horseback) watching Marianne be carried off by Brandon in marriage. In one scene in the film, Elinor convinces Marianne that Willoughby's love would have faded under the strain of their relative poverty. Austen is more equivocal, allowing Willoughby a degree of happiness in life, as Mrs. Smith restores his fortune, and "he found no inconsiderable degree of domestic felicity" (*SS* 379). Ironically, he must live with the knowledge that had he chosen to marry Marianne, "he might at once have been happy and rich," for his benefactress eventually restored his fortune, since her "clemency" was conditioned on his marrying "a woman of character" (*SS* 379).

Cinematic Technique: Reading the Visual Elements of the Film

Visualization of Inner Consciousness. Jane Austen's novels are written in omniscient mode. The movement is from a general to a more limited omniscience, centered in the mind of the heroine. Lost in the films is the voice of the narrator, which provides the unique perspective on characters and the ironic distance that allows for satiric commentary. The visual medium of film can re-create interior consciousness through focus on characters in moments when we imagine their thoughts. Some scenes where we view characters in thought or observation include Elinor looking out the window as Edward fences with Margaret (looking fondly) or watching Marianne play the piano (noting her sadness, feeling her own loss); Brandon watching Marianne play the piano (sharing her passion for music); or Willoughby riding up to the hill to witness Marianne's wedding (regretting his loss). One reviewer, David K. Jeffrey, credits Ang Lee's direction for providing the "visual equivalent of Austen's ironic narrative stance" in the way he positions his actors and creates visual symbols. He cites the long shots of the grand house at Norland and the vine-covered cottage to which the Dashwoods remove as symbolic of their decline in the world. Jeffrey also singles out for distinction Ang Lee's filming of Marianne alone on the windy hillside to "suggest her terrible loneliness and threatened position after Willoughby has left her" and using close-ups of Willoughby to "suggest his muscular thrusting of himself into the Dashwoods' life" (Jeffrey). A visual representation of the self-indulgence of "sensibility" can be read in the scene in which Marianne, her mother, and Margaret go into separate rooms and slam shut the doors, leaving Elinor alone on the step. Sitting alone and drinking a cup of tea she wished to share dramatizes the pain caused by a selfish indulgence in feeling. The three shut doors also visually demonstrate the closing off of communication. Elinor has a pained heart as well as the others, but the "doors" to consolation are closed to her.

The "sensibility" of Edward Ferrars and Colonel Brandon is more difficult to envision as their restraint subverts passionate display. Alan Rickman's approach to the scene at Marianne's bedside in Cleveland was to think of the character as "a man thawing out after having been in a fridge for twenty years. The movement of blood and warmth back into unaccustomed veins is extremely painful" (Thompson 251). Cheryl Nixon cites the "visual grammar of metonymic exchange" as Emma Thompson's means of defining their characters (38). For Edward the gifts of the atlas and his handkerchief express his emotional attachment to Elinor and her family; for Brandon the gift of the pianoforte to Marianne suggests his understanding and appreciation of her refined sensibility. When Marianne agrees to learn the song requested by Brandon, Nixon sees a presaging of the exchange of wedding vows that follows shortly (39).

Parallel Scenes. Austen's novels make use of bipolar elements to foster comparative analysis. In the film the courtship of Marianne first by Willoughby and then by Colonel Brandon invites comparison. Sample parallel scenes show the lovers admiring Marianne's music, reading her poetry, rescuing her in the rain, and bringing her flowers. Marianne, in the novel, moves from a self-indulgent, excessively strong-willed, and emotional attachment to Willoughby to a more reasoned, prudent acceptance of Colonel Brandon. In the film, the transference is from one dashing rescuer to another. The film also makes use of mistaken identities and unexpected appearances. Colonel Brandon appears when Willoughby is expected, foreshadowing Brandon's replacement of Willoughby in Marianne's heart. Lucy Steele is mistakenly believed to have married Edward Ferrars, when in actuality she is wed to Robert Ferrars. Miss Morton, first discussed as a likely match with Edward Ferrars, is as willing to marry his brother Robert—the choice dependent on which son Mrs. Ferrars chooses to disinherit at the moment. There is also some confusion over who is being courted by Brandon—Marianne or Elinor. While some of these mistaken identities and surprises are in the novel, the film adaptation plays up the "comedy of manners" motif. One wonderfully comic scene is Edward Ferrars's calling on Elinor Dashwood in London, while Lucy Steele is visiting her. Neither lady is clear as to which of them is the object of his attention, while Edward is unsure of the degree of intimacy the two women share. Not only comic, these plot twists and confusions suggest the difficulty of courtship in this decorous world.

Metaphoric Use of Landscape. Most of Jane Austen's settings are indoors. In the film the scenes at Norland Park and in London are mostly interior scenes, which image order and refinement. Occasionally, characters are seen looking out the window at nature. Elinor, when seen out of doors, is set in landscaped nature, ordered and refined. Sue Parrill writes that the growing relationship between Edward and Elinor at Norland is conducted in an "Arcadian" setting. "The formal, placid beauty of Norland supports and reflects the character of the developing relationship between Edward and Elinor. Both are rational, restrained people whose love is warm but not passionate and whose behavior is as ordered as the setting in which they appear" (Parrill 34). Marianne, especially at Barton Cottage, is seen in nature that is wild and free, often in bad weather. Violent weather projects a sense of turbulent emotions. At Barton Cottage, the women are often seen out of doors, and often working, on the lawn, in the garden, or near the rushes. Their costumes, including aprons and straw hats, are less fine, more practical, reflecting their lower position in the world of Barton Cottage. Colonel Brandon's gift to Marianne of hothouse flowers suggests his conventional nature, while Willoughby's wildflowers symbolize a nature that flouts convention. At Cleveland, the Palmers' estate, Ang Lee's camera makes use of "a strange, twisted hedge which the filmmakers nicknamed the 'Brain Hedge.'" Symbolically, the misshapen hedge represents "Marianne's physical and emotional deterioration" (Thompson 286–87).

Houses. The homes of the characters are visual representations of their class and character just as Austen intends through her verbal descriptions. The panoramic views of Norland Park, with its large, expansive rooms, represent the daughters' open prospects for marriage. Barton Cottage, with its small spaces and isolated location, represents the narrow prospects of the daughters. Margaret's treehouse suggests "a room of her own." Margaret "owns" her treehouse, and her future prospects are wider, more open, than the narrow ones of Marianne and Elinor. Emma Thompson described the treehouse in the film as "palatial" (217). We can read it as representing Margaret's carefree youth, unbounded by the social conventions that restrict her older sisters.

Men and Horses. The film increases the sense of male virility, energy, and spirit with scenes of men on horseback. Likewise, men are more often out of doors than in the drawing room. Willoughby appears in the rain on a white horse, like a knight rescuing the maiden in distress, rather than walking with his hunting dog as he does in the novel. Emma Thompson's screen direction evokes a romantic hero: "Crash! Through the mist breaks a huge white horse. Astride sits an Adonis in hunting gear" (85). Likewise, Colonel Brandon gallops his horse away from his picnic to rescue Eliza and later rushes off to collect Mrs. Dashwood and bring her to Cleveland. Earlier he is viewed cleaning his guns while in conversation with Sir John Middleton. Edward Ferrars attempts to confess his engagement to Lucy in the stables among horses and later rides over to Barton Cottage to propose to Elinor.

The horses and guns intensify the robust physical presence of the male protagonists.

Music. In the novel music is an essential feature of Marianne Dashwood's sensibility. Likewise, it is a shared pleasure with Willoughby, a register of the degree of their intimacy, for they sing together regularly. According to Kathryn Libin, male performance was not revered in the period in the same way that musical accomplishment was for young women (190). Thus, Willoughby's "considerable musical talents" would suggest a frivolous and pleasure-seeking character, according to Libin. In the film, musical appreciation is assigned to Colonel Brandon, who falls in love with Marianne as he hears her sing and play. He is an accomplished musician, who offers himself symbolically to Marianne through the gift of the square piano. As Libin sees it, the film producers wished to show Willoughby in a negative, promiscuous light through other improper activities with Marianne since musical performance would not be seen in contemporary minds as untoward. Our culture tends to think of a man's love and appreciation of music as a sign of culture, refinement, and sensitivity. Thus, Brandon appeals to a contemporary audience as a more suitable match for Marianne because of their shared love of music.

Reading the Film
—Questions for Discussion and Writing

1. Analyze the character of Elinor Dashwood. How is her "sense" represented in the film through the performance of Emma Thompson? What other characteristics does she bring to the role? Does she appear on-screen as you imagined her in the novel? How is she more or less attractive than Austen's character?

2. Analyze the character of Marianne Dashwood. How is her "sensibility" represented in the film through the performance of Kate Winslet? What other characteristics does she bring to the role? Does she appear on-screen as you imagined her in the novel? How is she more or less attractive than Austen's character?

3. How do the performances of Hugh Grant as Edward Ferrars and Alan Rickman as Colonel Brandon enhance your understanding of the "romantic heroes" of the film? Are their performances consistent with Austen's description of the male characters? Are they made more or less attractive than Austen's characters?

4. What invented or additional scenes contribute to a fuller characterization of Edward Ferrars and Colonel Brandon in the film? What additional scenes suggest indiscretions and intimacy between Willoughby and Marianne?

5. How well matched are Edward Ferrars and Elinor Dashwood in the novel? Compare your perceptions with the Hugh Grant and Emma Thompson performances in the film. Are their film characters equally matched? Consider also the Colonel Brandon and Marianne Dashwood relationship from the novel and through the film presentations of Rickman and Winslet. Are they convincing?

6. Analyze the settings of the Norland Park scenes and later at Barton Cottage. How does the film visually represent class and wealth? What symbolic elements in the setting contribute to the understanding of characters?

7. Analyze how Margaret's character is enhanced in the film. How does she represent "the new woman" or feminist view in Thompson's screenplay? How does she misrepresent Austen's characterization of her as representing the dangerous influence of excesses of sensibility?

8. Consider the parallel scenes that contrast Brandon with Willoughby. How is the transfer of Marianne's love from one "heroic lover" to the other visualized in the film through invented scenes and other details?

9. What is the effect on the film of eliminating the scene from the novel wherein Willoughby visits Cleveland to explain his behavior to Elinor? Why did Austen choose to include this scene? How does it change or enhance your understanding of Willoughby's character?

10. Does Elinor change during the course of the film? If so, how is she changed? Is "sense" or "sensibility" a factor in her development of character in the film? How does the film manage this development? How do these changes reflect contemporary attitudes toward emotion, self-assertiveness, and restraint?

11. Analyze what Marianne learns from her experience with Willoughby in the film. How does she grow from the heroine of strong feeling, visible emotion, and self-indulgence to the mature but wounded Marianne who accepts the love of Brandon in marriage? How does the film manage this transition? How do these changes reflect contemporary attitudes toward emotion, self-assertiveness, and restraint?

12. What changes in the theme of romance and courtship were made to accommodate the taste and values of contemporary audiences? What is the overall effect of such changes? Look closely at the violations of courtship rituals in the Willoughby-Marianne case as presented in the novel. How would they be portrayed today? How does the film represent their courtship?

13. Analyze Edward Ferrars's relationship with Lucy Steele as played by Imogen Stubbs. How is Lucy characterized in the film? How is her lower economic and social class visually detailed? How is her rivalry with Thompson's Elinor Dashwood presented through gesture and facial expression?

14. Analyze the determinants of class in the film. How does a contemporary audience watching the film distinguish the highest classes from the lower, such as Fanny Dashwood versus Lucy Steele, or Fanny and the Dashwood sisters? Does the film use Austen-era determinants of class, or are contemporary determinants also evident?

15. A trend in the 1990s' film adaptations is the removal of characters from the drawing room to the lawn. What scenes are invented or changed to give the film a more out-of-doors look? What is the effect of these changes on character or theme? Do these changes seem an improvement over Austen's settings? What is gained or lost?

16. How would you account for the popularity of the Thompson *Sense and Sensibility*, even with viewers who have never read Jane Austen? Does the film glamorize Austen's world? Does the film depict a negative or unattractive side to life for the gentry? Are the lower and working classes or the poor represented in the film? What about Austen's world is made to appear more attractive on film?

17. Analyze the feminist implications of Austen's novel and the film adaptation. Consider how Marianne's qualities early in the novel would be evaluated today. Would she be considered as needing "correction" or praised for her fresh, expressive openness and emotion? Would Elinor be thought "wrong," in need of revision for her control, "sense," and self-denial? How has the Thompson film changed these characters' fates to comply with contemporary attitudes toward feminism? Are they consistent with Austen's views?

18. Examine the relationships between women in the novel and the film. Consider Marianne and Elinor, who are often at odds over essential issues, such as love, courtship, manners, money, and principles. Consider Lucy Steele and her relationship with Elinor. What motivates each in how she relates to the other? Consider Mrs. Dashwood and her relationship with her three daughters. Who is she most like? Whom does she most trust and admire? Consider Fanny Dashwood in relation to her half sisters-in-law, to her mother, to Lucy Steele, and to her stepmother-in-law. What motivates her behavior? Are the characterizations in the film adaptation consistent with Austen's presentation in the novel?

19. How is literature used in the film? Examine how novels, plays, or poetry are incorporated into the film. What seems to be the purpose of the literature? How does it enhance character or action? Are these same literary elements in the novel? How would you account for the changes from novel to film?

20. Austen's novels are told from an omniscient point of view with limits on the degree of interior consciousness. In other words, we know Elinor's thoughts in great detail throughout the novel, but we have no knowledge of what Edward, Willoughby, or Brandon are thinking except as revealed through their spoken words. How does the filmmaker handle this limited point of view? How does the film use the camera eye as a kind of limited omniscience? How does the filmmaker reveal Elinor's interior consciousness, and how is the omniscient narrator's commentary treated through visual or other means in the film?

21. Austen's novels are spare in their description of landscape, houses, and other settings. How is landscape used in the film? Is it merely a backdrop to the action or can it be read as symbolic in some way? Is it designed to captivate our interest in English countryside? Give examples.

22. In Austen's novel music plays a subtle but essential role. Marianne's love of music is a feature of her sensibility. Analyze how the novel uses music; then compare the novel with the film in terms of the scenes within the film where music has importance. Also, analyze the musical score and how it contributes to mood, character, and theme.

Film Credits

Sense and Sensibility
Adapted from the novel by Jane Austen.

Columbia Pictures Presentation. A Mirage Production 1995.

Screenplay by Emma Thompson.

Directed by Ang Lee.

Produced by Lindsay Doran.

Cast

John Dashwood	James Fleet
Mr. Dashwood	Tom Wilkinson
Fanny Dashwood	Harriet Walter
Marianne Dashwood	Kate Winslet

Elinor Dashwood	Emma Thompson
Mrs. Dashwood	Gemma Jones
Edward Ferrars	Hugh Grant
Margaret Dashwood	Emilie Francois
Mrs. Jennings	Elizabeth Spriggs
Sir John Middleton	Robert Hardy
Thomas	Ian Brimble
Betsy	Isabelle Amyes
Colonel Brandon	Alan Rickman
John Willoughby	Greg Wise
Curate	Alexander John
Charlotte Palmer	Imelda Staunton
Lucy Steele	Imogen Stubbs
Mr. Palmer	Hugh Laurie
Pigeon	Allan Mitchell
Maid to Mrs. Jennings	Josephine Gradwell
Robert Ferrars	Richard Lumsden
Miss Grey	Lone Vidahl
Doctor Harris	Oliver Ford Davies
Mrs. Bunting	Eleanor McCready

Pride and Prejudice

4

Between October 1796 and August 1797, Jane Austen composed *First Impressions*, which her father offered to Cadell for publication on November 1, 1797. *Pride and Prejudice* was published in 1813, after substantial rewriting during the previous year. Austen said of her revisions, "I have lop't and crop't so successfully, that I imagine it must be rather shorter than *Sense and Sensibility* altogether." What is uncertain, but likely, is that the earlier text she revised was *First Impressions* (see Chapman, "Introductory Note to *Pride and Prejudice*" xi–xiii).

Pride and Prejudice is undoubtedly Austen's most popular novel. Its heroine, Elizabeth Bennet, lives out the Cinderella story of the middle-class woman of small fortune who marries the handsome, rich "prince," Fitzwilliam Darcy. Elizabeth Bennet is often cited as the favorite Austen heroine and one of the most admired and beloved in the history of the novel. Her wit and intelligence, charm and beauty, and unwillingness to be compromised make her a role model for many young readers. Darcy, too, becomes for readers a dashing hero who possesses wealth, power, intellect, and sophistication but also strength of character in his willingness to admit his faults and correct his pride. More than a romance, the novel is appealing for the wit, vibrancy, and intellectual play of its characters and the ironic humor of its narrator. The central issue is how to marry for love and mutual esteem in a world that thinks of marriage primarily as a business proposition. Elizabeth Bennet asserts not only her right to choose her partner in marriage, a marriage of affection, but also her rights to respect, independence, and individuality. Who could not like the charming heroine who defends her sister at the possible expense of marriage to one of the richest men in England. At the same time, the hero, Mr. Darcy, grows more appealing as we see his growing fascination with Elizabeth. Like Elizabeth, we admire a man who values a woman not for beauty alone, but for "the liveliness of her mind." The dramatic play of the characters is further enhanced by the challenges of judgment and authority and the dangers of unregulated pride and prejudice. The novel also has some of the most delightful comic characters, including Mr. Collins, Mrs. Bennet, Miss Bingley, and Lady Catherine. Reading the novel makes us feel the care Austen has taken in the creation of even her flawed characters, from Mr. Bennet to Lydia and Mr. Wickham. On the whole, it is Austen's most accomplished performance.

Viewing the Novel
—Approaches to Teaching *Pride and Prejudice*

I include here a general discussion of the main issues, themes, and ideas in *Pride and Prejudice*. My "Approaches to Teaching *Pride and Prejudice*" complement the analytical questions that follow this discussion.

Courtship and Marriage. The subject of marriage is introduced in the famous opening sentence of the novel: "It is a truth universally acknowledged, that a single man in possession of a good fortune, must be in want of a wife" (*P&P* 3). The author's approach to the "truth" that opens the novel is ironic. The exaggeration of "universally acknowledged" points to comic undercutting; it is the families in the immediate neighborhood with single daughters of marriageable age who hold this view, and later we learn that it is specifically Mrs. Bennet, with five marriageable daughters, who acknowledges this as truth. The second sentence of the novel introduces another element into the marriage theme: the young man is considered "the rightful property" (*P&P* 3) of the families with single daughters. And later, the narrator tells us "the business" of Mrs. Bennet's life "was to get her daughters married" (*P&P* 5). *Business* and *property*, we learn, are very important elements in the marriage arrangements of this world.

Austen's tone is satiric, with the intended effect to mock those whose approach to the "business" of marriage is either of two extremes: to marry to make one's fortune or to marry out of passion or lust without regard to provision. As Lord David Cecil remarked, "It was wrong to marry for money, but it was silly to marry without it" (qtd. in Bluestone 126). Austen sets up contrasting models of the mercenary and the prudent, the avaricious and the discrete in her comic display of young people on the verge of matrimony.

One approach to the subject of courtship and marriage is to compare examples of couples married, rumored to be marrying, or courting with marriage ensuing. The fine line between the "mercenary" or "avaricious" intent of marriage and the "prudent motive," the marriage for comfort or security, can be explored, as well as the dangers of marrying out of passion or lust, without forethought regarding provisions for living. The Bennets are contrasted with the Gardiners while Elizabeth and Darcy are compared with Jane and Bingley, Charlotte Lucas and Collins, and Lydia and Wickham. Also, rumors of engagements and impending marriages between Miss King and Wickham, Elizabeth and Wickham, Bingley and Georgiana Darcy, Darcy and Anne de Bourgh, and Collins and Elizabeth make interesting explorations of the marriage issue and its relation to "business."

The stages of courtship are also detailed in the novel: true affection or love results from respect, esteem, and gratitude that are allowed to grow and develop over a period of time. Had Elizabeth accepted Darcy's first proposal of marriage, it would have been without real respect on either side. Respect and mutual esteem form the foundation of successful relationships. The examples of the marriage relationships of the Collinses, the Wickhams, and especially the Bennets reveal the failure to achieve true affection because of lack of esteem for the marriage partner. Choices based on intelligence and good sense are revered, as in the case of Jane and Bingley who are compatible in their easy candour and amiability, while the Gardiners are both intelligent and sensible. Elizabeth sees how her playful manners, her "lively mind," can benefit Darcy, while his knowledge, education, and understanding will improve her mind. Austen privileges the rational choice, based on sound judgment and developed over time, in matrimonial decisions.

Related to the courtship/marriage plot is the role of parental responsibility or interference. Mr. Bennet evades responsibility with his daughter Lydia, while Mrs. Bennet's interference with Jane almost destroys her happiness and future with Bingley. Mr. Gardiner's aid in finding Lydia and arranging the marriage with Wickham as well as Mrs. Gardiner's advice to

Elizabeth concerning her attachment to Wickham are examples of responsible adult involvement. Lady Catherine's "usefulness" to Darcy and Elizabeth is an accident that grows out of her attempts to manipulate her nephew into marriage with her daughter.

Austen's theme for her marriage plot might be stated as "mutual respect and affection constitute the best and safest basis for marriage."

Issues of "Pride" and "Prejudice." As in *Sense and Sensibility*, Austen examines the problem of judgment in understanding those around us and especially in social relationships within a mannered and restrictive society. Knowing who is trustworthy is difficult for even "a studier of character" (*P&P* 42), as Elizabeth admits to being. She herself becomes a "study" in how wounded pride or vanity can distort normally sound judgment. Her "first impressions" of Mr. Darcy become a much more fixed judgment of his character than the prejudice he brings with him into the Hampshire countryside.

The novel's plot is organized around the progress of pride and prejudice and the eventual humbling and improved judgment of both characters, a complement to the growth in respect and affection that constitutes the marriage plot. Dorothy Van Ghent's diagram (105) of the plot of *Pride and Prejudice* is useful for showing the relationship of the two themes. She writes that the novel has a "pattern of antithetical balances" that constitutes its style (Van Ghent 104).

The conflict begins at the Assembly Ball with Darcy's insult to Elizabeth, pronouncing her as "tolerable; but not handsome enough to tempt [him]" (*P&P* 12), a remark that wounds Elizabeth's vanity and begins her prejudice against Darcy. The insult itself is a revelation of Darcy's pride. The rising action shows, as Van Ghent phrases it, "simultaneous opposition and union" (105). While Darcy believes his first impressions will be lasting, it is not long before "he began to wish to know more of her" (*P&P* 24). He watches her with fascination and discovers her face "rendered uncommonly intelligent by the beautiful expression of her dark eyes" (*P&P* 23). Within a few more days, he realizes he "had never been so bewitched by any woman as he was by her" (*P&P* 52), and even fears he might be in "some danger" of falling in love. Elizabeth's prejudice grows as she learns from Wickham of Darcy's purported ill-treatment and as she watches Jane suffer separation from Bingley. Meanwhile, Darcy's pride, born out of a prejudice against the middle classes, grows as he observes Mrs. Bennet's behavior and as he congratulates himself on separating Bingley from Jane, who doesn't appear to be in love.

Coincidentally, the relationship between the principles of pride and prejudice can be traced. Elizabeth "prides" herself on judgment and discernment, on her family, especially Jane and her father, and on her own value. This pride is the basis of her "prejudice" against Darcy, for her wounded vanity clouds otherwise good judgment. Likewise, Darcy's pride—in his family, his education, his fortune, and his value—predisposes him to see only the faults of the Meryton community, including Elizabeth.

At the same time, familiarity and mutual attraction lead to the climax of the novel, Darcy's first proposal. In a moment of heightened pride, he asks Elizabeth to marry him while reminding her of her inferiority. In her moment of greatest prejudice, she declines his offer and tells him that he is "the last man in the world" she "could ever be prevailed on to marry" (*P&P* 193). As Mary Lascelles writes, "This pattern is formed by diverging and converging lines, by the movement of two people who are impelled apart until they reach a climax of mutual hostility, and thereafter bend their courses towards mutual understanding and amity" (160).

After the marriage proposal, the characters appear to be at the point of greatest separation, but Darcy's letter prompts Elizabeth to examine the past and form a more favorable opinion of Darcy, lessening her prejudice. Darcy's opinion of Elizabeth is changed after her rejection of his proposal and their subsequent meeting at Pemberley. His willingness to write a letter explaining his behavior shows a lessening of his pride.

Once again, further separation seems likely with the elopement of Lydia and Wickham. However, it actually gives Darcy an opportunity to show Elizabeth how much he cares for her. For Elizabeth he humbles himself to the point of submitting to Wickham's blackmail so as to avert further damage to the Bennet sisters. Elizabeth understands his actions, and her gratitude reflects her changed feelings toward him, leading to the resolution, a second proposal, and union. The theme might be stated as "vanity as well as pride can distort good judgment."

Feminism and Education. The correlation of the pride and prejudice plot with the marriage theme results in changes in gender roles, for both Elizabeth and Darcy must be educated in relational politics as well as in moderating pride and overcoming prejudice. Elizabeth Bennet is her father's favorite daughter and closest to him in temperament and understanding, perhaps assuming the leadership role the absence of sons necessitated in the family. She prides herself on her "discernment," and on being a good judge of character. She is generally self-aware, but her own confidence in knowing and judging compels her to make quick and sometimes inaccurate judgments. Thus, her education involves refining her powers of judgment and at the same time learning more about herself.

Darcy's education is much more radical, for his failures to involve himself in social discourse, to restrain his judgments of people outside his circle, and to withhold presuppositions about class and character require serious adjustment. Ironically, it is Elizabeth who educates Darcy in how to act the "gentleman" and how to "please a woman worthy of being pleased" (*P&P* 369). Unconventional for novels of the time is the gender role reversal, for it is Darcy, with not only the power of his family, wealth, and position but also the authority that comes from being male, who must be schooled in social intercourse and courtship ritual by a young woman, one seemingly with little power, experience, or authority. This is perhaps the greatest source of Darcy's attraction to Elizabeth, that she is unconventional within her society and that she will not conform to the passive and submissive female role of "pleasing" the man. Her irony, impertinence, and playful, lively manners disguise an active and confident intelligence that overpowers and masters Mr. Darcy, educating him in ways his patriarchal father failed to do. He learns to think less well of himself, to involve himself with those outside his family circle, and to appreciate the partner he finds in a social class not his own.

Manners and Morals. Jane Austen, writing out of the tradition of the Comedy of Manners, uses wit and humor to mock affectation, hypocrisy, and pretensions. While the playwrights of the tradition in England employed caricature, exaggeration, stock characters, and elaborate and convoluted plots to satirize the follies of social behavior, Austen's moral intent addresses issues of human and social behavior on a more realistic plane. Her satire addresses the follies and vices of the middle and upper classes of all ages and professions in a fairly democratic way. Her characters are more fully developed than the caricatures or stock characters of the stage, and the problems of appearance and reality are played out in a realistic fashion. As in life, some of Austen's characters who appear amiable and well behaved prove to have the worst morals. The difficulty of knowing character in a world with highly defined social codes of behavior is evident. Having good manners becomes more complex than merely observing courtesy and ritual.

Some of the worst behavior can be found in the Bennet family. Lydia Bennet is an obvious example, for she is loud and unrestrained at home and in public. When her lack of restraint results in her elopement with Mr. Wickham, she exhibits no sense of shame and shows no evidence she will mature and become a responsible adult. She is incapable of improvement. Her mother is not much better. She, too, is loud, gossipy, self-indulgent, and, worst of all, mercenary in her attempts to marry her daughters to men of fortune. Like her youngest daughter, she feels no shame for what Lydia has done and even flaunts the patched-up marriage to her neighbors. Mr. Bennet's manners appear acceptable within his society, but in actuality, they prove costly to his daughters. His unwillingness to exert himself as a husband and father is his major flaw. He chooses the leisure of a country gentleman, preferring his library to the drawing room, allowing his wife the education of his daughters. His philosophy— "For what do we live, but to make sport for our neighbours, and laugh at them in our turn?" (P&P 364)—is very cynical and an abnegation of his responsibilities. Elizabeth, like her father, loves to laugh, but to see one's purpose in life as mocking others and enduring their scorn in turn denies the moral dimension in human relations. Mrs. Bennet's counterpart in the upper classes is Lady Catherine. She, too, is a mother who wishes to marry her daughter well: engaging her to Darcy while both are in the cradle epitomizes the scheming for fortune some parents resorted to. Her promotion of her daughter is equally as bad as Mrs. Bennet's, but she excels in bad manners through her self-importance and domination as she interferes in her nephew's affairs, controls the Collinses' household after insisting Mr. Collins marry, and attempts to rule Elizabeth's life as well. She is ostentatious and showy in her home and dress, ungracious and critical of those beneath her, domineering over her equals, and trivial and officious in her conversations.

In another category are two of Elizabeth's suitors, whose manners on the surface seem to be amiable and generous. Mr. Wickham, Elizabeth recalls, "must always be her model of the amiable and pleasing" (P&P 152). Later, he becomes the model of the mercenary as she learns of his attempted elopement with the wealthy Georgiana Darcy, efforts to secure Miss King's fortune, and eventual elopement with Lydia Bennet to extort money from Darcy once again. Elizabeth's early summation of his pleasing manners must be taken in the context of her prejudice against Darcy, for his poor manners in deriding Darcy behind his back and his hypocrisy in representing himself as the wronged party make even the generous Jane Bennet wary. If Charlotte Lucas and Mrs. Gardiner suspect his motives, Elizabeth should have mistrusted them as well. Eventually, Elizabeth reevaluates Darcy and Wickham and declares, "One has got all the goodness, and the other all the appearance of it" (P&P 225). While not so immoral as Wickham, Mr. Collins rivals him for hypocrisy. Austen creates in Collins the model of the toady, as he practices compliments to toss off casually to his patroness, appearing humble while thinking himself clever. "Not a sensible man," but "a mixture of pride and obsequiousness, self-importance and humility" (*P&P* 70), Mr. Collins is one of the great comic fools of literature, original and complex in his ability to surprise readers with new examples of his undeserved sense of good fortune while maintaining the guise of servile humility.

Finally, the manners of the novel's hero and heroine require examination. As discussed above, Darcy must learn to exert himself to please others if his manners are to be considered "gentleman-like." What defines his "heroism" in the novel is his willingness to change, to humble himself, to consider how his manners affect others, especially Elizabeth. He feels embarrassed by his aunt's domineering behavior and understands how Elizabeth must feel in the context of her own family. He identifies with the shame of having a sister elope with a man of questionable worth. Elizabeth attests to his value when she says of him, "in a cause of compassion and honour, he had been able to get the better of himself" (*P&P* 327). Darcy combines intelligence, judgment, and education with moral responsibility.

The same qualities are what make Elizabeth so attractive a character. She, too, is proud, but when she learns how blind she has been in judging her own family, and especially in recognizing the worth of Mr. Darcy, she experiences mortification and shame. She tempers her wit and avoids the cynicism of her father. Elizabeth takes responsibility for her bad manners and reconsiders her relationship to others in society—qualities of a socially responsible adult. At the same time, Elizabeth is admirable because she demands respect, importance, and independence within a society that sets strict rules for social behavior.

Viewing the Novel —Questions for Analysis and Discussion

The questions below address the larger issues of each volume and are designed to promote analytical thinking as the basis for discussion. These questions ask students to "see" into the text and complement the central issues of "reading the film" that follow.

Volume I

1. How are the five Bennet daughters distinguished from each other? How do you envision each?

2. What scenes most reveal Elizabeth Bennet's dominant character traits? What is the basis of her friendship with Charlotte Lucas?

3. How are Mr. Darcy and Mr. Bingley distinguished from each other? What are the strengths and weaknesses of each? Which scenes are most revealing of their characters? What is the basis of their friendship?

4. What is Charlotte Lucas's attitude toward courtship and marriage? Is her philosophy "sound"?

5. Why does Elizabeth find Mr. Collins so unattractive? What is particularly offensive in his proposal to her? What reasons does he give for wanting to marry Elizabeth?

6. What does Elizabeth's rejection of Mr. Collins reveal about her attitudes toward marriage and a marriage partner? Why is marriage to Collins "impossible"?

7. Why does Elizabeth find Mr. Wickham so attractive? Is there evidence that he is not forthright and honest about his history with Mr. Darcy? How is her pride and prejudice a factor in her judgment?

8. How is the Netherfield Ball an embarrassment for Elizabeth? How does it further Darcy's pride? How does the Netherfield Ball further the "courtship" of Elizabeth and Darcy? What changes in their initial feelings and first impressions are evident? Consider how Elizabeth's embarrassment for her family relates to her feelings for Darcy.

9. Why does Charlotte Lucas accept Mr. Collins' marriage proposal? Why does Elizabeth first think it "impossible" that Charlotte would marry Collins? How will her marriage to Collins benefit her and the Lucas family?

10. Examine Mr. and Mrs. Bennet as parents. How do they promote or harm their daughters' chances for marriage and happiness?

Volume II

1. When Elizabeth visits the home of the Collinses in Hunsford, what is her perception of their married life and situation? Is it different from her expectation?

2. What is the role of Lady Catherine in the Collinses' domestic life? How does Lady Catherine's parenting compare with the Bennets'?

3. How are Lady Catherine's manners an embarrassment to Darcy? Examine the scenes at Rosings. What are her prejudices?

4. How is the "courtship" of Darcy and Elizabeth furthered by their being away from their homes? What changes in their attitudes and feelings occur during this period?

5. How does Darcy's proposal represent the pinnacle of his pride? What is offensive to Elizabeth in his proposal?
6. How does Elizabeth's rejection reveal her prejudices? What is offensive to Darcy in her rejection? What does her rejection reveal about her attitudes toward a marriage partner?
7. Mr. Darcy's proposal has much in common with Mr. Collins.' Examine how the proposals compare and contrast. Include Elizabeth's responses in your analysis.
8. What does Mr. Darcy reveal about his character and his feelings for Elizabeth in writing her a letter? What evidence of his pride and his prejudices does it reveal? Is there evidence of the abatement of pride?
9. Is Darcy just in his defense of breaking up Bingley and Jane? What is the evidence he used to make his judgment?
10. In how many ways has Elizabeth, who "prided herself on her discernment," been blinded by prejudice? Who has she misjudged? Why was she so blind? Where did she place her "vanity"?

Volume III

1. How do the Gardiners provide surrogate parenting to Elizabeth and Jane Bennet?
2. How do you envision the house and grounds of Pemberley as compared with those of Rosings? How does Pemberley reflect Darcy's character?
3. Why is the testimony of Mrs. Reynolds so important to Elizabeth's understanding of Darcy?
4. How is Darcy changed at Pemberley? What is the role of the Gardiners?
5. How is Georgiana Darcy different from Elizabeth's expectations of her? What does Elizabeth learn about her own judgment and the nature of prejudice through this meeting? What more does Elizabeth learn about Darcy through her meeting with his sister?
6. Trace the progress of Elizabeth's feelings for Darcy after her admission that "until now I never knew myself." What is the role of "gratitude" in her changed feelings?
7. Why does Elizabeth fear the elopement of Lydia and Wickham will end Darcy's attachment to her? How does it actually become the means to a second proposal of marriage from Mr. Darcy? What is Lady Catherine's role?
8. How does Darcy's involvement in the "saving" of Lydia show the abatement of his pride? How does it relate to his own experience with his younger sister?

9. In what ways has Elizabeth proven herself most like her father? In what ways is she different? Why does Mr. Bennet warn Elizabeth against marrying Mr. Darcy? What has he learned from his marriage to Mrs. Bennet and the elopement of Lydia?

10. How does the marriage of Elizabeth and Darcy represent the ideal of marriage? What are the roles of "esteem," "respect," and "gratitude"? Why is their marriage superior to the relationship of Jane and Bingley?

Reading the Film
—Approaches to Teaching the Film

Choosing a Film Adaptation

Film analysis of the adaptations of *Pride and Prejudice* presents special problems. First of all, there are three excellent videos to choose from, each with its own strengths and weaknesses. Thus, it may be difficult to decide on a single film to use in class. Second, two of the adaptations are TV mini-series, intended for viewing over several sittings. The 1979 version was originally divided into five parts, spanning 226 minutes, and the 1995 version was shown in six parts, covering approximately 300 minutes. Unless there is opportunity for showing the films outside of class, most courses would be limited to showing only segments of the films. The third problem is that the one feature film adaptation, while only 114 minutes long, is from 1940 and considerably dated. While it is truer to Austen in many respects than the longest, most inclusive version (1995), it reflects the values, political and aesthetic, of a very different era. The debate continues over which of the films is superior.

1940 Feature Film. Elsa Solender, in the keynote address at the 2002 JASNA conference, quoted Joseph Epstein from a review called "Reel Literature" as saying the 1940 *Pride and Prejudice* was "the best movie ever made from a novel" (Solender 105). While some viewers may object to the lack of fidelity to the original, the film has what Epstein thinks is far more important: "It's magic . . . pure magic" (Solender 105). The most egregious violation is the "eros ex machina," Solender's term for the Lady Catherine collusion with Darcy to bring about his marriage to Elizabeth. This version also deletes the visit to Pemberley since the Greer Garson Elizabeth has already fallen in love with Darcy before the visit to the Collinses, thus rendering the visit to Pemberley unnecessary (Ellington 102). As George Bluestone notes in his excellent analysis of this film, the changes and addenda to the film "do not . . . alter any of the essential meanings in the original. The Huxley-Murfin additional dialogue bears an unusual ring of probability. It represents the kind of thing which Jane Austen *might* have said" (130). Indeed, this fidelity to the spirit and ideas of the original is its main strength. Overall, it does an excellent job of consolidating scenes to fit everything into two hours. Scenes that are taken from the first sixteen chapters are conflated into the Assembly Ball sequence (Bluestone 131). Bluestone's analysis focuses on the dance as the key to all relationships, events, and themes in this film, an excellent study of the use of the visuals of film to carry the weight of the language of the novel. Elsa Solender also notes the high comic spirit of the film. This version is undoubtedly the funniest of the three (Solender 106).

1979 BBC Mini-series. Most "critics" and "fans," judging by the various responses on Internet listservs, strongly favor one mini-series version over the other, but the comments seem to fall into two broad categories. The 1979 version is more popular with those who favor fidelity to the original. This version is cited for its interior drawing room settings, which is more consistent with Austen's novel, giving the film a theatrical stage appearance. The preference for Elizabeth Garvie as Elizabeth Bennet is the other strong response, while detractors argue that David Rintoul's reserved and haughty Darcy lacks appeal. Elizabeth Garvie's singing is a beautiful element of the film. Her music is a siren's call, and as she sings and plays, Mr. Darcy's fascination with her is manifest in his gaze and movements toward the piano. Critics of this production fault the performances as stiff and unemotional, lacking the overt passion and sexual energy of the 1995 version. In terms of fidelity to the spirit of Austen's novel, this restraint of the visible display of emotion would be considered the best manners. It is also consistent with the Austen text where the powerful sexual and emotional attraction between Darcy and Elizabeth is hidden from everyone, even themselves. Elsa Solender praises the BBC serialization of *Pride and Prejudice* in 1979 as the only successful adaptation of the BBC series begun in 1971: "For me, the 226 minutes of *P&P* . . . pass all too quickly" (107). Like the 1940 film, the Fay Weldon script has "the ring of possibility," and created dialogue is often indistinguishable from the language of the Austen novel. On the negative side, the series is faulted for the cinematic simplicity, which gives the appearance of an amateurish video or low-budget production, lacking the glamour and glitz of the more elaborate and costly Birtwistle production.

1995 BBC Mini-series. Those who favor the 1995 version of *Pride and Prejudice* admire it for the grandeur of its scenes, the costumes and great houses, and other production features. Colin Firth's Darcy, handsome, brooding, and sexy, complements the paler, smiling Jennifer Ehle as Elizabeth. The Firth Darcy is often given top billing in promotions. One reviewer derides Ehle's depiction of Elizabeth as "cuddly" (Alleva 18), while I find her a bit too confident and smirky. In production this series was referred to as "a six-part adaptation of simply the sexiest book ever written" (Birtwistle vi), and the series follows up this claim with scenes of Darcy in his bath, Darcy diving into a stream to quell his passion, Wickham as a young rake at university, and Wickham and Lydia in bed together in London. Language has been modernized, making it more "readable" or accessible than the earlier mini-series. The lesser characters—Mrs. Bennet, Lydia Bennet, and the Bingley sisters especially—tend toward caricatures of their novel counterparts. Their bad manners are made more extreme for comic effect, intensifying for modern audiences their lack of propriety in Austen's decorous society.

Using Film in the Classroom

While choosing one version over another begins as a matter of preference, the decision is also based on what purpose an instructor has in using the film. My approach is partly determined by the course I'm teaching at the time. I have a preference for the 1979 version because of its fidelity to the spirit of the original and its appealing cast. Due to the length of the video, I use three representative segments: the opening scene through Jane Bennet's illness and recovery, which provides an opening into reading the text as students can visualize characters, dress, and settings, and can hear the language. The second segment I show is Elizabeth's visit to the Collinses and Darcy's first proposal through the reading of his letter to Elizabeth. The clownish Mr. Collins and Charlotte serve to contrast for students Elizabeth's relationship with Mr. Darcy. Darcy's first proposal and Elizabeth's response brilliantly expose the hostility of each at this climactic moment in the novel, and Darcy's voice-over as Elizabeth reads his letter begins the softening of the pride and prejudice each has displayed. The film is an excellent representation of Elizabeth's spirit and Darcy's passion. Finally, the visit to Pemberley, which shows the more civil, "gentlemanly" Darcy, is valuable for students. They will have seen Lady Catherine's ostentatious home at Rosings, and the contrast with Pemberley reveals Darcy's more natural self.

Another approach I find successful is to select a specific scene, such as the Netherfield Ball, Darcy's first proposal, or the visit to Pemberley, and view that scene from the two mini-series. For example, I show Mr. Collins' proposal scene from all three films and compare the film scenes with the text. I then show Mr. Darcy's proposal scene from the three films and compare the film scenes with the text and with the Collins' proposal. Another option I might use is to compare one scene from the novel, such as Mr. Darcy's proposal, with the same scene from one film. The class then discusses how Darcy's indirect speech from the novel's proposal scene is "invented" for the film versions. We also discuss how Mr. Darcy's "pride" and his passion collide during his proposal and how Elizabeth is both flattered and offended by his mode of proposing. Many options are possible here, depending on what outcome you set for your students. Not only is comparison with the novel valuable, but also comparison among the adaptations is possible as well with this approach.

Individual Film Analysis

Because the 1995 mini-series is the most recent adaptation, I give it the most extensive analysis.

1940 Feature Film

Casting and Characterization. I find the Laurence Olivier Darcy (1940) to lack both the hauteur of David Rintoul's Darcy (1979) and the sexual attractiveness of Colin Firth's (1995). Olivier as Darcy tends to laugh too easily, suggesting he is too quickly won over by Elizabeth. Greer Garson is beautiful, poised, and charming but a bit old for the part of Elizabeth. Certainly the change in Lady Catherine in the same film is a violation of the character Austen created, for she conspires with Darcy to convince Elizabeth to hear his second proposal. As a whole, the obstacles to their marrying seem less formidable than in either mini-series. The 1940 Jane Bennet, played by Maureen O'Sullivan, is my preference as the most beautiful, sweet, and attractive Jane. Mrs. Bennet is a silly, nervous, hypochondriacal busybody, well played by Mary Boland. Her Mrs. Bennet is an excellent comic portrayal of the conniving mother competing to marry off her daughters. Edmund Gwenn as Mr. Collins is delightful, although his role has been changed from clergyman to librarian, more suited to the high comedy of this film and in keeping with the Production Code of the time (Bluestone 142). One of his excellent comic scenes is his examination of the merits of the Bennet sisters through his monocle.

Notable Deletions. The Gardiners and their journey with Elizabeth to Pemberley are eliminated. By deleting the Gardiners and their visit to Pemberley, the contrast between the grandeur and ostentation of the Rosings estate and the simple elegance and naturalness of Pemberley is not visually represented. George Bluestone contends, "everything we need to know about the taste and luxury of Darcy's life we learn from the physical trappings at Lady Catherine's house in Hunsford" (140). I would call this a misreading of Austen's novel, since at Pemberley, Elizabeth learns how very different Lady Catherine's taste and lifestyle are from Darcy's. This visit is an important part of her moral education, for here she begins to understand how character is reflected in lifestyle. The association of Elizabeth with her well-mannered and intelligent relatives, the Gardiners, is also part of Darcy's education.

The most radical change involves Lady Catherine's collusion with Darcy, which the film uses as an opportunity to prove Elizabeth is not a gold digger, for Lady Catherine threatens to cut off Darcy's fortune if he marries her. If this is Darcy's concern so late in the game, we would wonder if his respect for her is really sufficient for a second proposal.

Happy Ending. The film ends on a happy note with not only the dual marriages of Elizabeth and Jane but also the seeming financial success of Lydia and Wickham with their coach and liveried servants, and the prospects of good marriages for Kitty and Mary as well. The ending of Austen's novel is not so hopeful, as marital strife, economic problems, and unhappiness mark Lydia's marriage to Wickham. The other two Bennet daughters are left without prospects when Jane moves north with Bingley to escape the interference of her mother, leaving the two girls to fend for themselves without the assets of beauty and intelligence that Elizabeth and Jane capitalized on in their marriages.

Costuming. Costumes resemble those of the later Victorian era with full-skirted, cinched-waist gowns. Elizabeth does show an empire gown (popularized by Georgiana, the Duchess of Devonshire) in her collection when visiting Charlotte, telling her she couldn't let her mother see it. The dresses overall are very modest, unlike the exposed bosoms of the racier 1995 miniseries.

Visual Symbols. The dance sequences and gaming are metaphors for the ritual of courtship. Also, the carriage race at the opening suggests the competition for husbands that Mrs. Bennet and Mrs. Lucas wage. Another early scene of Mrs. Bennet strutting like a clucking hen through Meryton followed by her flock of daughters is visually echoed in the 1995 film as the Bennets with all five daughters parade through town on their way to church. The archery scene in the 1940 film has Darcy attempting to teach Elizabeth the sport, but she bests him, suggesting not only gender equality but also that the pointed barbs of her wit have hit the mark.

1979 BBC Mini-series

Casting and Characterization. For me, Elizabeth Garvie, with her "fine eyes," and David Rintoul, with his distant but obsessive gaze, generate a kind of chemistry that makes them the quintessential Elizabeth and Darcy. Rintoul's haughty, distant, and awkward Darcy seems in keeping with Austen's creation, although he has a formality and stiffness that is often uncomfortable to view. His feisty arguments with Elizabeth testify to the attraction/resistance that is the essence of their courtship. Only the 1979 version retains a Darcy with a heightened sense of his own worth, a posture solidified by his reticence to speak and his arrogance when he does. The performances of Jane (Sabina Franklyn) and Mrs. Bennet (Priscilla Morgan) are excellent, and fidelity to the original characterization is a strength of this production. Sabina Franklyn is a sweet, pretty Jane, not unintelligent but less of a presence than her lively sister. Priscilla Morgan's fits of nerves and high voice are just annoying enough for the part, but not over the top. Her comedy is foolish without losing the realism of her character.

I would single out the casting of Malcolm Rennie as Mr. Collins for particular praise. This Collins avoids excess while portraying the foolish but arrogant and self-righteous clergyman. Austen's irony in her characterization is that he is "Christian," a holy man, yet intolerant, narrow, and avaricious. He is a comic fool, not "a sensible man" but not a clown either. While not repulsive, he is both arrogant and humble, foolish yet a not "impossible" match for Charlotte Lucas. Rennie's performance captures that fine line remarkably well. Likewise, Bingley is a wonderful creation, as he must be handsome, intelligent, and affable but not clownish or arrogant. He must represent less than Darcy but more than Jane and, at the same time, be not too much different from either. This Bingley has some dignity and much affability. The wry, irascible Mr. Bennet, portrayed by Moray Watson, is often hiding behind a book or away in his library, a kind of eighteenth-century scholar-gentleman. Watson plays the role with the emotional distance necessary to depict Austen's figure of a father who fails to be actively concerned for his daughters' welfare. He delivers his lines in a wry, satiric way that is consistent with the novel. Likewise, Judy Parfitt's Lady Catherine is perfectly domineering, superior, and overbearing in her interference in the lives of those around her.

Narration and Point of View. The voice-over is used in the 1979 mini-series to depict what is rendered as indirect thoughts in the novel and especially for the many letters in the novel. An effective example is the scene in which Darcy's voice-over is heard as Elizabeth reads his letter following the first proposal. While Elizabeth sits alone in the park at Rosings, the camera follows Darcy as he walks farther and farther away from her. The increasing physical distance between them as Elizabeth reads his defense of his behavior suggests the widening emotional distance between them. Elizabeth's thoughts are presented as voice-over as she recalls the incidents he alludes to. At the same time, superimposed images, such as the smiling face of Wickham or her sisters' wild behavior at Netherfield, appear to indicate her memory of the events. Since the novel contains many letters, the voice-over is used often as we view the writer at her desk or the recipient reading the letter.

Music. Like many Austen heroines, Elizabeth Bennet is proficient at the piano. In the novel we read of performances by her sister Mary, by Mrs. Hurst, and by Georgiana Darcy. In this adaptation, Darcy's fascination with Elizabeth is dramatized through his attention to her singing and playing the piano. As she plays, the camera pans to Darcy and follows his slow movements closer to the instrument. He appears mesmerized by her song. The moody piece she plays at Hunsford Parsonage reflects her as-yet-undiscovered feelings for Mr. Darcy. There are also conversations about musical accomplishments that occur with Miss Bingley, Mr. Darcy, and Lady Catherine de Bourgh, who brags, "If I had ever learnt, I should have been a great proficient" (*P&P* 173). These conversations highlight the class differences between Elizabeth's more middle-class education and the sophisticated training provided to the Bingley sisters and Georgiana Darcy. The many balls, musical performances, and country dances also contribute to the courtship motif of the novel.

1995 BBC Mini-series

Casting and Characterization

Jennifer Ehle, in the 1995 mini-series, is an attractive Elizabeth Bennet. She exudes confidence and intelligence, setting her apart from all her sisters and her mother. She never appears intimidated or frightened by Mr. Darcy and his set, perhaps displaying a bit more security than her situation merits. In fact, I would fault her performance for fitting Darcy's declaration about Jane: "she smiled too much" (*P&P* 16). Instead of confidence in her own judgment and intellect and an ironic view of the world that makes her laugh at follies, this Elizabeth tends to smirk and sneer as if she knows exactly how this story will end. And in spite of the intense gaze of the Colin Firth Darcy, I failed to discern a charisma or attraction between them. A characteristic gesture of Ehle's is free use of her hands. She never carries a parasol or bag or parcel. Often she holds her arms behind her, swings her arms freely, or crosses them in front of her (as in the library after Collins' proposal). The gesture seems more appropriate to the manner of a contemporary woman than one from this era and symbolizes her freedom, spirit, independence, and feminist lack of restraint. Her predominant facial expressions, the visual component of the repartee or inner consciousness of the novel, include a smirk, a sneer, a pursed lip, a roll of the eyes, a raised eyebrow, or a huff of exasperation. She sometimes simply walks away from someone in mid-sentence. While these are film gestures designed to portray irony, annoyance, or distance from those around her, they can also be construed as bad manners in this or any period, and Austen's Elizabeth conforms to the best manners of her age. Her pacing and agitation, walking and running, are designed to represent cinematically her sexual energy, which in the Austen novel is rendered through intellectual or verbal energy, her wit and "the liveliness of [her] mind" (*P&P* 380).

For many viewers, the Colin Firth Darcy is the strongest feature of the 1995 adaptation. His smoldering Byronic figure, struggling to repress his sexual attraction to Elizabeth, is perhaps a reflection of the contemporary emphasis on strong, virile men of feeling. Rather than a struggle to humble his pride, the battle appears to be to repress his sexual longings. In the novel we learn that Darcy admires and watches Elizabeth constantly. In the film he states in his first proposal, "almost from *the earliest moments* (italics mine) of our acquaintance, I have come to feel for you a passionate admiration and regard" (Davies script). Unlike the novel where we learn, as does Elizabeth, only gradually of Darcy's attraction to Elizabeth, in the film the disclosure is visible from the start. As Cheryl Nixon notes, "The films prematurely resolve rather than heighten . . . conflicts; masculine emotional display makes the final pairing of hero and heroine obvious, removing the narrative suspense of a relationship hindered by social restraint" (25). Thus, Austen's standard of male conduct, of restraint in expressing emotion in courtship, is removed: "Each hero equates courtship with emotional restraint and proves his worth by enacting that equation until a climactic event forces an emotional display that, in turn, forces courtship into marriage" (Nixon 25).

Because we share Elizabeth's point of view in the novel, we observe that Mr. Darcy is a gentleman of class and consequence because he is self-controlled; he masters his feelings and longings, at least on the surface. His self-restraint is so strong that even Elizabeth is taken by surprise with his proposal. Darcy's battle with control is the primary conflict we see in this film as his struggle is depicted through the many added scenes. This Darcy is much more athletic and more often seen out of doors or in stages of undress than in the other film versions. His dominant facial expression is a scowl, which can be interpreted as either his sense of the wrongness of Elizabeth or his own "wrong" feelings of admiration and passion. Occasionally, he sneers, but he rarely laughs or smiles unaffectedly. Three times he is associated with water: once in his bath as he sees Elizabeth on the lawn playing with a dog, once as he bathes his face after writing the letter to exonerate himself of her charge of not behaving in a "gentleman-like" manner, and lastly as he dives into the lake at Pemberley. The three water scenes show Darcy at crucial stages of the battle between his passions and his reason, each marking progress toward a more open, civil, and feeling character willing to admit feelings for a woman considered less than his equal. In the novel, we are not privy to this development although we learn that it goes on off the page.

Among the performances of the supporting cast, I find Susannah Harker's Jane as one of the weakest. It is hard to believe Bingley would think her the most beautiful woman in the room, as she seems too lethargic and simple. Jane should have "excellent understanding" and be, at least, companionable to Elizabeth. Crispin Bonham-Carter as Bingley also smiles a great deal and has a fresh-faced youthful exuberance but not much more. I cannot imagine him as capable of a strong and deep affection. David Bamber's Mr. Collins is a bit overplayed, a bit too greasy, too smug and leering to fit the self-righteous Collins of the novel. Benjamin Whitrow as Mr. Bennet is somehow too small for this role. Austen's father figure is faulted for lack of involvement in his family, and the scenes created around Mr. Bennet in this version show him sitting with the family, reading among them, and walking into town together. I don't believe this warm and comforting father figure would tolerate the highly obnoxious and loud behavior of his daughters, which goes beyond silly to downright rude and obnoxious.

Changes from Novel to Film
(Significant Deletions, Additions, and Revisions)

Sexualized Darcy. The additional Darcy scenes in the 1995 mini-series are the obvious changes. Darcy is seen in his bath, playing at billiards, hunting, fencing, washing his face, and diving into a stream to quell his passion for Elizabeth. The scenes are designed to give Darcy more presence onstage than the novel affords. Louis Menand, writing in the *New York Review of Books*, notes that Darcy is given "a body," "a physical presence," "the erotically enhanced Darcy" (qtd. in Nixon 23). Cheryl Nixon's analysis of why the 1990s adaptations include more physicality and masculine presence concludes that the changes are concerned as much with the emotional display of feeling as with the interest in the flesh. "The films use a visual, indeed a bodily, vocabulary to express what is essentially an emotional redefinition of each character" (Nixon 24). For Nixon, the dive into the pool at Pemberley is a visual expression of Darcy's connection to nature, the cleansing of social prejudices, and the "rebirth of love for Elizabeth," a dramatization of the development of character to satisfy our contemporary need for "masculine emotional display" (24).

Lisa Hopkins, writing on the Darcy factor in this adaptation, asks the perennial question, "What do women want?" She answers, "Women authors [of romance] have delighted in creating male characters who crave the love of the heroines with an intensity . . . real men rarely experience. Perhaps, the deepest appeal of *Pride and Prejudice* lies in the extent to which it has exploited the medium of television to lend physical actuality to that fantasy" (120). Our need is not to understand Darcy in the abstract but to see him looking at and wanting Elizabeth. This interpretation of the "extra Darcy" suggests that the real shift in emphasis in this version is toward romance—the love story—away from the story of a man's pride and a woman's prejudice.

Addition of Servants. In the novel only Hill is mentioned as the housekeeper at Longbourne. In the film the staff is expanded as two servants assist in dressing Elizabeth and Jane, a manservant appears in the drawing room, and a gardener is seen tending the flowers and grounds.

Conceptual Integrity (Themes, Ideas, Spirit of Austen's Novel)

"Pride" and "Prejudice." The courtship and romance issues are central to all of the Austen film adaptations of *Pride and Prejudice*. What is less prominent is the "pride and prejudice" theme. The problem may be that in efforts to increase the presence of Darcy, his aloofness, distance, and superiority must be diminished. In the novel, Elizabeth has little exposure to Darcy, and when she does, they meet in settings that increase their awareness of the disparity in their rank and consequence. By putting them together in more everyday situations, the film diminishes Darcy's aura of consequence and Elizabeth's sense of inferiority. Thus, the filmmakers demote the importance of humbling pride and soothing wounded vanity and instead privilege the romantic quest to know the heart of the person. The "humanizing" of Darcy is less a humbling than a normalizing of the hero.

We might question whether the new Darcy and the changed Elizabeth in the 1995 mini-series aren't actually counter to Austen's ideas of sensibility. Austen's novels demonstrate that the open display of feelings, the failure to restrain violent emotions, was dangerous and fraught with consequences. In Austen's earlier novel *Sense and Sensibility*, Marianne Dashwood suffers physically and emotionally for her unrestrained passions and, especially, for revealing them so freely. Darcy, in this adaptation, is shown more often as a figure fighting to quell his passions, a man of nature more comfortable in the pool or engaged in athletics than in the drawing room or reading a book.

Elizabeth, too, is much more physically active in this adaptation than in earlier films or the way we generally think about her from reading the novel. Sue Birtwistle believes this is actually the creation Austen had in mind, for she writes, "she is a very active, lively girl, not just mentally but also physically. Again and again she is described as running out of the room, or rambling through the countryside, and so on. So there is this kind of tomboyish almost gypsy-ish quality to her, which we wanted to get across" (4). She goes on to say that this is probably what attracts Darcy: her "sexual energy" (Birtwistle and Conklin 4). As Nixon writes, "Watching these film adaptations, I cannot help but conclude that sensibility has won its battle" (41). While contemporary audiences find such a hero and heroine to be more attractive and "balanced," the fidelity to Austen's heroes is called into question.

The moral education of the heroine is also less prominent a feature in this film. While Ehle's Elizabeth appears not to like Darcy very much, she is quite early aware of his glance and of his presence. And while the film makes her change in feeling toward him obvious, the sense of her own wrongness in judgment, her "prejudice," seems not a major fault to be corrected. If she has "courted prepossession and ignorance" (*P&P* 208) in her relationship with Darcy, she appears not overly bothered by the sensation. The difficulty with any film is depicting introspection, self-analysis, and insight. In this film the bedroom chats between Elizabeth and Jane attempt to present this, but most often they merely advance the plot. We fail to see in this script the intelligent and contemplative Elizabeth.

Cinematic Technique: Reading the Visual Elements of the Film

Metaphoric Use of Landscape. While the 1979 mini-series is filmed more as a theatrical adaptation, with mostly interior scenes, the 1995 adaptation moves much of the film out of doors, and we see the Ehle Elizabeth skipping, running, and walking in all kinds of weather. Elizabeth, like Darcy, who plunges into the pool at Pemberley, is represented as one with nature, part of the natural rather than the artificial world. When he emerges from the pool, he walks through a field of wildflowers and meets Elizabeth. The indoor scenes of the earlier adaptation suggest a more formal, artificial drawing-room world than the romanticized nature scenes of the later film. In the 1995 mini-series, a church tower looms over the Longbourne house during many of the outdoor scenes. The tower is a backdrop to conversations that relate to marriage, such as after the tea party given to welcome Mr. Wickham to the neighborhood; when the Gardiners arrive at Longbourne to take Jane off to London, hoping to further her connection to Bingley; when Wickham and Eliza talk of Mr. Darcy as betrothed to Anne de Bourgh (tower bells sound); and when Mr. Bennet discusses Lydia's marriage arrangements with Elizabeth. Later, the double wedding of Elizabeth to Darcy and Jane to Bingley takes place in what we assume is the same church. Thus, the prospect of marriage to secure the future of the Bennet family is symbolized through the church tower rising over the landscape and the roofline of the house.

Houses. Houses are carefully chosen to reflect not only the wealth and consequence of the owners but also their attitudes toward themselves and their position in life. In the 1979 mini-series the contrast between the lifestyle of Rosings and Darcy's home at Pemberley makes the point that while Darcy is rich and worldly, he is not ostentatious and showy about his wealth as Lady Catherine is at Rosings. The 1995 adaptation shows Pemberley as a much grander estate than Rosings, but the naturalness of the house, the simple elegance, is not as dramatically contrasted as in the 1979 film.

Mirrors and Windows. Lisa Hopkins examines Darcy's looking out of windows at Elizabeth: "a recurrent and compelling image to build insight into his character and to build up a powerful erotic charge" (114). Looking out the window suggests also the movement out of the drawing room, into nature. The message is that sexual feelings are natural, while reason suppresses passion and natural urges. Thus, the film privileges nature and sensibility over artifice and sense. During the proposal scene, Hopkins notes that Darcy is seen in front of a mirror, but he does not look into it (114). Looking into a mirror is a conventional symbol for self-examination, and at this stage Darcy has not closely examined his own psyche.

Men and Horses. Austen rarely refers to men on horseback, but in the 1995 mini-series we see Darcy and Bingley on horseback on several occasions. Darcy's horse while at Netherfield is a dark brown, while Bingley rides a white horse, symbolic of the legendary hero knight who frees the poor lady from the tower. Later, when Darcy travels to Pemberley from London, he, too, is riding a white steed, emblematic of his approaching heroic "rescue" of Elizabeth. The scenes on horseback are wilder than in the 1979 version where Bingley is seen approaching Longbourne at a slow, steady pace. In this earlier adaptation, Darcy meets Elizabeth in the park at Rosings on foot, while the 1995 adaptation has him on horseback, making for a somewhat awkward encounter. These scenes can be read as representing sexuality, virility, and spirit, qualities demanded in a contemporary hero but less evident or missing entirely from the novel's characterization. In another example, as Elizabeth is returning by coach from her stay at Hunsford, she recalls Darcy's face as he spoke his love for her in his proposal: "I admire and love you." This visual memory is superimposed over the galloping feet and legs of the horses, a suggestion of her fomenting sexual energy.

Sports and Other Business. The men in this production are depicted as more athletic than in the previous films or the novel. We see Darcy as he is fencing, playing at billiards, hunting, riding, and swimming. In one scene at Netherfield, Elizabeth's presence distracts him, causing him to "scratch" at billiards. This is a visual allusion to a scene from the 1940 film where Bingley scratches the table because of his preoccupation with Jane. Elizabeth, too, is seen out of doors more often than in previous film adaptations: in addition to walking, we see her gathering and arranging flowers but seldom sewing or playing the piano as in the 1979 production. At one point we see Lydia and Kitty in a swing together with two officers, one behind and one in front. The girls are gleefully flirting with the officers as their bare legs are exposed. Sexual symbolism can be read in the swinging motion and the position of the officers. Lydia and Kitty are almost always in motion: running, bouncing, dancing, laughing, and giggling noisily. Increasing the sexual tone of the film, several scenes are shown in the girls' bedrooms as they are dressing or preparing their hair. In one scene Mr. Collins runs into Lydia in her underclothing on the stairs at Longbourne; only Mr. Collins is embarrassed.

Music. In this film adaptation, music serves a variety of functions quite consistent with the importance of music to the novel. Kathryn L. Shanks Libin sees this production as "musically the most successful" of the Austen films and notes that the "sound" of the eighteenth-century pianoforte is captured (192). (All piano pieces are performed by Melvyn Tan.) Her observations enlighten us about how music in film can represent the nuances of social class in Austen's novel. The country-dance band at the Red Lion represents a "different social plane" than the string and wind ensemble at the Netherfield Ball (Libin 192). Various pianos showcase the class of the homes in which they appear, from the square parlor piano in the middle-class homes of the Bennets, Lucases, and Phillipses to the grand style of piano seen at Netherfield, Rosings, and Pemberley (Libin 192). The contrast of Mary's "off-key renditions of humble sentimental tunes" to Mrs. Hurst's "too fast, flashy performance" of a Mozart piece vividly points to the class differences and the relative nature of "accomplishments" (Libin 193). In addition, the piece Elizabeth Bennet plays at Rosings is from the same sonata, played with more composure and expression, suggesting that Elizabeth is in the same sphere as Mrs. Hurst, only of a different style (Libin 193). Most famously, Elizabeth's performance of "Voi che sapete" from Mozart's *Marriage of Figaro*, which "describes the sensations of being in love for the first time," is most appropriate when sung at Pemberley on Georgiana's fine new instrument (Libin 193). Libin goes on to note that no musical performance is mentioned in *Pride and Prejudice* at Pemberley, yet this scene is consistent with the talk of music and is a symbolic representation of Elizabeth's "ennoblement," as Darcy must perceive (193).

Narration and Point of View. In the 1995 adaptation, more scenes from the letters are visualized. Since the scene is in the letter writer's memory, the rethe effect of the letter on the reader. For instance, when Darcy is writing to Elizabeth after the rejected proposal, his struggles to put his thoughts on paper are enacted. Then we see the flashback to the Cambridge days when Wickham's lascivious behavior and debauchery were first evident. Also, the scenes of Wickham's attempted seduction of Georgiana Darcy are re-created, giving her more of a presence in the film as well (Birtwistle and Conklin 11). When the scene shifts to Elizabeth reading the letter, Darcy's role in the breakup of Bingley and Jane is the visual subject. Lisa Hopkins suggests a connection between Darcy's memories of the overt sexual relations of Wickham and the apparent lack of sexual response he witnessed from Jane. According to Hopkins, "the whole question of sexual attraction and female desire is thus sharply highlighted" (116).

Andrew Davies reversed the order of the letter in the 1995 adaptation, putting the story of Wickham's debauchery first and his interference with Bingley second. Davies felt that Darcy began writing the letter out of anger, spurred by Elizabeth's defense of Wickham. In the film the visual begins with Darcy writing about Wickham, and scenes from Darcy's memory are reenacted; then Elizabeth is shown reading about Jane and Bingley, and the visuals represent what she remembers (Birtwistle and Conklin 10). This puts the camera focus first on the issue most important to Darcy, his past relationship with Wickham, and then on Elizabeth, who is most concerned with Darcy's treatment of Jane and Bingley.

To increase the presence of Darcy in the 1995 adaptation, the point of view is split between Darcy and Elizabeth. Darcy is shown watching Elizabeth with a brooding, longing gaze. In the novel both Elizabeth and Charlotte notice that Darcy is often watching her. While the novel's point of view is limited mostly to Elizabeth's mind, in the film we also see into Darcy's thoughts. His gaze, what he sees, becomes like a point of view shift away from the omniscient narrator and the female point of view that is Elizabeth's. Andrew Davies writes of "going backstage" to show the preparations his female characters make to appear beautiful in public and to hear their "behind the scenes" conversations. But a broader invention is the backstage scenes of Mr. Darcy and Bingley when Elizabeth is not present. Davies says, "I've really been telling [this story] as if it's a story about Mr. Darcy" (qtd. in Birtwistle and Conklin 3). Thus, we get such added scenes as Darcy with Wickham at Cambridge (shown as flashback), at home fencing, in London warning Bingley away from Jane, on the road to Pemberley, and in London again at the wedding of Wickham and Lydia.

Reading the Film
—Questions for Discussion and Writing

Note: these topics for discussion and writing are geared to the 1995 Andrew Davies film version of *Pride and Prejudice* unless otherwise noted. They can be adapted to the other film versions.

1. Note the casting of the characters, especially that of the two oldest Bennet sisters, and Bingley and Darcy. Are they appropriate to your "vision" of the characters from the novel? Are their speech and actions faithful to the novel? What gestures, facial expressions, and postures are used to reveal character?

2. Choose a proposal scene from the novel, and compare the screenplay with the novel. Mr. Collins' proposal in the novel is rendered entirely in direct speech almost as it appears in a screenplay. What wording or text is eliminated in the film, and what is added? Examine both Elizabeth's speech and Mr. Collins', and note changes. For instance, why do you think the term "rational creature" (*P&P* 109) was eliminated in the film version?

3. Trace the theme of pride and prejudice in the film. How is Darcy's pride visually presented? When does his pride lessen? Does he appear humbled at any single point, or is it revealed over time? How is Elizabeth's prejudice visually presented? The novel is essentially an indictment of Elizabeth's prejudice—her vanity, her misjudgments, her blindness to her family's faults as well as Wickham's. How does the film actually diminish Elizabeth's self-examination and "shame"? Consider Elizabeth's examination of her errors in judgment after reading Darcy's letter. Why is her self-examination with its emphasis on "reason" and "the rational" reduced in the film version? Analyze other instances where the theme of pride and prejudice is lessened in favor of the romantic story of courtship.

4. Examine the scenes of Darcy "at play" or involved in sports. What do these scenes contribute to your sense of his character?

5. Examine the symbolism of water used in the film. Consider whether it represents cleansing, quelling "fire" or passion, rebirth, or associations with the natural world.

6. Examine the "sexual" appeal of Darcy in the novel. While his presence is less obvious than in the film, he has a strong hold on the imagination. Consider his attraction to Elizabeth's face and "fine eyes," his fascination with her singing, his watching her from a distance. What about Darcy attracts Elizabeth to him (excluding of course the grounds of Pemberley!)? How does the film depict his fascination with her?

7. What role does music play in the film? How does music fit into the conception of the "accomplished" woman? How do Elizabeth, Georgiana Darcy, Miss Bingley, and Anne de Bourgh compare as musicians? How are they represented in the film?

8. Examine how scenes are removed from the interior setting of the novel to the exterior in the film. What opportunities for character development or enhancement do these exterior scenes provide? How does the movement out of doors enhance or detract from the world of the Austen novels, where we see young men and women dancing, reading, or playing cards but not much else?

9. Lydia's and Kitty's loud manners among the officers is "over the top" in the film. Mrs. Bennet, too, is loud and giddy. Why do you think the filmmakers played the characters this way? You might consider how the "bad manners" they exhibit in the novel would be judged today. Would the flirtation with the "red coats" be construed today as anything more than being "boy crazy"? Would their interest in walking to Meryton and buying new hats be any more than cruising the mall? How does the film make their bad manners fit a contemporary sense of bad behavior?

10. How does the feminist appeal of Elizabeth Bennet in the novel reveal itself in the film? How are her spirit, her rebellion, her independence, and her intelligence portrayed visually? Are these characteristics from the novel enhanced or diminished in the film?

11. How are the other female characters portrayed, especially Jane and Charlotte? Do they have the same "principles" in the film as we read in the novel? Early in the film Elizabeth and Jane talk about marrying for love. Jane hopes she will be able to marry for love, while Elizabeth asserts she will only marry someone she deeply loves. Austen sets Charlotte Lucas up as the woman forced by age and circumstances to marry for "security" and "a comfortable home." Is Jane's philosophy of marriage in the film closer to Elizabeth's or to Charlotte's? Do you think Jane would have married without love if her situation demanded it? Luckily, Jane finds the man who offers love *and* money, but does the film convey a sense that this is her choice, that she was an active participant in making Bingley fall in love, or does she appear to be a pawn in her mother's "chess matchmaking"? How consistent is the film's Jane with the Austen conception of her?

12. Examine the homes and settings in the film. How are the homes of Longbourne, Netherfield, Rosings, and Pemberley differentiated? Does Longbourne seem an appropriate home for the middle-class Bennets? Do the number of servants present in the Bennet home correspond to those in the novel? Would the

Bennet sisters have been likely to have separate bedrooms as in the film and maidservants to dress their hair, etc.? How does Netherfield Park compare with Longbourne? How does Rosings compare with Pemberley? How are the furnishings of the various houses signs of class and fortune? Does the film use houses and other settings as a revelation of character as well as class?

13. Consider the determinants of class in Austen's novels and the late eighteenth century: money, property, titles, ancestry, and inheritances. How are these conveyed through the contemporary medium of film? Note the luncheon the Bingley sisters serve Jane, with the lobsters and shrimp contrasted with the more prosaic meat and potatoes of the Bennet luncheon on the same day. How are the dresses of the Bingley sisters made more elegant than the gowns of the Bennet sisters? How is Lady Catherine dressed to entertain her guests versus Mrs. Bingley's dress at home? Is the film's visual of Mr. Bennet poring over bills and worried about expenses consistent with the Austen novel?

14. Does the film make visual reference to the working classes of the time? If so, how are they depicted and in what roles? Are these consistent with the novel?

15. How are the letters, reading and writing, treated in the film? What literary references and activities are incorporated into the film? Is Elizabeth characterized (visually) as a "great reader"? Are these additions or changes from the Austen novel?

16. Sue Birtwistle referred to Jane Austen's *Pride and Prejudice* as "simply the sexiest book ever written" (vi). What makes it sexy? Her film adaptation is designed to appeal to this interest in contemporary audiences. What from the novel that you would deem "sexy" is transferred to the film? What is added? How is Elizabeth's "sexual energy" visually portrayed? How is Darcy's?

17. One year elapses from the time Mr. Bingley first appears at Netherfield and the proposals of Bingley and Darcy. How is the passage of time rendered visually (and aurally) in the film? Is there a comparable narrative description in the text? What emotional effect do the scenes of time passing create?

18. How is Austen's satiric purpose revealed? Is the comic tone heightened or diminished in the film? What examples stand out?

Viewing the Novel/Reading the Film
—Comparative Screen Analysis

Marriage Proposals

The proposal scenes in the three film versions of *Pride and Prejudice* invite comparison and analysis. The three adaptations can be compared (or two similar scenes in the two mini-series); the proposal scene from the film can be compared to the novel's textual version; and one can compare the proposal of Mr. Collins with that of Mr. Darcy. In *Northanger Abbey, Sense and Sensibility,* and *Mansfield Park,* we learn of the proposals after the fact; in *Emma,* like *Pride and Prejudice,* the main character receives two proposals. In both of these novels, the first proposal is from a clergyman, is unexpected, and is unwanted. In *Pride and Prejudice,* we have the longest and most directly reported marriage proposals in all of the Austen novels. Coupled with the fact that Elizabeth rejects Darcy's first proposal, we have a second offer to consider.

The Proposals. While Elizabeth rejects both Mr. Collins and Mr. Darcy, she has more obvious reasons for rejecting Collins than for declining Darcy. While Darcy's character and qualities are certainly of greater merit than Collins,' Darcy's manner of proposing is not much more acceptable to Elizabeth than Collins.' Collins' insulting proposal is as offensive as the man himself, but Mr. Darcy's failure to propose in a "gentleman-like" manner demeans and insults Elizabeth in an even more discrediting way. Although Elizabeth is flattered by Darcy's proposal and eventually comes to understand him, and herself, well enough to accept a second offer, she is insulted and embarrassed by the proposal of Collins and never changes her opinion of him. The key element in the proposals of both Collins and Darcy that rankles Elizabeth is the lack of respect for her as a rational person with self-worth and value. Both Collins and Darcy fail to unite the rational and the passionate, the essential foundations of true affection.

Mr. Collins' "Rational" Offer. Mr. Collins begins by acknowledging Elizabeth's reluctance to hear him and flatters her (and himself) that her attractive "modesty," "a natural delicacy" (*P&P* 105), prompts her to spurn his attentions. But he then undercuts his compliment by reminding her that he has "authority" to speak from her mother. This reference is a reminder that Elizabeth has little power or choice in the matter of marriage. Mr. Collins puts his *reasons* for marrying first because his decision to marry is rational, based on arguments, not on feeling. He explains that he must give his reasons first, "before I am run away with by my feelings" (P&P 105). Elizabeth finds this laughable considering his attentions were first aimed toward Jane and only moved to her by default and that he has known her for only eight days. When he lists his reasons for marrying, it becomes clear, if Elizabeth doubted it before, that Mr. Collins is weak, controlled, and avaricious, and his emotions are bogus. First, he believes a clergyman should set a good example for his parish by marrying although it is unclear what kind of example it sets. Second, he says, "it will add very greatly to my happiness" (P&P 105). Of course, the conventional belief is that marriage and especially sexual relations were to please the man; it would be expected that Elizabeth's happiness would be in adding to his. And finally, he declares the real motive: Lady Catherine has ordered him to marry. Because Mr. Collins is not a relative or even a friend of Lady Catherine, he is at the mercy of her whims, for she can withdraw her patronage at her pleasure. Thus, Mr. Collins must court her favor to the point of allowing her absolute control over his (and his future wife's) life. His livelihood truly depends on submission to her will, and his proposal of marriage to Elizabeth is under her command. Mr. Collins presents his case as an advantage, for his wife will share in his bounty. She, too, will be recognized by Lady Catherine and thus share with him the fruits of patronage.

Debasing Elizabeth. Collins does caution Elizabeth that she may not be exactly the wife Lady Catherine would have chosen for Mr. Collins, and, therefore, she will have to make adjustments to suit Lady Catherine; "an active, useful sort of person" (P&P 106), frugal, silent, and respectful, is demanded. Collins is perceptive enough to know this is not truly the Elizabeth who sits before him, but he has other compelling reasons for choosing her: the fact that she is one of five Bennet daughters, likely to be somewhat desperate for a husband and desirous of keeping the entailed property in the family, furthers his suit. Thrice he refers to her as "my fair [or dear] cousin," a rhetorical address not so much of endearment as designed to prompt in her a sense of obligation to provide a means of keeping the estate in the Bennet family.

And Last but Not Least, His Feelings. Finally, Collins remembers to profess his feelings, actually relayed indirectly: "And now nothing remains for me but to assure you in the most animated language of the violence of my affection" (P&P 106). This is deliciously vague because we hear no actual statement of those sentiments. In fact, Collins never really recommends himself to Elizabeth. Instead, his mind races back to money, and he professes a disregard for dowry. This, too, is undercut by his full awareness of how paltry her share of family monies will be and how little her father can give, details that contrast unfavorably with the violent affection he professes to feel. Incredibly, he has calculated carefully not only her value to himself but also her lack of value to anyone else.

Elizabeth's Response. Elizabeth is remarkably patient in hearing him out, but when he presumes a favorable response— "when we are married"—she reminds him, "you forget that I have made no answer"(*P&P* 106). More likely, Collins, believing he has presented an extremely persuasive case, assumes that her answer is positive and thus need not be spoken. Elizabeth politely declines, expressing gratitude for the compliment of the offer, but twice she tells him it is "impossible" (*P&P* 107), "absolutely impossible" (*P&P* 109) that she would marry him. Later, when hearing that her friend Charlotte has accepted Collins, she exclaims, "impossible!" (*P&P* 124). Elizabeth cannot fathom that her friend Charlotte, or any *rational* woman, would consider such an offer. Elizabeth demands that she be heard as a woman of judgment and discrimination. Luckily, she has recourse to a voice that will be heard. She trusts her father for a "decisive" negative that will be believed. Unlike many young women of the time, she has her father's parental power and authority to authenticate her thoughts and feelings.

The Film Adaptations

Rational "Creature" or Elegant Female. The Andrew Davies script (1995) maintains much of the original dialogue from the novel. Some of the omissions are mere redundancies, which serve only to increase the comedy of Mr. Collins' arguments. However, lines that express Elizabeth's struggle to be heard are omitted. In the novel she pleads with Collins: "You must give me leave to judge for myself, and pay me the compliment of believing what I say. . . . This matter may be considered, therefore, as finally settled" (*P&P* 107–8). Later, she says, "I would rather be paid the compliment of being believed sincere. . . . Do not consider me now as an elegant female intending to plague you, but as a rational creature speaking the truth from her heart" (*P&P* 108–9). Calling herself "a rational creature" is Elizabeth's plea for equality in rational argument. It is an avowal of her unwillingness to be silenced or to be thought insincere and unfeeling.

This juxtaposition of the "rational" and the "elegant" or refined female appears in the later novel *Persuasion*. The hero of *Persuasion*, Captain Wentworth, assumes that women of refinement could not withstand the arduous life on board a ship. His sister calls this thinking nonsense and contrasts "fine ladies" with "rational creatures" (*P* 70). The determiners of "fine" or refined include submission, reticence, docility, modesty, and "sweetness of manner." Conversely, rational would suggest strength of mind and will, decisiveness, confidence, intellect, and judgment. Mr. Collins persists in thinking of Elizabeth as a refined lady, whose "delicacy" will bring her to submission, and therefore, not a woman of will and judgment. Deleting her claim to "rationality" from the Davies script makes Elizabeth's rejection less forceful in anticipating the proposal by Mr. Darcy. Darcy, like Mr. Collins, approaches Elizabeth confident of her acceptance, submission, and silence. Not surprisingly, he, too, faces the resistance of a "rational creature," unafraid to speak the truth from her heart.

Darcy's Passion. If Collins' proposal is a sustained argument without regard to feelings, Darcy's proposal to Elizabeth is an acknowledgment that passion has overcome rational argument. Darcy's proposal, unlike that of Mr. Collins, begins with a profession of feelings: "After a silence of several minutes he came towards her in an agitated manner, and thus began, 'In vain have I struggled. It will not do. My feelings will not be repressed. You must allow me to tell you how ardently I admire and love you'" (*P&P* 189). While Collins defers expression of his runaway feelings and violent affections until late in the conversation, Darcy's blunt statement "in an agitated manner" suggests real and violent emotion.

However, his expression of love and admiration is hopelessly undercut by the nature of the struggle he has undergone and his compulsion to recount it to Elizabeth. He confesses that his passions ("inclination") could not be subdued by his reason ("judgment") *(P&P* 189). In essence, Darcy is approaching his offer in the reverse of Mr. Collins,' for Collins laid out the rational plan for marriage to Elizabeth, the "wisdom" of it, prior to expressing his feelings, which we can assume were of little merit anyway. For Darcy the problem is that the "rational" course for a man such as himself would speak against involvement with a woman who is his inferior. It is a testament to the strength of his passion for Elizabeth that his reason could not overcome his feelings.

Debasing Elizabeth. While Collins strives to make an argument for marriage to Elizabeth by counting off the reasons in its favor for both of them, Darcy feels compelled to detail all the reasons against the marriage. In both cases, Mr. Collins and Mr. Darcy argue for Elizabeth's insufficiencies. In Collins' case it is to strengthen his argument; in Mr. Darcy's it is to disclose the strength of his passion. Neither case is likely to flatter Elizabeth. Furthermore, true affection in Austen's novels is not based on passion or strong feeling alone, nor is it solely a rational decision, substantiated by argument. If Collins' proposal is all argument, the listing of reasons, Darcy's is an avowal of the failure of his reason to support his passion. True affection results from an equal balance of strong passion and good judgment.

Direct, Indirect, and Narrated Speech. After the initial expression of Darcy's ardent love and admiration, Austen renders the remainder of his proposal indirectly as free indirect speech (for a more detailed discussion of free indirect discourse, see Flavin, "Free Indirect Discourse and the Clever Heroine of *Emma*"):

> He spoke well, but there were feelings besides those of the heart to be detailed, and he was not more eloquent on the subject of tenderness than of pride. His sense of her inferiority—of its being a degradation—of the family obstacles which judgment had always opposed to inclination, were dwelt on with a warmth which seemed due to the consequence he was wounding, but was very unlikely to recommend his suit. (*P&P* 189)

Speech that is rendered indirectly tends to have less credibility than speech rendered directly. Indirection allows for the listener's response to be included, and it seems here that the effect of the speech on Elizabeth is more important than Darcy's words themselves. In addition, Austen may have felt that having Darcy state directly the degrading nature of Elizabeth's connection to him in marriage would be too negative for readers to forgive and forget later in the book. In other words, Elizabeth must put the image of Darcy's pride aside when he becomes humbled by her correction of his demeanor. Having him speak directly the language of "degradation," "family obstacles," "wounded consequence," etc., might make the reformation of his character and Elizabeth's change of perception less plausible to readers. In any event the direct rendering of his "ardently I admire and love you" has the romantic effect on readers of a man conquered by love.

Interestingly, both the 1979 and the 1995 film versions convert the indirection into direct speech. Thus, the brutal honesty of Darcy's perception of Elizabeth's family is presented. In the 1995 version, we hear Colin Firth say:

> In declaring myself thus, I am fully aware that I will be going expressly against the wishes of my family, my friends, and I hardly need add, my own better judgment. The relative situation of our families is such that any alliance between us must be regarded as a highly reprehensible connection. Indeed, as a rational man, I cannot but regard it as such myself, but it cannot be helped. Almost from the earliest moments of our acquaintance, I have come to feel for you a passionate admiration and regard, which despite all my struggles has overcome every rational objection, and I beg you most fervently to relieve all my suffering and consent to be my wife.

Colin Firth's performance here is that of a tortured, suffering soul. His manner in proposing suggests someone in deep pain, even confusion. The language created by the screenwriter is almost too literate, that is, it has the sound of premeditated composition. The three references to the rational and to judgment suggest that Davies wanted this to be seen as the struggle between passion and reason. Somehow it does not ring true, for it seems a man in the throes of passion would not have at the tip of his tongue such artfully constructed arguments to present. I am also unconvinced that a man of Darcy's "pride" and sense of superiority would "beg" a woman to marry him. Granted, the conventional belief was that woman's role was to support a man's emotional and physical well-being, so his desire for her to relieve his suffering would have been an acceptable one.

One other claim in the Davies rendering of Darcy's profession of love is that he has felt "admiration" and "regard" for her "almost from the earliest moments" of knowing her. While Austen builds into the novel early on Darcy's obsessive watching of Elizabeth, his attraction to her fine eyes and pretty face, it is not clear that this can be construed as "passionate admiration and regard." Instead, this echoes Collins' absurd claim that "almost as soon as I entered the house I singled you out as the companion of my future life" (*P&P* 105). In Darcy's case there may be some degree of truth, but its believability is threatened by the extravagance of the claim.

By way of comparison, this is the text of the 1979 BBC mini-series in which David Rintoul as Darcy proposes to Elizabeth:

> In spite of all my endeavors I found it impossible to conquer the strength of my feelings. The *inferiority* of your family, the miserable connection, the *degradation*, the lack of *judgment* I display, the harshness by which I shall rightly be judged by my own family and connections—all these count as nothing. Even the damage, for damage it must be to my sister, and the insult to Anne de Bourgh and her mother mean nothing in the face of my attachment to you. Miss Bennet, I have struggled greatly and endured great pain. I hope I will now be rewarded. Miss Bennet, will you accept my hand in marriage?

In this Fay Weldon script, Rintoul's Darcy borrows language (in italics) from the original Austen indirect summary of his remarks. The speeches from the Andrew Davies and the Fay Weldon scripts are approximately the same length with the same degree of sentence complexity. Comparatively, Weldon accentuates the problem Darcy has with their class and family differences while Davies puts more emphasis on Darcy's struggle with his passions, the "judgment/inclination" opposition Austen references.

Elizabeth's Response. In the 1995 Davies script, Jennifer Ehle's responses as Elizabeth match closely the dialogue Austen presents with redundancies removed. Her performance seems to me to have a mean intensity, a desire to wound. In the novel Elizabeth sits and weeps over the conversation for half an hour. I suspect the Ehle Elizabeth is unlikely to be shaken for long.

Enlightenment. Darcy is much more willing to allow Elizabeth her own voice and never threatens parental intervention as Collins does; in fact, he asks for explanation of her refusal: "I might, perhaps, wish to be informed why, with so little *endeavour* at civility, I am thus rejected" (*P&P* 190). I find it interesting that Darcy is unaware of his own lack of civility in the proposal itself— Elizabeth must teach him how his manners offend. Later, she adds that his "manners," his behaving less than in a "gentleman-like manner," revealed his character from the beginning of their acquaintance. His manners early on impressed her with his "arrogance," "conceit," and "selfish disdain of the feelings of others" (*P&P* 193). We see here the progress of Elizabeth's prejudice after her "first impression" of Darcy and how she has construed his manners to be a revelation of his character. Her misjudgment of Darcy parallels her overly trusting acceptance of Wickham based on his amiability.

Elizabeth voices firmly her rejection of Darcy as she had to Collins. Telling Collins that marriage to him is "impossible" is a sentiment she echoes when she tells Darcy, "You could not have made me the offer of your hand in *any possible way* [italics mine] that would have tempted me to accept it," and she adds, "you were the last man in the world whom I could ever be prevailed on to marry" (*P&P* 192–3). Her surety is a revelation of the degree of prejudice she has nursed against Darcy.

Mutual Esteem, Regard, and Affection. In both proposals Elizabeth is not threatened, seduced, and certainly not swayed. Just as Darcy has struggled with passion and sense, so Elizabeth is sensitive to the compliment of his expression of strong feelings for her, while her own sense reminds her that his consequence is greater than hers. He does not, as Collins does, deny her the power of refusal, but his offer of both intense feelings, plus wealth and consequence, is a compelling case. What he cannot give her at this point is equality of being, a sense of self-worth and value. Nowhere in his proposal does he consult her feelings; he only expresses his own. True respect for her would have silenced his obsession with the disparity of their situations and prompted a regard for her consequence as well. True affection results from mutual respect and esteem.

Dramatic Effects of Refusal. By looking ahead to the immediate consequences of their proposals, we can see that Collins is unchanged, while Darcy will act on what he has learned. His letter is an attempt to show Elizabeth the truth of his character by explaining his relations with Wickham and Bingley. Elizabeth's words, saying his manner was not "gentleman-like," have an immediate effect on him; he humbles his pride and grows to understand his faults and Elizabeth's merits. Starkly contrasting, Collins leaves believing still in his own merits and doubting that Elizabeth is as valuable as he once thought. After all, a woman who speaks, expects to be heard, and has thoughts and feelings would hardly be acceptable to Lady Catherine. We can assume that he presents his "case" to Charlotte in exactly the same way he argued it to Elizabeth. After all, nothing has changed except the woman. And Charlotte, not "romantic," will see the good sense in marrying a man with so much to offer.

Darcy's Second Proposal. Darcy's second proposal comes, ironically, after his family and Elizabeth's encroach on their relationship in such a way as to actually bring them closer together. The same individuals who so embarrassed both Darcy and Elizabeth now become the means of their renewed courtship: Lydia, Wickham, Mr. Collins, and Lady Catherine. The second time Darcy begins much more cautiously: "You are too generous to trifle with me. If your feelings are still what they were last April, tell me so at once. *My* affections and wishes are unchanged, but one word from you will silence me on this subject for ever" (*P&P* 366). The power dynamic has shifted in Elizabeth's favor, as she now has the power to silence a man of Darcy's consequence with "one word." Austen renders Elizabeth's "sentiments" and Darcy's "assurances" indirectly, leaving to our imagination what words could have induced such delight and pleasure.

The 1995 mini-series is disappointing in its dramatization of the second proposal. For one thing, I would expect Mr. Darcy to at least remove his hat when proposing. Firth seems to have lost the passionate attraction he struggled with throughout the film. In fact, he has only a vague smile as he and Jennifer Ehle's Elizabeth continue their saunter down the lane to Meryton. While a public kiss would be unexpected (although in keeping with the other current Austen adaptations), some show of intimacy, such as taking Elizabeth's hand, would demonstrate the real feeling we know Darcy should have at this juncture. On the other hand, David Rintoul in the 1979 production removes his hat and takes Elizabeth's arm during the proposal. The scene fades out as they disappear behind the trunk of a huge old tree, leaving us to imagine the long-awaited kiss to confirm their mutual affection. This ending is more emotionally satisfying than the kiss in the carriage leaving the church after the marriage ceremony in the 1995 adaptation.

All that remains in the novel after the proposal is for the characters to revisit the year of courtship. Direct speech is reserved for the conversation that returns to the earlier proposal and the mistakes each readily admits. Primarily, the lack of civility of manner has produced the greatest pain on both sides, leaving us to conclude that the feelings of each for the other were essentially founded in love and regard. In other words, each is guilty of the failure to understand that manners and principles or "proper feeling" can be two distinct components of conduct. Darcy later tells Elizabeth that he "was given good principles, but left to follow them in pride and conceit" (*P&P* 369). While Darcy has always been in essentials "a gentleman," and Elizabeth "a gentleman's daughter," their conduct has not always been consistent with the code of behavior associated with this distinction of class. Darcy learns "how insufficient were all [his] pretensions to please a woman worthy of being pleased" (*P&P* 369). And Elizabeth admits, "My manners must have been in fault, but not intentionally I assure you. I never meant to deceive you, but my spirits might often lead me wrong" (*P&P* 369). For both of them, manners and demeanor contributed to their inability to properly judge and value the other. Had the first proposal been met with a positive response, the marriage of Elizabeth and Darcy would have been based on a blind assumption of regard and a delusion of equality. In actuality, they would only experience much later the mutual esteem and respect which is the basis for true affection and enduring love.

Film Credits

Pride and Prejudice

MGM 1940.
Screenplay by Aldous Huxley and Jane Murfin.
Directed by Robert Z. Leonard.
Produced by Hunt Stromberg.

Cast

Elizabeth Bennet	Greer Garson
Fitzwilliam Darcy	Laurence Olivier
Jane Bennet	Maureen O'Sullivan
Lydia Bennet	Ann Rutherford
Mrs. Bennet	Mary Boland
Mr. Bennet	Edmund Gwenn
George Wickham	Edward Ashley
Mary Bennet	Marsha Hunt
Kitty Bennet	Heather Angel
Charles Bingley	Bruce Lester
Mr. Collins	Melville Copper
Lady Catherine de Bourgh	Edna Mae Oliver
Anne de Bourgh	Gia Kent
Charlotte Lucas	Karen Morley
Caroline Bingley	Frieda Inescort
Lady Lucas	Marjorie Wood
Sir William Lucas	E. E. Clive
Mrs. Philips	May Beatty
Mr. Denny	Marten Lamont

Pride and Prejudice

BBC television series produced in 1979.
Five parts (226 minutes).
Screenplay by Fay Weldon.
Directed by Cyril Coke.
Produced by Jonathan Powell.

Cast

Elizabeth Bennet	Elizabeth Garvie
Fitzwilliam Darcy	David Rintoul
Mr. Bingley	Osmund Bullock
Jane Bennet	Sabina Franklyn
Lydia Bennet	Natalie Ogle
Mrs. Bennet	Priscilla Morgan
Mr. Bennet	Moray Watson
Mary Bennet	Tessa Peake-Jones
Kitty Bennet	Clare Higgins
Mr. Collins	Malcolm Rennie
Lady Catherine de Bourgh	Judy Parfitt
Charlotte Lucas	Irene Richard
Mr. Wickham	Peter Settelen
Georgiana Darcy	Emma Jacobs
Caroline Bingley	Marsha Fitzalan
Mrs. Hurst	Jennifer Granville
Mr. Hurst	Edward Arthur
Colonel Fitzwilliam	Desmond Adams
Mrs. Philips	Shirley Cain
Mrs. Hill	Janet Davies
Sir William Lucas	Peter Howell
Captain Denny	Andrew Johns
Mr. Gardiner	Michael Lees

Mrs. Gardiner	Barbara Shelley
Lady Lucas	Elizabeth Stewart
Mrs. Reynolds	Doreen Mantle
Anne de Bourgh	Moir Leslie

Pride and Prejudice

BBC/A&E mini-series 1995.
Six parts (300 minutes.).
Screenplay by Andrew Davies.
Directed by Simon Langton.
Produced by Sue Birtwistle.

Cast

Fitzwilliam Darcy	Colin Firth
Elizabeth Bennet	Jennifer Ehle
Mr. Bennet	Benjamin Whitrow
Mrs. Bennet	Alison Steadman
Jane Bennet	Susannah Harker
Lydia Bennet	Julia Sawalha
Mary Bennet	Lucy Briers
Kitty Bennet	Polly Maberly
Mr. Bingley	Crispin Bonham-Carter
Caroline Bingley	Anna Chancellor
Mrs. Louisa Hurst	Lucy Robinson
Mr. Hurst	Rupert Vansittart
Lady Catherine de Bourgh	Barbara Leigh-Hunt
Anne de Bourgh	Nadia Chambers
Mr. Collins	David Bamber
Mr. Wickham	Adrian Lukis
Sir William Lucas	Christopher Benjamin
Lady Lucas	Norma Streader
Charlotte Lucas	Lucy Scott

Maria Lucas	Lucy Davis
Georgiana Darcy	Emilia Fox
Colonel Fitzwilliam	Anthony Calf
Mr. Gardiner	Tim Wylton
Mrs. Gardiner	Joanna David
Alice Gardiner	Natasha Isaacs
Kate Gardiner	Marie-Louise Flamank
William Gardiner	Julian Erleigh
Robert Gardiner	Jacob Casselden
Mrs. Philips	Lynn Farleigh
Denny	David Bark-Jones
Colonel Forster	Paul Moriarty
Mrs. Forster	Victoria Hamilton
Mrs. Reynolds	Bridget Turner
Hill	Marlene Sidaway
Mary King	Alexandra Howard
Mrs. Jenkinson	Harriet Eastcott
Hodge	Roy Holder

Mansfield Park

Mansfield Park was begun around February 1811 and finished after June 1813. Publisher Egerton announced it as "by the author of *Sense and Sensibility* and *Pride and Prejudice*" when it was published in May 1814 (Chapman, "Introductory Note to *Mansfield Park*" xi–xii).

Mansfield Park, Austen's third published novel, was the first written at Chawton. Often considered her "problem novel," its subject is less focused on courtship and marriage. Instead, Austen explores such themes as tradition and modernity, principle versus expediency, and choosing a profession. Fanny Price is a heroine considered by many to be the least likable in Austen's canon and the only one we see as a young child. Adopted away from her life of poverty and noise in Portsmouth, she grows up at Mansfield to become a pretty, intelligent, and principled young woman. As a kind of *bildungsroman*, the novel depicts the scenes of Fanny's life as she learns to quell her envy, rouse her spirits, fight depression, build strength, and retain virtue. The battle is fought in an environment where her two beautiful cousins outshine her, and a modern "woman of spirits," Mary Crawford, uses her "lively" manners to win the admiration of Edmund Bertram, Fanny's secret love. Fanny's inner consciousness is shared through free indirect discourse, and the insights into her mind and heart reveal a quiet soul who watches and judges. What makes her a "problem heroine" is that we as readers identify with her values but not with her personality. The family at Mansfield eventually learns to appreciate Fanny's character, and Edmund learns to realize that "a very different kind of woman" (*MP* 470) than Mary Crawford might be preferred. The novel celebrates "early hardship and discipline, and the consciousness of being born to struggle and endure" (*MP* 473). With a heroine so often found lacking, this Cinderella story shares the struggles of the future princess, but her triumph in winning the prince is left to our imaginations.

Viewing the Novel
—Approaches to Teaching *Mansfield Park*

I include here a general discussion of the main issues, themes, and ideas in *Mansfield Park*. My "Approaches to Teaching *Mansfield Park*" complement the analytical questions that follow this discussion.

The Heroine and the Rival. Fanny Price is often cited as the Austen heroine most difficult to like. While her virtue is unassailable, she seems stodgy, unimaginative, dogmatic, physically weak, and "creep mouse." Not only is she contrasted with her more lively cousins, but her rival for the love of Edmund, Mary Crawford, makes Fanny appear dull and insignificant. We learn directly what is in Fanny's mind through the free indirect discourse, and it most often reveals a watchful, jealous soul (see Flavin *"Mansfield Park"*). For example, when Fanny is saved from acting by Mrs. Grant's willingness to take the part of Cottager's Wife, Fanny is told she owes gratitude to Mary Crawford for the favor. Through free indirect discourse we learn how Fanny feels about this event: " . . . for it was Miss Crawford to whom she was obliged, it was Miss Crawford whose kind exertions were to excite her gratitude, and whose merit in making them was spoken of with a glow of admiration" (*MP* 159). Instead of exciting Edmund's admiration of her for resisting acting, Fanny must listen as Edmund sings Mary's praises, directing his respect for her principles at her rival. Her insignificance as a heroine derives from Fanny's position as "audience" rather than actor in the "performances" at Mansfield. She watches Mary ride, fearless and brave, the mare given to her by Edmund. At Sotherton Court she trails along with Edmund and Mary; then abandoned and alone, she watches as Maria and Henry escape through the fence, with Julia and Rushworth in pursuit. She watches the actors rehearse, especially the "indefatigable" Maria and Henry, and soothes the jealous glances of Rushworth. She witnesses the rehearsal of Mary and Edmund as they play-act the expression of love, a scene that animates and arouses the actors. For over half of the novel, Fanny's jealous perceptions are shared through the narration, making readers feel her weakness and trepidation. Jealousy abounds in the hearts of other characters as well. Both Maria and Julia are jealous of the attentions of Henry Crawford, Rushworth feels justifiable jealousy of Crawford's attention to his espoused, and Mary fears the Owen sisters may have won over Edmund. Only Fanny suffers in silence, fighting the tendency to be overwhelmed by jealous feelings.

Edmund refers to Fanny's rival, Mary Crawford, as "lively," a phrase used to describe Elizabeth Bennet as well. She characterizes herself during the game of Speculation: "There, I will stake my last like a woman of spirit. No cold prudence for me. I am not born to sit still and do nothing. If I lose the game, it shall not be from not striving for it" (*MP* 243). Mary does not compromise her demand that Edmund choose another profession if she is to marry him. She stakes her claim on her power to charm and her unwillingness to live a quiet life. In the same game of Speculation, Henry says to Fanny, "The game will be yours . . .—it will certainly be yours" (*MP* 244), a prophecy proven true when Fanny wins Edmund in the matrimonial game with Mary. If Mary's liveliness, wit, and intelligence mark her for comparison with Elizabeth Bennet, her principles and moral values differentiate her from any Austen heroine. Edmund finds Mary very attractive but ultimately realizes what her true nature is: "it does appear more than manner; it appears as if the mind itself was tainted" (*MP* 269). Blinded by love, Edmund is slow to realize that Mary's playful wit and clever abuse of religion and morality are evidence of her principles and not just her manner. The ever-watchful Fanny witnesses Mary's power over Edmund and knows her ability to charm and seduce. Fanny's comparative silence and failure of spirit disadvantage her as a heroine, although her unwavering principles mark her as the archetypal Austen heroine. Her manners and her morals are consistent, and her appearance of virtue is her reality.

While Mary Crawford's thoughts are never revealed except through conversation, we suspect she has her own jealousies, perhaps subconsciously seeing Fanny as the rival for Edmund's more than "cousinly" love. She plays Edmund's favorite musical piece when performing for Fanny. She flaunts her sexual attractiveness in front of Fanny, especially asking her to watch the rehearsal of the love scene with Edmund. She promotes Henry as a lover, knowing that Henry's intentions were to make Fanny love him without involving himself. We cannot help but wonder how Mary could not know how much Fanny feels for Edmund, for Edmund himself praises her for "great discernment" (*MP* 198). Perhaps her scheme is to remove a rival through marriage to her brother so as to secure her place with Edmund. In any case, Fanny appears comparatively less of a heroine because she is physically weak, reserved, and quiet. Her real heroism is in maintaining her principles and integrity when tempted by Henry to a life of riches, especially in the face of her exile to Portsmouth. She, like Mary, is "a woman of spirit," albeit a spirit that does not reveal itself in lively manners.

Ordination. Jane Austen announced that her newest novel would be about the subject of "ordination." Edmund Bertram, as a youngest son, is "designed for some profession," and he chooses to be a clergyman rather than a lawyer, soldier, or sailor (*MP* 91). Mary Crawford attempts to argue him away from his chosen profession to one with more "distinction" and later attempts to sway him away from the life of the active and involved clergyman that Edmund intends. He defends the role of the clergy for its power to influence morality and conduct (*MP* 92–93). More problematic for Mary, Edmund, endorsed by his father, intends to be a resident clergyman, one who will "live among his parishioners and prove himself by constant attention their well-wisher and friend" (*MP* 248). Their conflict is based on "her acknowledged disinclination for privacy and retirement, her decided preference of a London life" (*MP* 255). In Mary's imagination, the parsonage at Thornton Lacey would be modernized, the role of the clergyman diminished, and Edmund would live the comfortable life of a respectable gentleman.

Edmund realizes that Mary's acceptance of him is likely to be "deprecated, demanding such sacrifices of situation and employment on his side as conscience must forbid" (*MP* 255). At the same time, seduced by Mary's charms, he tells Fanny, "I cannot give her up. . . . She is the only woman in the world whom I could ever think of as a wife" (*MP* 421); Fanny expects "her acceptance must be as certain as his offer" (*MP* 367). We are left to wonder how Edmund could be so blinded, even if by love. Mary's speech and manners, her dislike by Fanny, her brother's indiscretions around his sisters—all have been witnessed by Edmund, and yet he so little suspects the degree of her faults. One would expect a clergyman, a man whose judgments and sense of right and wrong should be highly refined, to see the dangers of bringing such a worldly wife to his parsonage. Luckily for Edmund, before he is put to the test, his sister Mrs. Maria Rushworth elopes with Henry Crawford. When Mary exposes her feelings about the morality of their affair, Edmund is fully cognizant of her "blunted delicacy and a corrupted, vitiated mind" (*MP* 456).

The novel furthers the discussion of the power of the clergy to influence and inspire parishioners when Henry Crawford, the best actor among the young people, suggests that he too would like to be a preacher, albeit only to an educated London audience and only on a few Sundays a year (*MP* 341). Since his discussion is intended to impress Fanny Price with his sincerity and knowledge of the liturgy, it can be seen as another example of Henry's duplicity, his ability to speak and act well but without the underlying integrity to act upon his ideas. It also continues Austen's critique of the subject of ordination, especially the worldly temptations faced by a young man with a religious vocation and the abuses of the position by those without a true vocation.

The pattern of temptation, seduction, and resistance is evident not only in Edmund's relationship with Mary but among the other characters as well, suggesting Mansfield Park as a kind of Edenic garden into which the serpent brings an apple of temptation. Maria Bertram is tempted by the wealth and power of marriage to Rushworth; she succumbs. She is tempted by Henry's seductive charms; she succumbs, but he resists *hers*, arousing her pride, jealousy, and vengeance. Later, she tempts Henry; both succumb. Henry attempts to seduce Fanny, first as a game, but he succumbs to *her* charms. Although she resists his offer of marriage, she is tempted: marriage to Henry would be a means to escape Portsmouth, to provide her sister Susan with a home, to repay gratitude for William's promotion (and perhaps gain other favors for him in the future), and to secure a home of her own once Edmund has married Mary Crawford. Fanny resists. As Edmund said of her after the temptations of the theatrical adventure: "Fanny is the only one who has judged rightly throughout, who has been consistent" (*MP* 187). Fanny is the moral heroine who resists pride, anger, jealousy, and vengeance to win the game (and her version of Paradise) in the end.

Theatricals. The scheme to set up a theater at Mansfield Park is controversial on many levels. The Austen family itself engaged in theatrical ventures, so Austen could not be said to disapprove of family acting generally. Edmund voices the particular reasons the acting scheme is wrong for Mansfield: "In a *general* light, private theatricals are open to some objections, but as *we* are circumstanced, I must think it would be . . . more than injudicious, to attempt any thing of the kind." He says it would be insensitive to their father, whose life is endangered, and "imprudent" given Maria's "extremely delicate" situation (*MP* 125). In addition, he concludes that "it would be taking liberties with my father's house" both as an innovation to the structure and as an expense (*MP* 127). Edmund strictly resists involvement in acting himself.

As the theatrical scheme develops, many of Edmund's concerns are realized. The strict "sense of decorum" (*MP* 127) forbidding the grown-up daughters to be acting in plays is violated by Maria's play-acting the role of a fallen woman, Agatha. Cast opposite Henry Crawford as Agatha's son, she speaks lines of affection to, and embraces, a man not her espoused. The acting out of her maternal love becomes for Maria a means to illicit sexual embracing. The dangers are evident when Rushworth complains of "Maria's avoidance of him [Mr. Rushworth], and so needlessly often the rehearsal of the first scene between her and Mr. Crawford" (*MP* 165). Mary Crawford, too, playfully notes " . . . the theatre is engaged of course by those indefatigable rehearsers, Agatha and Frederick" (*MP* 169).

Even Edmund is tempted to involve himself, on the pretext that he will be excluding outsiders from taking part if he himself takes the role of Anhalt, a clergyman who professes his love to Amelia, played by Mary Crawford. According to David R. Carroll, Edmund's agreement to act is "wish-fulfillment in which he can reconcile his profession and his love of Mary: Anhalt, the part he plays, permits him to be both a clergyman and the accepted lover" (Duckworth, *Improvement* 63). Specifically, the scene between Amelia and Anhalt contrasts the marriage of convenience, for property or situation, with the marriage for love. Fanny anxiously anticipates the third act, which "would bring a scene between them which interested her most particularly. . . . The whole subject of it was love—a marriage of love was to be described by the gentleman, and very little short of a declaration of love be made by the lady" (*MP* 167). Mary Crawford's own discomfort with the scene exposes her feelings: "There, look at *that* speech, and *that*, and *that*. How am I ever to look him in the face and say such things?" (*MP* 168). For Mary to suffer discomposure suggests the prurient nature of the scene, and Fanny, forced to watch Mary and Edmund rehearse, becomes distracted and "agitated by the increasing spirit of Edmund's manner" (*MP* 170). Both couples, Maria with Henry and Edmund with Mary, act out relationships they dare not experience in actuality.

Other future events are foreshadowed in the play chosen, *Lovers' Vows*, and the casting of the characters. The discussion on the marriage of convenience directly reflects on Maria Bertram and Rushworth: "When convenience and fair appearance joined to folly and ill-humour, forge the fetters of matrimony, they gall with their weight the married pair. Discontented with each other—at variance in opinions—their mutual aversion increases with the years they live together" (*Lovers' Vows* 505). Were Maria and Rushworth more attentive to the message of the play, they might have averted the catastrophe of their marriage and its eventual demise. Mr. Yates occupies his time in consoling Julia and later reenacts his role as the seducer baron when he elopes with her. His insensitivity to the absent Sir Thomas reflects his earlier callousness to the Ravenshaws in wishing that notice of the death of a grandmother be delayed for the three days needed to complete the acting of the play.

Finally, the issue of acting in the theatricals reflects on the theme of appearance, sincerity, reality, and flattery. Fanny astutely identifies Henry's talents for acting: "Mr. Crawford was considerably the best actor of all" (*MP* 165). Likewise, Julia mistrusts Henry's sincerity when he "supplicates" her to take the part of Amelia: "was he only trying to soothe and pacify her, and make her overlook the previous affront? She distrusted him. . . . He was, perhaps, but at treacherous play with her" (*MP* 135). Indeed, Henry is not only at "treacherous" play with her, but also with her sister, Maria, and later with Fanny Price. Henry, like Mary, is a flatterer, a smooth talker, a worker of appearances. Duckworth says of Crawford, "What makes his wish and ability to act a multiplicity of parts dangerous . . . is that these are not his avocation, but his vocation, not his recreation, but his profession" (*Improvement* 65). Fanny, as audience not only to the play but to the real scenes enacted around her, is a keen witness to Henry's duplicity and knows his ability to please and soothe through flattery, preparing her for his later assaults on her heart. Fanny herself repeatedly asserts that she cannot act, suggesting her inability to be duplicitous, to play a role.

Improvements. The late eighteenth century was noted for its landscape and home improvements, a kind of makeover that often resulted in a classically beautiful space being modernized into one with no particular style or aesthetic. As R. W. Chapman notes, "Our ancestors a hundred years ago had little of the modern taste for the antique, and were all for Improvement" ("Improvements" 557). The excursion to Sotherton, seat of the Rushworths, lends itself to a discussion of improvements. One possibility is to demolish an avenue of oaks to improve the approach to the home. Fanny laments the loss: "Cut down an avenue! What a pity!" recalling the late eighteenth-century poet Cowper, "'Ye fallen avenues, once more I mourn your fate unmerited'"(*MP* 56). But as Edmund notes, "the avenue stands a bad chance" of surviving the improvers (*MP* 56). Humphrey Repton, "then the head of his profession," is the landscape designer of choice alluded to in *Mansfield Park* (Chapman, "Improvements" 558). According to Alistair Duckworth,

Repton's "principles of landscaping often seem close to Jane Austen's own views," especially when he emphasizes "utility" over purely aesthetic improvements (*Improvement* 42). However, Austen was generally disapproving of "radical improvements" or "drastic alterations to landscape" which sacrifice practicality, real elegance, and taste for trendy but not necessarily aesthetically pleasing styles (Duckworth, *Improvement* 44).

Just as Sotherton is threatened by the introduction of sudden improvements, the appearance of the "modern" and urbane Crawfords at Mansfield Park poses a threat to the stately and conservative traditions of Sir Bertram's country manor. Their worldliness, London ways, wit, and vitality are contributions that might have enlivened and regenerated the world of Mansfield, but their presence instead hastens the corruption of values already showing signs of decay. Economically, Sir Thomas's fortune, built on the profits of slave labor on plantations in Antigua, is eroding, partially due to the reckless habits of his eldest son, Tom. The stagnation of culture and society is emblemized in the indolent Lady Bertram, who dawdles on the sofa, working a useless, and endless, needlework fringe. Tom Bertram has already wasted much of his and his younger brother's fortune, prompting his father to say, "'I blush for you, Tom.' . . . 'You have robbed Edmund for ten, twenty, thirty years, perhaps for life, of more than half the income which ought to be his'" (*MP* 23). The eldest daughter, Maria, is induced to marry the dull but wealthy Mr. Rushworth. Selfishness and envy bind the sisters, Maria and Julia, producing a rivalry that nearly destroys both their lives. The Crawfords, while possessing fortune, beauty, intelligence, and manner, are flawed by habits of self-indulgence, lack of discipline, and a corrupt domestic example. Their modernity does not improve but further adulterates the estate of Mansfield.

Ironically, it is an outsider who infuses Mansfield with moral principle and integrity, its best hope for "improvement." Fanny Price experiences "the advantages of early hardship and discipline" (*MP* 473), and is sustained through her ordeal by the kindness and guidance of her cousin Edmund. Both Edmund and Fanny are tempted to join the Crawfords' world of ease, liveliness, and wealth. Mary Crawford, who unintentionally falls in love with a clergyman, hopes to "improve" Edmund's parsonage through not only a "modernization" of the building but a makeover of the parson as well. Her vision of the future Thornton Lacey is "to shut out the church, sink the clergyman, and see only the respectable, elegant, modernized, and occasional residence of a man of independent fortune" (*MP* 248). As R. W. Chapman notes, "In Mary Crawford's picture of Edmund's future residence *modernized* figures as a term of approbation with *respectable* and *elegant*" ("Improvements" 558). Mary's modernity considers adultery as an indiscretion, a folly, to be glossed over with the appearance of respectability. As Edmund eventually discovers, Mary's manners mask "faults of principle" (*MP* 456). Likewise, Henry Crawford thinks that "acting" like a responsible man is sufficient to win the heart of Fanny Price. While Fanny admits to his being "altogether improved" (*MP* 406), he fails to sustain the part and ultimately resorts to his favored role, the seducer. Fanny Price, the newcomer to Mansfield, becomes the daughter Sir Thomas always wanted, and her marriage to Edmund secures the future "improvement" of the estate in ways more essential than the outward appearance of change.

The Slavery Issue. In *Mansfield Park* Austen alludes to the issue of slavery only once, when Fanny Price's question to Sir Thomas regarding the "slave trade" was followed up with "such a dead silence" (*MP* 198) that the subject is not broached again. The very fact of the Bertram plantation in Antigua and the necessity of Sir Thomas's journey there to shore up his fortune make the slavery issue larger than this one reference. In a review of the Rozema film *Mansfield Park*, Alistair Duckworth summarizes the Austen family's involvement in issues of slavery, including Jane Austen's father's role as a trustee of a plantation in Antigua and her brother Frank's abolitionist fervor. Duckworth notes also a parallel between the dependency of single women of small fortune in Austen's novels and the subjection of slavery ("Film Review" 566). As with the slave trade, Fanny Price is displaced, taken from the familiarity of her home in Portsmouth, forcibly separated from her parents and siblings, two of whom she misses greatly, and is relocated at Mansfield Park, where her status is closer to a servant than a family member. Even her bedroom is located in the attic where the governess and the servants were housed. Jane Fairfax in *Emma* equates the position of governess to "the sale—not quite of human flesh—but of human intellect" (*E* 300). Fanny Price is never put in the actual position of having to sell her talents for survival, but her choices are severely limited by her birth and economic position, and she is pressured by Sir Thomas to marry Henry Crawford for economic advantage in spite of her feelings. While Sir Thomas, reluctantly, offers Maria a means to escape her engagement to her wealthy suitor, Fanny's feelings are never consulted in the matter of her alliance with Henry. Sending Fanny back to

Portsmouth to reacquaint her with the value of her Mansfield friends is somewhat akin to the torture and separations of slave families designed to discipline and instill fear. Fanny nearly breaks under the experiment.

Viewing the Novel —Questions for Analysis and Discussion

The questions below address the larger issues of each volume and are designed to promote analytical thinking as the basis for discussion. These questions ask students to "see" into the text and complement the central issues of "reading the film" that follow.

Volume I

1. What are the motives of Mrs. Norris and Sir Thomas in bringing Fanny Price to Mansfield Park? Are they worthy motives? Are they in Fanny's best interest? Why did they choose a girl over a boy?
2. What kind of education and upbringing have the young Bertrams been given? What has been the result of their education?
3. Evaluate Sir Thomas and Lady Bertram as parents.
4. How is Edmund Bertram distinct from his brother and sisters? How do you explain his kindness to Fanny?
5. How would you characterize Mary and Henry Crawford? What kind of education and upbringing have they had? What is likable and attractive about the Crawfords? What is unlikable?
6. Why does Fanny not like Mary Crawford? Are there subconscious reasons for her aversion?
7. What does the visit to Sotherton reveal about Henry and Mary Crawford? About Julia and Maria Bertram? About Edmund Bertram? What is the symbolism of the caged starling?
8. What is "wrong" about the theatricals? How does the choice of *Lovers' Vows* reflect on the actors? Why does Mrs. Norris so readily approve and involve herself? How are all of the young people "tested" through this venture?
9. What does the first volume reveal about Sir Thomas and his investments in Antigua? What is his business there?
10. Why does Maria Bertram engage herself to Mr. Rushworth?

Volume II

1. How does Sir Thomas appear changed as a parental figure after his return from Antigua?
2. Why do you think Maria did not accept his offer to break off the engagement to Rushworth?
3. Why do you think Henry Crawford did not propose marriage to Maria?
4. How does William Price's visit advance Henry's courtship of Fanny? Is there evidence that Henry feels more for Fanny than he acknowledges?
5. Why does Fanny not like Henry Crawford? How do you justify Sir Thomas's acceptance of Henry as Fanny's suitor?
6. Is there any scenario for compromise between Mary Crawford and Edmund Bertram over his choice of profession and lifestyle? Do you think each is sincerely in love with the other? What evidence do you see to support your belief? Could a strong and sincere love sustain them through some sort of compromise? What does their refusal to compromise suggest about the true nature and character of each?
7. Do you think Edmund ever thinks of Fanny in a sexual or conjugal way? Do you think he knows her true feelings for him? What evidence do you see to support your view?
8. Do you see any indications that Mary Crawford thinks of Fanny as a rival or knows Fanny's feelings for Edmund? Why does she so strongly promote the union of Henry and Fanny?
9. At the ball for Fanny she wears a cross from William, a chain from Edmund, and a necklace from Henry. What are the symbolic implications of each item?
10. Is there a defense for Sir Thomas's persistence in promoting the marriage of Fanny and Crawford? How does "gratitude" toward her uncle and toward Henry complicate Fanny's decision?

Volume III

1. Is Henry Crawford truly in love with Fanny? Do you think he would have made a loving and faithful husband?
2. What definition of "heroism" does Fanny display in rejecting Henry, especially when she is returned to Portsmouth? What does her home life there suggest about her future? How realistic are the plans she and William make to live together in a little cottage?

3. Is Fanny responsible in any way for Henry's elopement with Maria?
4. What does Mary Crawford's response to the elopement tell us about her character?
5. Is there a possibility that Fanny might have accepted Henry over time, especially if Edmund had married Mary Crawford? If Fanny had accepted Crawford's proposal, what would have been her reasons?
6. We know that Fanny has loved Edmund consistently and passionately. Why do you think Edmund has never thought of her as anything other than a sister? How convincing is the eventual marriage of Edmund with Fanny? Is your estimation of Edmund's judgment and character lower by his infatuation for Mary Crawford?
7. How does Fanny become the moral center of Mansfield?
8. If her upbringing with her corrupted uncle is the reason given for Mary Crawford's lack of moral principles, how does the novel explain Maria's corruption? Or Tom's?
9. Given their home life in Portsmouth, with an alcoholic parent and slovenly mother, how are Fanny and William Price's moral character and ethical behavior explained?
10. Why did Edmund choose to be a clergyman, when so many more glamorous professions were possible? Does he seem to have a spiritual or intellectual calling to the church?

Reading the Film
—Approaches to Teaching the Film

Choosing a Film Adaptation

Patricia Rozema's *Mansfield Park*, more than any other Austen film adaptation, has fueled the debate over the issue of a film's fidelity to the original novel versus its originality and success as a film in its own right. The film is said to be "Based on Jane Austen's Novel," suggesting that it does not intend to be a faithful rendering of *Mansfield Park*; thus, we viewers are invited to analyze and evaluate the film based on what Rozema has taken from Austen, what she has changed, and what she has created. I like the film in many ways as a work of film art. I like the new and improved Fanny Price, the setting and stylized cinematic technique, and what it says about women's independence and freedom. I fault the film as an adaptation in what it leaves out, especially the values and moral distinctions that are so important to Austen's novel about "ordination." Thus, I conclude that some of the spirit or essence of the author's original novel is treated in an excellent way, while other elements are lost or muddled. Admirers of the film include Claudia Johnson, who praises it as "a stunning revisionist reading of Austen's darkest novel" ("Run Mad"). Johnson rates it highly among the Austen adaptations: "Finally a director has taken risks with Austen, treating her work not as a museum piece or as a sacred text but as a living presence whose power inspires flight. *Mansfield Park* is an audaciously perceptive cinematic evocation of Austen's unblinking yet forgiving vision and its own accomplishment of dazzling imagination and originality" ("Run Mad"). Alistair Duckworth calls it a "brilliantly tendentious adaptation" ("Film Review" 565) and "the most creative, as well as the most provocative, of the film adaptations of Austen's novels" ("Film Review" 570). Dissenters include Elsa Solender, who "disliked the film," feeling that "Rozema's agenda stifled Austen's." Solender says Rozema "betrayed the spirit of Jane Austen's fiction." She is especially disturbed by the inclusion of Austen's *Juvenilia* and other writings never intended for publication (108).

Using Film in the Classroom

Like many others, I find *Mansfield Park* a difficult novel to like or to teach. However, the Rozema film so energizes the character of Fanny Price that I find myself reading the text in a new way. Fanny's strengths—her principles, unseducible virtue, discernment, loyalty, and integrity—are more apparent in the novel after watching the film. I use the film as a resource for helping student readers get past the perception of Fanny as weak, whining, and jealous; the film allows her beauty as a character to be appreciated. In essentials, this cinematic Fanny Price is still Austen's timid heroine, but she is contemporized as a woman who not only survives the misfortunes of her birth and home life but *chooses* the direction of her life without dependence on the benefits of wealth or opportunity. Once viewers get past the jarring change in the surface characterization of Fanny Price, the film prompts new interest in her story and invites a reinterpretation of the problematic heroine.

My focus here is on four general issues of film analysis that may serve as the basis for analysis and discussion of the film adaptation, and my discussion is limited to the 1999 *Mansfield Park*, written and directed by Patricia Rozema.

Casting and Characterization

Rozema's makeover of Fanny Price is perceived as an improvement over Austen's reserved, quiet, observant heroine, who is physically weak and painfully conscious of any kindness shown her. The new Fanny is physically strong and active, an author modeled on Jane Austen herself, who achieves her self-fulfillment through the writing of her own story, *Mansfield Park*. According to Troost and Greenfield, the shift in Fanny Price "from a silent, emotional sufferer to an active figure who can create her own success" is due to the change in focus from "the effects of particular upbringings on individual happiness and morality into a film concerned with the effects of broader social forces on . . . entire classes of people" (188). Rozema's Fanny Price is a representative of the contemporary feminist spirit, while Mary Crawford is a model of the "modern" woman of Austen's day, with very liberal ideas about the clergy, adultery, and morality in general. Fanny is a woman seeking liberation from the rules imposed by a society in which marriage, especially marriage for fortune, is the only option. In the film her mother cautions her against a marriage for love, with herself as example, but Fanny sees as much entrapment in marriage to a man she cannot trust or love, Henry Crawford. In both the novel and the film, Henry sets out to "make" Fanny love him, to be so persistent as to wear down her power of refusal. He is joined in his endeavors by the authority of Sir Thomas. In the film, more so than in the novel, Sir Thomas acts not so much in Fanny's interest as in his own in joining his niece to a man of fortune. His attitude toward young women in the film is equated with his treatment of his slaves. Sir Thomas speaks of bringing home a mulatto slave girl, for purposes not explained, much as he had taken in Fanny, who is depicted as a servant in the film. Frances O'Connor's Fanny balks at the notion of herself as a prize piece of livestock on the market to the highest bidder. Harold Pinter, in the role of Sir Thomas, has the lecherous, greedy look of a sexual predator who would sell his own niece as he does the slaves whose suffering supports his lifestyle.

Fanny is also a more sexualized woman in the film. While we know from the novel that she is capable of strong feelings, we are not aware of her sexual energy. Frances O'Connor's Fanny Price is conscious of the sexual appetites that the Crawfords bring to Mansfield. She witnesses the hugging and fondling of Henry and Maria during the rehearsals; she learns from Mary Crawford the sensual power of touch as Mary uses Fanny as her acting partner before Edmund. She also perceives the change in the somber and scholarly Edmund as he is aroused by Mary's speech and gesture. At Fanny's "coming out" ball, a slightly tipsy Fanny dances charmingly and seductively with both Henry Crawford and her cousin Edmund. The dance itself, with its commingling and shifting of partners, foreshadows the partner exchanges that conclude the film. At this juncture it is unclear who will couple with Edmund, Fanny, Henry, Mary, Julia, or Maria.

A fault I find in the Rozema characterization of Fanny is her lack of consistency. In an attempt to make her more independent and less morbid and "creep mouse," Frances O'Connor plays Fanny as a cheerful, unaffected woman who tends to laugh too easily. Whether playing tag with Edmund or dancing with Henry, she is smiling and eager to please. Moreover, her vacillation in relation to Henry adversely affects her character. If her purported reason for refusing his offer of marriage is because she knows him to be untrustworthy and false with the power to act, charm, and seduce, we have to question why she accepts him in the first place. Is it because she sees his as her only and best offer? An escape from the dirt and poverty of her Portsmouth home? When she thinks Edmund will marry Mary Crawford, she not only says "yes" to Henry, she does so with smiles and giggles, a strong hug, and a passionate kiss. This scene, even though she recants the next day, shows her to be as changeable and opportunistic as Maria Crawford in marrying Rushworth. After all, Maria's reasons for marrying were much the same: to escape home and parental authority and to become mistress of her own beautiful homes. This characterization ignores the moral struggles endured by Austen's Fanny Price.

Next to Frances O'Connor's vibrant Fanny Price, the characterization of Sir Thomas Bertram, played by Harold Pinter, is the most dramatic departure from the novel. Young Fanny Price grows up in fear of her uncle's authoritarian ways, but the film casts him as a lecher who tortures and sexually abuses his slaves. The novel hints at his relief in marrying Maria to the wealthy Mr. Rushworth, but the film emphasizes his eagerness to promote Fanny through a ball given in her honor and to push his son Edmund into marriage with Mary Crawford for her fortune. Pinter's lusty glances at Fanny make of him more than a tyrant. His lasciviousness has no source in the novel, unless we derive it from his pride in Fanny's growth into a young beauty. Pinter's Sir Thomas "is terrifying when he chastises Fanny for rejecting Henry" (Troost and Greenfield 196). Furthermore, the Rozema film foregrounds his moral conduct as setting the tone for Mansfield, with his corruption through the approval of slavery permeating his family life. Claudia Johnson agrees with Rozema's characterization: "Sir Thomas's misrule abroad sullies his authority and leads to the moral turpitude at home. Spurred on by the searing power of Harold Pinter's Sir Thomas, Rozema is unrelenting on this point" ("Run Mad"). According to Troost and Greenfield, Austen's readers should appreciate this association: "the institution of slavery degrades both slave and master, and it also corrupts family life in England" (196). As in the novel, Sir Thomas eventually acknowledges the superior moral authority of Fanny Price and, in the film, relents even as to his plantations, turning to tobacco, a seemingly less controversial source of income.

Making Sir Thomas more villainous in the film serves another point. In the novel Fanny's rejection of Henry Crawford is built on an early dislike, predicated by his flirtation with her two cousins, and fueled by her feelings for Edmund, "her pre-engaged heart" (*MP* 326). She is suspicious of his sincerity, knowing his ability to flatter and please. However, when Fanny believes Edmund will marry Mary Crawford and after Henry persists in courting her, she weakens her resolve to resist his proposal. For most of us, and especially for first-time and student readers, Henry Crawford appears a changed man, one Fanny admits is "altogether improved" and "so *near* being agreeable (*MP* 406). Considering Fanny's prospects and Henry's apparent reformation, it becomes increasingly difficult to see her resistance as a viable plot option. The film solves this problem by making Henry an attractive character, one viewers would not object to seeing Fanny marry, but making Sir Thomas less attractive. Instead of the kindly uncle who has his niece's best interests at heart, his judgment is called into question by his lechery in Antigua among his slaves, his tyranny over his children, and his leering interest in Fanny herself. Such a villain, changed as he is from the kindly but authoritarian uncle of the novel, is one Fanny must resist. As viewers of the film, we instinctively mistrust his principles in matters matrimonial or sexual. Thus, the rejection of Henry, even after her initial acceptance (reminiscent of Austen's own change of mind in the Bigg-Wither affair), is accounted for in her understanding of Sir Thomas's weaknesses for money and for sexual gratification. Fanny knows she must rely on her own perceptions and judgment. Claudia Johnson writes that Fanny's initial acceptance of Henry in the film brings her "under the influence of the moral and erotic confusion elsewhere, without sacrificing our sympathy for her struggle to do and feel as she ought" ("Run Mad"). In the novel no such confusion is apparent.

Mary Crawford is played beautifully by Embeth Davidtz. She has a mature look, a woman of the world, slightly exotic and elegantly dressed. Her smiles are not flirtatious but seductive. In dress and manner, smoking her brother's cigarette and shooting pool, she appears "modernized" into a 1930s woman. Henry Crawford, played by Alessandro Nivola, is equally successful. While the novel suggests Henry is not tall or handsome, Nivola is a bit smallish next to Frances O'Connor's Fanny Price, but he too is attractively seductive. The change from lover to avenger after Fanny recants her acceptance of his marriage proposal is masterful. In the end neither is punished for transgressions, and the film ends with a scene suggesting a potential partner swapping, somewhat reminiscent of a comic drama from the Thirties.

Jonny Lee Miller plays Edmund Bertram as a scholarly, choirboy lover. His character is modified to show sexual feelings for Fanny that are not evident in the novel. While his attraction to Mary Crawford is evident, he appears to have a feminine and romantic longing for her. Dressed in a kind of schoolboy costume, Miller seems immature and not overly intelligent beside either Frances O'Connor's Fanny or Embeth Davidtz's very worldly Mary. The bold, independent Fanny portrayed in this film, emancipated from patriarchal authority through her writing, seems hardly a match for the sedate and angelic clergyman represented by Miller's Edmund Bertram.

As in so many Austen novels, *Mansfield Park*'s character pairings invite comparisons. The three sisters, Mrs. Norris, Mrs. Price, and Lady Bertram, have come to different destinies through marriage. Casting Lindsay Duncan as both Mrs. Price and Lady Bertram sets off a comparative look at how much alike the two sisters are. Austen describes both as "naturally easy and indolent" (*MP* 390). As Mrs. Price, Duncan is drawn and haggard, as lethargic and ineffectual as her sister in her role as parent, spouse, and housekeeper. Lady Bertram sits all day working an endless piece of fringe, while Mrs. Price is caught in a cycle of laundry and child rearing. The film explains Lady Bertram's indolence by making her an abuser of opium, a habit she later gives up to signal the regeneration of Mansfield occasioned by Fanny and Edmund's union. For modern audiences, being a "couch potato" might be an insufficient character flaw, but Lady Bertram as a user of opium visually conveys moral corruption.

Changes from Novel to Film
(Significant Deletions, Additions, and Revisions)

The Slave Issue. Although Austen wrote that the subject of *Mansfield Park* was "ordination," the Rozema film makes much of the slave issue. In the novel itself we know that Sir Thomas's extended stay in Antigua is to solidify his plantation holdings to finance the debts of his eldest son, Tom. Fanny asks

Sir Thomas one question about the slave trade upon his return but is met by silence among the family members (*MP* 198). Hardly the center of the novel, the issue of the slave trade is foregrounded by Rozema. In an added sequence, in which the young Fanny Price is seen at home in Portsmouth and on her journey to Mansfield, she hears the mournful wail of "black cargo" aboard a ship anchored in the bay. The "darkies," she is told, are a gift brought home by a captain for his wife. We might see identification here with Fanny, who is being brought to Mansfield as a kind of "gift" to Lady Bertram. Fanny's existence in the house of Mansfield is not unlike that of the mulatto slave Sir Thomas considers bringing there to work as a servant (and potential mistress). Another of Rozema's additions is Edmund's reply to Fanny's query about abolition: "We all live off the profits [of slavery], Fanny, even you." The quote was added to the original screenplay to bring the slave issue more emphatically to the center of the film (Troost and Greenfield, note 9, 202). Further, Fanny rebels against Sir Thomas's plans for her marriage to Crawford with "I won't be sold off like one of your father's slaves." In a later added sequence, Rozema has Fanny finding Tom's drawings of Sir Thomas in the act of brutalizing his slaves in Antigua, a sight that turns her against the uncle to whom she owes so much gratitude for bringing her to Mansfield. Rozema effectively links Sir Thomas's responsibility for the abuses of the slave trade and his role in the domestic life at Mansfield Park. However, for Alistair Duckworth, the "coarsening of Sir Thomas's character . . . is a travesty of the fictional character" ("Film Review" 566). Rozema is also forcing an analogy between the dependency of women, especially in their limited power of choice in marriage, and the bondage of the slaves.

Explicit Sexuality. Some viewers have objected to the inclusion of sex scenes not explicit in the novel, such as the lesbian touching of Fanny by Mary Crawford, Fanny's discovery of Tom's drawings of Sir Thomas in fellatio with a slave woman, and a scene of Fanny discovering Henry and Maria having sex. While these scenes seem shockingly inappropriate for a Jane Austen film adaptation, we must acknowledge that sexuality is pervasive in a novel with seven young adults brought together without a mature adult chaperone. From the home life of the Crawfords, where an uncle lives openly with his mistress after his wife dies, to Mary's expressed "unintentional" pun on "*Rears*, and *Vices*" (*MP* 60), to the rehearsals of the suggestive play *Lovers' Vows*, and finally Maria's elopement with Crawford, we are reminded that this world is suffused with sexuality and decadence. Mary Crawford's sexual caresses of Fanny in the film contribute to the characterization of Mary as one who, like her brother, "takes her pleasure wherever she pleases, without any regard for the feelings of those she wishes to 'play with'" (Troost and Greenfield, Note 6, 202). While Austen puts scenes of illicit sexuality "off stage," the film brings these scenes to the forefront and highlights the subject as a central component of Austen's theme: Moral corruption destroys the social and economic world of English country life. One further change is in the "crime" that prompts Edmund to disengage his interest from Mary Crawford. In the novel, Mary's moral depravity is evidenced in her acceptance of adultery, whereas in the film her additional fault is a callous attitude toward Tom's illness and the prospect of his death opening the way for Edmund's inheritance. In the film Fanny and Edmund's relationship is also much more sexual than it is in the novel. Edmund secures the first dance of the ball with Fanny, not Mary. When Fanny is returned to Portsmouth, the novel is explicit in denoting their relationship: "she knew he was giving her the affectionate farewell of a brother" (*MP* 374), but in the film when Edmund brings Fanny back to Mansfield, they embrace and almost kiss. While this sexualizing of their relationship makes the belated proposal from Edmund more plausible, it is a decided change from the "spiritual" relationship of Fanny and Edmund that Austen created.

The change in Fanny's personality and characterization is discussed more thoroughly under "Conceptual Integrity," but some other notable changes in the plot as it relates to Fanny are relevant. For one, Fanny accepts Henry Crawford's proposal after his persistent visits in Portsmouth, but recants in the morning. Since this Fanny is a retooled Jane Austen as author, the scene suggests Austen's own change of heart in accepting, then rejecting Harris Bigg-Wither's proposal of marriage. Conceptually, Troost and Greenfield like this addition as personifying Fanny as an author who can imagine or envision alternative endings, not like the novel's Fanny who is inflexible regarding Henry and Edmund (190). However, Rozema has Fanny declare, "I have no talent for certainty," which may align her with the inventive author but not with the Fanny Price of Austen's novel who knows with true certainty the difference between an Edmund and a Henry. Ultimately, Austen has Fanny called home to Mansfield because the family feels the loss of her moral integrity after Maria's elopement with Henry, while in the film she is called home to nurse Tom back to health. This change is consistent with Rozema's characterization of Fanny as a servant (or nurse in this case) at Mansfield, furthering the link between patriarchal authority over women and slaves.

In the film, those who commit adultery, and those who sanction it, are not punished. Instead, Henry and Mary Crawford's destiny, as well as Maria's, is treated with lighthearted humor. Henry and Mary entertain their spouses on the lawn of some mansion in a grand style, and, in keeping with their modern attitudes toward relationships, their mates exchange knowing glances, suggesting adultery and partner sharing are still approved. Maria, meanwhile, suffers the fate given her by Austen as she must endure exile with the loyal Mrs. Norris, but the tone of their final scene is more jovial than morose.

Characters Changed or Deleted. William Price is deleted entirely from the film. Duckworth regrets this loss, for he sees William as Austen's prime example of true heroism and the useful life, a contrast to Henry Crawford, Tom Bertram, Mr. Yates, and even Edmund. Duckworth rightly sees the fallacy of an attractive young naval officer in a film that censures imperialist exploits. In Rozema's feminist film, all the male figures are lacking in some way; only William displays "male energy and professional commitment" and is thus eliminated ("Film Review" 567).

Thomas Bertram is changed from a spendthrift who has squandered the family fortunes to a drunk. His redemption in the film is signaled through his art, which has no source in the novel. Like Sir Thomas, his son and heir is made much more profligate than Austen's character. His drawings of the torture of slaves in Antigua bring home to Fanny the degree of Sir Thomas's moral degeneracy and function to expose his sins to Fanny, increasing her moral authority. Duckworth sees the characterization of Tom Bertram as an early Branwell Bronte, part of the "Brontification" of Austen in this film ("Film Review" 567).

Conceptual Integrity (Themes, Ideas, Spirit of Austen's Novel)

The alterations Rozema makes in adapting *Mansfield Park* are many, yet several excellent critiques of the film find this adaptation conceptually true to the spirit or essence of Austen's novel. Claudia Johnson raises the essential issue: "Rozema's 'unfaithfulness' obliges us to think responsibly about what we want a director to be faithful to" ("Run Mad"). In this case the use of Fanny as narrator/writer, as the voice of Austen herself, re-creates the free indirect discourse we so often miss in Austen film adaptations. "On these counts, Rozema's film is faithful, for it gives us what many of us love about Austen in the first place, what other movies never deliver: Austen's presence as a narrator." As Johnson notes, the "funniness" of the novel is preserved in the film through the writing of Fanny Price. As author she can say what

Austen wrote in the narration and in the satiric and parodic stories of her childhood ("Run Mad").

In *Mansfield Park* we might say that Fanny's triumph is discovering herself to be the heroine of her own life. From waif to wife, she is twice removed from peril, first by Sir Thomas's willingness to take her from poverty in Portsmouth and raise her as his daughter and, second, by Edmund Bertram's willingness to take her from her servitude at Mansfield and make her his wife. In either case, Fanny is not the main actor in the drama of her life. Throughout her childhood, her brilliant and beautiful cousins outstrip her. In her young adulthood, she is overmatched by the lively and charismatic Mary Crawford. Fanny is a character of endurance and perseverance, who is belatedly discovered as the true heroine, the beloved of Edmund. Thus, when Rozema makes of Fanny an author writing her own story, one whose destiny is plotted through her childhood and adolescence with herself as heroine, we have a very different story than author Austen intended. For one thing, as a clergyman's wife, living on a limited income, a mother, a tender of gardens and livestock, Rozema's Fanny will have to give up the life of the writer, just as Austen must have anticipated her fate as wife to Bigg-Wither. In the remake of Fanny as a "compilation" of autobiographical details from Austen's life and her youthful writings, Rozema makes of Fanny's life a fairy tale, one that is inconsistent with the realities of the story *Mansfield Park* tells.

Another problem with the depiction of Fanny Price as self-confident writer of her own fate is the inconsistency in the way that the film shows her status in the Bertram household. Unlike other recent Austen films, the servants who maintain the lifestyle of Mansfield are never seen. Fanny is the only conspicuous servant, yet she seems to have the standing of a family member. She is dressed very simply through most of the film, almost in uniform, suggestive of a schoolgirl or even a nun, perhaps a servant, yet she partakes of the entertainments and speaks up boldly to Mrs. Norris and her cousins. Having a coming-out ball for the film's only visible servant is problematic at best. The film's excuse for recalling her to Mansfield is another point at issue: she is needed to nurse Tom back to health. We would expect qualified nurses or servants to nurse the heir to Mansfield Park; instead, Fanny is shown at his bedside, with sleeves rolled, caring for Tom, performing some of the less attractive tasks of the sickroom. And this occurs at the same time that she is being pressured to become Henry Crawford's wife. The film seems a bit unsure of how to position Fanny within the family, in part because Rozema is pushing the thesis of women as equivalent to slaves.

Cinematic Technique: Reading the Visual Elements of the Film

Mansfield Park. The setting of the film is highly symbolic. Unlike the great homes of other films that feature an ostentatious and grand display of wealth and privilege, Mansfield in Rozema's film is cave-like: cold, barren, faded, and empty. Instead of glamorizing the country estate, Rozema filmed the adaptation at the uninhabited Kirby Hall. The lack of furnishings, rich colors, and opulent display suggest, to Claudia Johnson, a world "corrupted by the moral crime on which it subsists and on which account it cannot thrive" ("Run Mad"). In the final scene Fanny and Edmund sit on the lawn in the shadow of the "ruins" of the west wing of Mansfield, representing the near ruin of the family brought on by its moral corruption.

Self-conscious Stylization. The Rozema film departs from the period-piece adaptations that attempt a near-exact recreation of Austen's rural Regency world. One of the things I like most about this film is its self-consciousness as it calls attention to itself as cinematic art, breaking the illusion of realism. By having Fanny be the author, supplying the narrative voice, we have the ironic distance from the subject that Austen herself supplies in the novels. Through the use of cinematic devices such as freeze frame, slow motion, voice-over, and direct camera address, the film disrupts the realistic illusion and reminds us we are viewing a film, just as the novel's narrator reminds us we are reading fiction. This technique is consistent with one of the film's themes: the role of acting and the difficulty of distinguishing sincerity from role-playing. While debating which play the young people will perform, Edmund defends the drama with a quote about novels from the narrator of *Northanger Abbey:* "it is . . . only some work in which the greatest powers of the mind are displayed, in which the most thorough knowledge of human nature, the happiest delineation of its varieties, the liveliest effusions of wit and humour are conveyed to the world in the best chosen language" (*NA* 38). Readers of Austen's fiction will recognize the quote and appreciate the film's conceptual vantage point. Just as *Northanger Abbey* is self-conscious about novel writing and the narrator's presence as the creator of a novelistic heroine, so the film addresses viewers about the creation of a cinematic heroine.

Another attribute of the Rozema film is its almost parodic approach to "The Austen Film Adaptation." A good example is the moment when the Crawfords are introduced at Mansfield. The dramatic music, slow motion, silent screen, and stylized movements suggest a dramatic "moment" in the story. Maria drops her cards—and her jaw—in exaggerated awe at the sight of Henry Crawford. When the camera pans to Fanny, as the narrative focus, we perceive with her the effect of the Crawfords on the Bertram family, a kind of foreshadowing of the havoc their presence will wreak. This stylized cinematic technique parodies other dramatic moments in Austen film adaptations such as the entrance of the Bingleys and Darcy at the Assembly Ball in *Pride and Prejudice* or Willoughby's dramatic rescue of Marianne Dashwood in *Sense and Sensibility*. Rozema's film invites viewers to engage in criticism not only of the novel it dramatizes but the entire canon of Austen film adaptations as well. Near the end of the film, narrating Fanny reminds us that she is the author of the story we are watching: "It could have turned out differently, I suppose." Claudia Johnson praises these "superb scenes that freeze the action and break the illusion of realism to call attention to the intervention of her art" ("Run Mad").

The theme of *freedom and confinement* in the film is visually represented through birds. In one scene Fanny is reading Lawrence Sterne's *Sentimental Journey*, and Henry Crawford reads aloud the passage of the caged starling who declaims, "I can't get out." The film eliminates the excursion to Sotherton, where Maria Bertram, confined by an engagement to the dull Rushworth, quotes the starling's plea to Henry Crawford, literally referring to a tall iron fence that blocks their progress into the wilderness. Maria says, " . . . unluckily that iron gate, that ha-ha, give me a feeling of restraint and hardship. I cannot get out, as the starling said." Henry replies, "for the world you would not get out without the key and without Mr. Rushworth's authority and protection." He offers as an alternative his "assistance" (*MP* 99). Henry Crawford's "assistance," either as a free sexual encounter with Maria or the offer of marriage to Fanny, is really about control. His chauvinistic pride demands power and authority over women, to play with their hearts for his own entertainment. In the film Henry courts Fanny by bringing an exploding donkey cart filled with encaged white doves. Henry's display is meant to charm Fanny into submission through the symbolism of freeing the doves just as he would free her from the "prison" of Portsmouth. Ironically, his offer of freedom and flight through marriage would only represent another kind of enclosure: marriage to a man Fanny neither loves nor trusts. The circling starlings that Fanny watches from Tom Bertram's sickroom are emblems of the freedom Fanny will achieve through marriage to the man she truly loves, Edmund Bertram. Bird imagery, from Fanny's quill pen to the circling starlings, is intended to symbolize female emancipation from patriarchal tyranny.

Reading the Film
—Questions for Discussion and Writing

1. Analyze the character of Fanny Price. How well are her virtues as *Mansfield Park*'s heroine retained in the film? What new qualities have been added to her characterization? Which of her film qualities have a basis in Austen's text?
2. Frances O'Connor's Fanny is more spirited and sexual than Austen presents her. Are there sources for this characterization in the novel? In what scenes is cinematic Fanny improved over Austen's heroine?
3. Analyze the characterization of the Bertram brothers. Why has Tom been changed into a drunkard and an artist? What purposes does this change in characterization serve? Does Edmund preserve the role of moral guide in the film? How is his relationship with Fanny changed in the film? Is there evidence of his sexual interest in Fanny in the novel?
4. Analyze Harold Pinter's portrayal of Sir Thomas. Why is he demonized in the film? Is there a basis in the novel for his lechery and debauchery?
5. Analyze the portrayal of the Crawfords. Is Mary as lively and charismatic as the novel suggests she would be? Is Henry so attractive and appealing that the Bertram sisters, and Fanny too, might be seduced by him? What, ultimately, does Mary say or do to enlighten Edmund about her character? Why is this changed from the novel?
6. What is lost in the elimination of William Price as a character? Define his role in the novel, and consider why Rozema excluded him from the film.
7. What visual symbolism is associated with feathers and birds in the film? Is there a counterpart in the novel?
8. How important is the slavery issue to the novel? How does it function in the film? How is slavery related to female emancipation in the film?
9. Jane Austen's *Juvenilia* and letters are incorporated into the film. How do the passages used reflect on the development of young Fanny Price?
10. What ironic commentary is provided through the narrative authorial voice of Fanny Price in the film?
11. Examine the setting of Mansfield Park. How is the setting symbolic? What colors predominate? How affluent or lavish is the decor?
12. Examine the setting of the Price home in Portsmouth. Is the film's vision consistent with the details provided in the novel? What other changes occur during the two Portsmouth sequences? Are these consistent with Austen's novel? How do the changes reflect on the heroine?

13. This film has been referred to as *Patricia Rozema's Mansfield Park*. What about the film would make it Rozema's and not Austen's? What is retained from Austen's novel?

14. Analyze the costuming, makeup, and hairdressing of Fanny Price and the other female characters. How do Fanny's costumes compare with those of the Bertram sisters and Mary Crawford? How do her costumes change from her youth to young adulthood? How do these costume changes reflect her character? What colors are predominant in the costuming of all the characters? What mood or tone is set through light and color?

15. How is music used in the film? Consider not only the music within scenes but the score as well.

16. *Mansfield Park* is often thought of as Austen's most serious novel. Does the film include comedy or comic moments? What characters, dialogue, or events suggest comedy? What is the overall tone of the film? What kinds of comedy are evident?

Film Credits

Mansfield Park

"Based on the novel by Jane Austen, her letters and early journals."

1999 BBC/Miramax, 112 minutes.

Written and directed by Patricia Rozema.

Produced by Sarah Curtis.

Cast

Young Fanny	Hannah Taylor-Gordon
Fanny Price	Frances O'Connor
Sir Thomas Bertram	Harold Pinter
Edmund Bertram	Jonny Lee Miller
Mary Crawford	Embeth Davidtz
Henry Crawford	Alessandro Nivola
Mrs. Price/Lady Bertram	Lindsay Duncan
Maria Bertram	Victoria Hamilton
Julia Bertram	Justine Waddell
Mrs. Norris	Sheila Gish

Tom Bertram	James Purefoy
Mr. Rushworth	Hugh Bonneville
Mr. Yates	Charles Edwards
Susan	Sophia Myles
Mr. Price	Hilton McRae
Betsey	Anna Popplewell
Young Susan	Talya Gordon
Carriage Driver	Bruce Byron
Young Maria	Elizabeth Eaton
Young Julia	Elizabeth Earl
Young Edmund	Philip Sarson
Teenage Fanny	Amelia Warner
Boy with Bird Cart	Danny Worters
Dr. Winthrop	Gordon Reid
Ballroom Dancer	Jack Murphy
Ballroom Dancer	Peter Curtis
Ballroom Dancer	Emma Flett
Ballroom Dancer	Wendy Woodbridge

Emma

Emma was written between January 1814 and March 1815 and announced as being "by the author of *Pride and Prejudice*" when it was published in 1816 by John Murray. *Emma* was reviewed by Walter Scott and dedicated to the Prince Regent (Chapman, "Introductory Note to *Emma*" xi).

Emma, the fourth novel published and the second written by the mature Jane Austen at Chawton, is decidedly different from those preceding it. It is the only novel Austen named for its heroine rather than concepts, places, or principles, and it has a decidedly less moral tone. The novel is Austen's most comic, with the heroine herself as the object of irony. As Austen declared, the heroine is one she believed only she would "much like," suggesting a flawed personality. She is also the only heroine who has beauty, fortune, and intelligence united with independence and a beloved circle of family and friends. The only dangers to complete happiness are Emma's propensity "to think a little too well of herself" (*E* 5), and "intellectual solitude" (*E* 7). In fact, the plot is driven by these twin evils, and Emma is shaken out of her complacency by unexpected revelations. On first reading, the book has many surprises, what Claire Thomlin calls "a detective story . . . added to the study of human psychology" (248). Emma learns to know her own mind and heart.

Viewing the Novel
—Approaches to Teaching *Emma*

I include here a general discussion of the main issues, themes, and ideas in *Emma*. My "Approaches to Teaching *Emma*" complement the analytical questions that follow this discussion.

Emma's Education: The Discovery of Self. Emma Woodhouse is described in the opening lines of the novel as "handsome, clever, and rich" (*E* 5). Tutored by Miss Taylor, who had long ago ceased to exercise authority over her charge, holding only "the nominal office of governess" (*E* 5), Emma has come to think herself a very fortunate and independent woman. For Emma the problem is that the gifts of intelligence, sense, and "cleverness" are combined with self-importance and too much time on her hands. If Miss Taylor fails to educate her, so also her indulgent father encourages her vanity and idleness. Only Mr. Knightley is willing to find fault in Emma. As mentor he attempts to check her matchmaking and flights of fancy and imagination, which endanger her place in the social world. Knightley understands Emma completely and assesses her character as such: "She will never submit to any thing requiring industry and patience, and a subjection of the fancy to the understanding" (*E* 37).

Perhaps more serious, Emma has become used to the exercise of power, over her father and her governess, and the management of the household of Hartfield. She rules not as a tyrant but as a benevolent and generous queen. With the marriage of Miss Taylor, she is threatened with "intellectual solitude" (*E* 7), a void Emma fills with an exercise of her power in less productive and even damaging ways. She takes on the improvement of Harriet Smith, dashing Robert Martin's hopes of marriage; attempts matchmaking with Mr. Elton only to suffer his proposal to her; plays at making Frank Churchill fall in love with her only to discover his own secret game with rival Jane Fairfax; and finally competes with Mrs. Elton for power over the community only to wound and offend the beloved Miss Bates. After suffering a series of painful "mortifications," Emma experiences an epiphany, delivered "with the speed of an arrow": "Mr. Knightley must marry no one but herself!" (*E* 408). She discovers "the blindness of her own head and heart" (*E* 411–12). At this same moment, Emma, so used to power, feels powerless to secure the love of Mr. Knightley as she thinks he intends to propose to Harriet Smith. A comic reversal occurs during Mr. Knightley's attempt to propose marriage to Emma, as she stops him at the crucial point thinking he is "within half a sentence of Harriet" (*E* 429). Instead, all ends happily when Emma encourages him to speak, and he acknowledges his love for her. The threat of further isolation is averted. Additionally, Emma will remain mistress of Hartfield, secure in the power over her home and the heart of her husband.

Although Emma "blunders" through a series of schemes that nearly end in disaster, she is not a character whose errors are serious moral failings. Mr. Knightley refers to her as "faultless in spite of all her faults" (*E* 433), a paradox that points to the "perfections" of Emma—her intelligence, independence, beauty, and strong feeling—and her misuse of the gifts and talents she has been blessed with. Emma herself says, "I always deserve the best treatment, because I never put up with any other" (*E* 474). Emma's "education" is not in matters of principle but in the acknowledgment of the claims of others to fair treatment as well, including Robert Martin and Jane Fairfax, the most wronged by her exercise of power. Emma is the only Austen heroine who cries over her own bad behavior, specifically the misuse of her wit at the expense of Miss Bates on Box Hill. While she never apologizes to Miss Bates directly, her visit to her home shows her acting on her awareness of how her cleverness may cause another pain. Her faults are never ones of selfishness as evidenced by the persistent care of her hypochondriacal father, which extends even to the delay of her marriage until he can be reconciled to change. She comes to an honest appraisal of the merits of Jane Fairfax, eliminating the envy that made her think Jane a rival instead of a worthy companion deserving of her sympathy. With Mr. Elton and Frank Churchill, she learns that, although she has the power to stimulate desire and inspire love, the feelings of others are not to be trifled with. Instead, she learns her lack of perception made her vulnerable to the control of others. Likewise, she realizes that her ability to manipulate an ignorant and emotionally vacuous girl like Harriet should not be exercised for the convenience of her own amusement. Through the example of Mrs. Elton, Emma is reminded of how ugly, inelegant, unappealing, and obnoxious is the exercise of pushing oneself forward and claiming superiority. While not herself publicly exposed as such, Emma privately thinks like a Mrs. Elton, and her rare lapses are quickly admonished by Mr. Knightley's "tell[ing] . . . truths" (*E* 375). The lesson of the novel, and the heart of Emma's education, is summarized in Mr. Knightley's proclamation that "every thing serve[s] to prove . . . the beauty of truth and sincerity in all our dealings with each other" (*E* 446). Mr. Knightley had earlier tempered Mr. Weston's compliment to Emma at Box Hill by saying, "*Perfection* should not have come quite so soon" (*E* 371).

Emma is close to perfection, but one more discerning than Mr. Weston is aware of her failings.

Issues of Classism and Feminism. Emma is the Austen heroine who is least concerned about marriage. Her wealth, independence, and position as mistress of Hartfield make marriage less of a necessity than it is for the other heroines. As she says, "I have none of the usual inducements of women to marry. . . . And, without love . . . I should be a fool to change such a situation as mine" (*E* 84). According to Claudia Johnson, critics of *Emma* are most focused on Emma's "authority," the control she exercises over others and her refusal to apologize for this control (122). She is defiantly independent in asserting her advantages: "Fortune I do not want; employment I do not want; consequence I do not want: I believe few married women are half as much mistress of their husband's house, as I am of Hartfield" (*E* 84). Johnson sees *Emma* as an exploration of "positive versions of female power" (126). This heroine's "sense of the privileges and duties attached to her station is legitimate" in spite of her obnoxious and overbearing snobbishness (Johnson 127). Austen's focus in *Emma* on the social hierarchy suggests that class, not gender, is the determiner of power, and most of the wielders of power in the novel are in fact women. Many of us, at least as modern readers, do not decry Emma's power or her independence. Overall, Emma's reign over Highbury shows her to be generous and socially responsible, a remarkable heroine whose smaller failings we tolerate because she is so much closer to perfection than those around her. Nor do we really feel the need for Emma's "reformation," so much as applaud her marriage to Mr. Knightley as a union (the novel's final word) that will enliven his world with her imagination and enrich hers with his wisdom, good judgment, and discipline.

While the actions of Mrs. Churchill, who uses illness and the threat of dying to control the life and movements of her adopted son, represent the abuse of power, we find that simple Miss Bates is a positive example of the power of good will over one's friends and community. Austen creates in Miss Bates a comparative model of behavior for Emma. Seeing something of herself in Miss Bates may account for some of the annoyance she generates in Emma. The novel's narrator, after listing the gifts and privileges united in Emma Woodhouse, invites comparison with Miss Bates in this descriptive passage:

> She had no intellectual superiority to make atonement to herself, or frighten those who might hate her, into outward respect. She had never boasted either beauty or cleverness. Her youth had passed without distinction, and her middle of life

was devoted to the care of a failing mother, and the endeavour to make a small income go as far as possible. And yet she was a happy woman, and a woman whom no one named without good-will. (*E* 21)

As Emma obsesses on social rank and attempts to set up an exclusive circle of friends, Miss Bates rivals her for popularity in the community through her inclusiveness, visiting and receiving guests from all ranks of life. Emma's exercise of her wit on Box Hill, when she "presides" over all, is a direct attack on Miss Bates, one that diminishes Emma and raises sympathy for her opponent. Miss Bates is like a mirror opposite of Emma, an alter ego or "other," that Emma perhaps subconsciously fears becoming as she ages.

When Emma fills her "solitude" with the exercise of her power of matchmaking and interference, she nearly secures the "exclusivity" of herself and her father by excluding all others: "If all took place that might take place among the circle of her friends, Hartfield must be comparatively deserted; and she left to cheer her father with the spirits only of ruined happiness" (*E* 422). Emma, however, is restored to the community, extending her good will to Jane Fairfax, whom she genuinely admires and loves, and to Harriet and Robert Martin, whom she receives at Hartfield. While social classes are not significantly altered in the course of the year in *Emma*, some inversions do occur: Mr. Weston happily marries a governess; Frank Churchill, heir to fortune, marries the penniless Jane Fairfax, averting her sale of "human flesh" (*E* 300); and Mr. Elton, a poor clergyman, secures the fortune of Miss Augusta Hawkins, whose connections include a lawyer (Isabella Woodhouse, too, is married to a lawyer). Even the "worthy" Coles, having risen "in fortune and style of living, second only to the family at Hartfield" (*E* 207), deign to entertain Emma and her father with their new fortune and grand piano. A more open and tolerant society is gradually emerging.

One other example of female authority is Mrs. Elton. Mrs. Elton complicates the plot with her arrival in the community, as she vies with Emma for control over the social life of Highbury. In many ways a caricature of Emma, Mrs. Elton's overreaching sense of superiority is self-involved, parading, even cruel. She torments Emma with her superior judgments, ease of manner, and mode of addressing near strangers in a familiar way. She takes on Jane Fairfax as her protégée as Emma had Harriet, promotes herself among Emma's rivals, the Coles and Bateses, and even attempts to advance Emma socially with introductions to Bath society. Her false elegance is marked by her assertion that Mr. Elton is her "lord and master," when it would be hard to imagine someone more in control than she. Although she resembles Emma, she is differentiated by her hypocrisy, insincerity, and vanity.

Narration and Irony. Emma is the most comic of Austen's novels, with the humor deriving not so much from plot elements or comic characters as from the dramatic irony of the narration. Emma's failures of perception, especially her inability to know her own mind and heart, create a dramatic irony as we, as readers, see more than she knows. Comic deflation is the result of a narration that allows us knowledge and insights denied the heroine. To heighten the dramatic irony, Austen makes use of a narrative device called free indirect discourse, a mode of speech or thought presentation in which the narrator recounts what a character has said while retaining the patterns and idiomatic qualities of her speech. In essence, the narrator exposes the thoughts or speech of the character in a way that undermines credibility and sincerity. (For a more complete analysis of free indirect discourse, see my articles, "Free Indirect Discourse and the Clever Heroine of *Emma*," and "*Mansfield Park*: Free Indirect Discourse and the Psychological Novel.") In this novel, the heroine herself is comically deflated through free indirect discourse as are other characters who are either lacking in knowledge and insight (Harriet Smith) or deceptive (Frank Churchill). This example of free indirect thought shows Emma's failures of perception when given over to "fancy":

> She was not struck by any thing remarkably clever in Miss Smith's conversation, but she found her altogether very engaging—not inconveniently shy, not unwilling to talk—and yet so far from pushing, shewing so proper and becoming a deference, seeming so pleasantly grateful for being admitted to Hartfield, and so artlessly impressed by the appearance of every thing in so superior a style to what she had been used to, that she must have good sense and deserve encouragement. (*E* 23)

In this example, Emma's praises of Harriet actually flatter Emma herself at the same time that they expose Harriet's shortcomings.

Other kinds of irony are evident in the situations of the plot, with its many surprises and discoveries. Obvious examples would be the promotion of Harriet, which convinces Mr. Elton that Emma is interested in him; the raising of Harriet's taste from Robert Martin, which makes her reject Frank Churchill as beneath her; and the good fortune of Frank Churchill, who is rewarded as a result of the deaths of his mother and aunt and whose deceptions eventually secure him the prize of Jane Fairfax. Character pairings, such as Emma and Mrs. Elton, or Emma and Jane Fairfax, also are a source of comic undercutting and irony.

Viewing the Novel
—Questions for Analysis and Discussion

The questions below address the larger issues of each volume and are designed to promote analytical thinking as the basis for discussion. These questions ask students to "see" into the text and complement the central issues of "reading the film" that follow.

Volume I

1. In chapter one the narrator states, "The Woodhouses were first in consequence there. All looked up to them" (E 7). Is this statement completely true? Are there indications that not everyone in the community shares this point of view? Examples?

2. What is the source of Emma's sense of superiority? Is it merited?

3. How does Mr. Knightley rate Emma's abilities? What is the danger of "imagination"?

4. What are Emma's professed reasons for remaining single? Are there subconscious motives? What is her relationship with Mr. Knightley?

5. Why does Emma take on the education of Harriet Smith? What is the basis of their friendship? What is the danger to Emma in such a relationship, and what is the danger to Harriet?

6. What does Emma learn from her miscalculation of Elton's affections for Harriet? Does she express publicly her error? How do you judge her behavior after this incident?

7. What is Emma's relationship with her father? Is there an explanation for why Emma has so much patience with her father and so little with Miss Bates? How do you judge her behavior to each?

8. *Emma* includes more gradations in social/economic class than previous novels. What are some examples? What role does class play in this novel?

9. Analyze Emma's relationship with Miss Bates. How much of her impatience with her is warranted? What motives might underlie Emma's intolerance? Contrast Miss Bates with Emma Woodhouse. Consider their ages and appearance and their social and economic rank in the community. How do you account for Miss Bates's popularity?

10. How is Emma unprepared for matrimony at the novel's opening?

Volume II

1. Mrs. Elton is faulted for her "ease of manners." Why is this a fault? What else about her manners distinguishes her class and upbringing?
2. Critics have referred to Mrs. Elton as a "wicked parody" of Emma. In what ways does Mrs. Elton mirror Emma? What essentials separate them? Why do you think Austen sets up this comparison?
3. Mrs. Elton's protégée is Jane Fairfax. How are these two young women comparable? What essentials separate them? Why do you think Austen sets up this comparison? How is Emma exposed through Mrs. Elton's friendship with Jane?
4. Mrs. Elton speaks of her husband as "lord and master." How would you describe their marriage relationship? How "liberated" is Mrs. Elton in marriage?
5. How is Jane Fairfax comparable to Emma? Why can they not be friends? Is this aversion mutual?
6. How successfully has Austen created the character of Jane Fairfax? What would improve her characterization in the novel?
7. Why does Mr. Knightley dislike Frank Churchill? Is his dislike warranted?
8. What are the clues to Frank Churchill's secret relationship with Jane Fairfax?
9. How is Emma reprehensible for her relationship with Frank Churchill? How is Frank at fault?
10. How does Mr. Knightley feel about Jane Fairfax?

Volume III

1. The incident at Box Hill may be considered the most important single scene in the novel. Which characters are affected by the experience? How has Miss Bates contributed to Emma's moral education?
2. Emma comes to realize she has created "a monster" in Harriet. Describe her creation. How is the new Harriet, in fact, a reflection of Emma herself?
3. What has been Harriet's role in Emma's education into her own mind and heart? Mrs. Elton's role? Jane Fairfax's role?
4. Does Emma's sense of social class change in the novel?
5. Emma refers to Frank as the "child of luck." In how many ways is this true? How much of Frank's good fortune is of his own making?
6. How are Frank and Jane reprehensible in their secret engagement? What risks did they take?

7. Why do you think Mr. Knightley suddenly realizes he loves Emma in ways other than as a sister? What has prompted his discovery?
8. Austen believed that she had created in Emma a heroine "no one but myself will much like." Is this true? Do you like Emma? Why or why not?
9. *Emma* is Austen's most comic novel. What are the sources of comedy? How is Emma a comic heroine?
10. Are tragic events included or alluded to? How do these events affect the overall comic tone? What are the "serious" issues in *Emma*?

Reading the Film —Approaches to Teaching the Film

Choosing a Film Adaptation

Three *Emma* film adaptations are transpositions of the novel: the BBC production from 1972 is a lengthy 257 minutes. In 1996 Miramax created the Gwyneth Paltrow *Emma*, and in 1997 Kate Beckinsale was the lead in a Meridian/A&E film called *Jane Austen's Emma*. *Clueless*, a Paramount production from 1995, is an updated version of the novel almost unrecognizable as an *Emma* transference except to those familiar with the novel. All of the films have strengths and weaknesses, and no one film is completely superior to any other. Elsa Solender, speaking to the Jane Austen Society of North America Conference in 2002, found "some winning scenes" in the 1972 production but wished for closer editing. Of the two 1990s productions, she writes that "neither . . . entirely succeeded" and that the Paltrow film "was little more than a rich, handsome, not-quite-clever-enough vehicle that jump started her career as a superstar" (107). Of the Beckinsale film she writes: "the low-cost production lacked the sparkle of the Paltrow competitor or the bite of Amy Heckerling's *Clueless*." She concludes that the "definitive film *Emma*" might have emerged from combining elements of the three films (Solender 108).

Using Film in the Classroom

I have used one-hour portions from each of the three "transpositions" in teaching *Emma*. This invites discussion as to how the performers, writers, and directors interpret *Emma* differently. For instance, from the 1972 film, I show the Christmas party at Randalls and the proposal scene by Mr. Elton. From the Paltrow 1995 film, I use the scene of the Donwell Abbey strawberry picking and the excursion to Box Hill. And from the 1996 adaptation, I choose the proposal scene and the harvest feast that ends the novel.

If I were to select only one film to show completely through in class, it would be the Beckinsale A&E film. I find the 1996 Davies script closer to Austen's conception of her heroine, especially with its interior fantasy dream sequences to cinematically reveal Emma's imagination and subconscious. Although unsatisfactory in many ways, it does have an interesting portrayal of Emma as a shrewd and manipulative heroine, one whose dreams and subconscious renderings give us a clue to her motivations and fears. Knightley is intense and a worthy match to Emma in intellect, influence, and power unlike the younger, weakened Jeremy Northam portrayal in the Miramax production. If time allows for more student viewing, the older 1972 BBC production offers a close reading of Austen, presented in a traditional and fairly accurate way. This production goes for the "letter of the text" rather than contemporizing or interpreting Austen in any fresh way, but it is serviceable. The only reason I would show the Paltrow Miramax film is to invite analysis of what went wrong. Exhibiting little understanding of Austen's ideas or the culture of the period, the film has only the characters' names and the basic plot to identify it as "based on Jane Austen's *Emma.*" The film is the most romantic and comic of the three transpositions. *Clueless* is another matter altogether. Students should enjoy not only matching the film characters to Austen's and relating plot events but also analyzing the ideas, cultural values, and other issues comparatively. Of the four film versions, this one has the most comedy, another source of analysis that invites students to look more closely at the comedy of the Austen novel as well.

1972 BBC Mini-series

This dramatization attempts to stay close to the original novel, with few appeals to contemporary tastes and values. At times scenes are conflated or rearranged, but not much is deleted in this over-four-hour production. Cinematically, the production has the look of a videotaped stage play (only a single "cameraman" is named in the credits). While most of the major scenes, characters, and dialogue are accurate, the dramatization does not interpret Austen so much as objectively present it. One critical piece calls this the "least interesting of the four" *Emma* adaptations: "it tells the story of *Emma* and not much more" (Phillips and Heal). *Emma* is more comedy than drama, and the film's poignant moments are few. For example, Emma's tears in the carriage from Box Hill need more preparation than the abrupt camera shot from Harriet to Emma in the carriage. The rainy day when Mr. Woodhouse and Emma lament their separate isolations is likewise an abrupt change of tone in this upbeat and energetic dramatization.

Casting and Characterization

Doran Godwin as Emma Woodhouse is lively, gracious, and clever. Occasionally, she is annoyingly cheerful or obnoxiously snobbish. Her scenes with Mr. Knightley have a "sauciness" that just escapes flirtation. John Carson portrays Mr. Knightley as a bit more refined than one would expect from the proprietor of a working estate like Donwell Abbey. His accent and dress are more suited to the drawing room, and we rarely see him out of doors, riding his horse or walking, as he is described in the novel. He seems most "natural" when lecturing Emma or noting her bad behavior. In Knightley's proposal scene, the potential for comedy is present in the Austen text as Emma stops Knightley in the midst of his proposal, fearing he is to speak of Harriet: "'Oh! then, don't speak it, don't speak it,' she eagerly cried. 'Take a little time, consider, do not commit yourself'" (*E* 429). In the film the comedy of the moment borders on buffoonery, as Knightley is rebuffed, then petitioned to begin again. Knightley is mortified, and Emma relents and asks him to continue, but the tenderness and romance of the scene are lost.

Ania Marson, playing Jane Fairfax, recalls the subject of a Vermeer portrait, pale and refined with carefully arranged hair and costume. Her halting, barely audible speech suggests shyness and lack of confidence. Instead of a depiction of "reserve," she appears depressed, silent, and slumping, almost drugged in her glassy-eyed stare. Given the energy and exuberance of Robert East as Frank Churchill, we doubt the companionship of this match. Critics Phillips and Heal disagree, singling her out as "a spirited, resolute woman who stands up for herself as best she can against the pushy Mrs. Elton.... She certainly is a character whose presence is felt." Jane's complicated coiffures suggest a hairdresser's assistance in arranging her hair although Miss Bates claims that she did it herself.

Harriet Smith, played as a wonderful naïf by Debbie Bowen, is perfectly credulous and a brilliant contrast to the clever machinations of the heroine. Seeing Emma's own impatience and, at times, annoyance with Harriet points out the disparity in their intelligence and consequence as well as proving Emma is aware of Harriet's inadequacies, heightening the comedy.

Mr. and Mrs. Elton provide some of the film's best comic moments, such as the one in the carriage on Christmas Eve when Mr. Elton "attacks" Emma with his proposal. Her surprise and annoyance are comically rendered with Emma as the ironic victim. Mrs. Elton, played by Fiona Walker, has lots of finery, bad teeth, a loud voice, and a sneering contemptuousness suitable for the character. Her bad manners take the form of shouting and talking over people, a display most likely to offend modern audiences, who might miss the more subtle ill-mannered use of familiar modes of address ("Knightley," "Mr. E.," and "Jane," for example) that characterize her in the novel.

Changes from Novel to Film
(Significant Deletions, Additions, and Revisions)

A significant change occurs because of the conflation of the strawberry-picking scene and the Box Hill excursion into an extended scene occurring during one day instead of successive days. Having Mr. Elton away to London on business is the pretext for Knightley's offer to bring the Highbury friends to Donwell Abbey to pick strawberries. Thus, Mrs. Elton is given ample opportunity to command and lead. However, because Jane is out of sorts and walks home from this gathering, she is not present for the later trip to Box Hill to witness Frank openly flirting with Emma. It is important to the development of their relationship that Jane witness both the flirtation and the insult to her aunt, Miss Bates. Austen makes Emma more reprehensible for exposing the aunt to ridicule before her niece. Eliminating Jane thus diminishes some of the shame and embarrassment Emma should feel as part of her moral education. Likewise, Mr. Elton is not present to hear Jane's response to Frank's remark about couples "marrying ... upon an acquaintance formed only in a public place" (*E* 372). Jane replies, "it can be only weak, irresolute characters, (whose happiness must be always at the mercy of chance,) who will suffer an unfortunate acquaintance to be an inconvenience, an oppression for ever" (*E* 373). This must surely register on the Eltons, whose own relationship was formed at Bath, but Mr. Elton's absence lessens the sting.

Another change occurs in the visit Emma makes to Miss Bates after the insult at Box Hill. In the novel the discussion during the visit centers on Jane and her acceptance of a governess position with Mrs. Smallridge, an acquaintance of Mrs. Elton. However, in the film Emma attempts an apology for her insulting remark the previous day. This change is notable because in the novel Emma never publicly admits her errors nor apologizes to the offended parties. A smaller change is in having Jane accept a position with a Mrs. Dixon. The film eliminates the word game with "blunder" and "Dixon" as well as the friendship with the Campbell daughter married to a Mr. Dixon, who

Emma imagines is in love with Jane and the source of the pianoforte.

At the end of the film Harriet brings Robert Martin to Hartfield to be introduced, and Emma invites Harriet to bring him again. This is not inconsistent with the novel, for "Emma became acquainted with Robert Martin, who was now introduced at Hartfield" and "attended Harriet to church, and saw her hand bestowed on Robert Martin" (*E* 482), indicating she has lessened her earlier resistance to the farmer whose class she considered so beneath her.

In the novel Austen has Emma playing with her niece, little Emma, to thwart more criticism from Knightley about her involvement in the Martin/Harriet affair (*E* 98). This film sets the scene in the nursery, with Emma finishing the feeding of the infant. She is posed as a Madonna with Child, and the acrimonious conversation with Knightley is thus toned down. I don't find this scene to be realistic for two reasons: for one, feeding an infant would have been the nanny's duty; and, second, Knightley's appearance in an upper nursery bedroom would have been inappropriate. The intimacy of the scene is uncomfortable although most likely designed to foreshadow a future family.

1996 Meridian-ITV Film

Jane Austen's Emma does many things that engage viewers in textual considerations. In its relatively short 107 minutes, the adaptation retains the key scenes of the novel and enough of the dialogue and minor characters to be a close representation of Austen's story. Additionally, its cast is engaging, and the psychological rendering of the inner consciousness of a few key characters probes the subtext of Austen's work. Not all critics were pleased with the Davies script. Elsa Solender thinks *Jane Austen's Emma* "lacks sparkle" (107–8). Lisa Hopkins disagrees: "Davies's film is not only, subjectively, a much more interesting and creative adaptation than McGrath's version; it is one that, objectively, shows more." William Phillips and Louise Heal call this film "perhaps the most important of the period adaptations."

Casting and Characterization

Kate Beckinsale is an interesting Emma. Not a great beauty like Gwyneth Paltrow, she features instead the intelligence, ironic wit, confidence, self-importance, and deviousness that is the essence of Austen's Emma. She holds her own against the Mark Strong Knightley, no easy task given the sharpness of his anger and force of his chastisements. Instead of pouting and hanging her head when reproved, Beckinsale's Emma fumes with a sense of her own rightness and a determination to have her own way, excepting of course the moments after she is almost forcibly thrown into the carriage at Box Hill. She never seems to think of Harriet as an equal or even as a friend so much as a project, which I see as consistent with the Austen text. This Harriet is sweet, simple, admiring, and very fragile, setting off by contrast Emma's smart confidence in her makeover scheme, the means of filling the void of her "intellectual solitude" (*E* 7). Beckinsale has an air of importance that never falters, and her scorn for Mrs. Elton, Miss Bates, and Jane Fairfax is subtly revealed in glance and gesture.

Mark Strong as Mr. Knightley seems right, not so old and stuffy as John Carson's 1972 Knightley nor so young and handsome as Jeremy Northam's in the Miramax adaptation. Strong is attractive and almost too forceful in reprimanding Emma. The film makes an interesting psychological study of Knightley as the jealous lover who does not know his own heart or mind any more than Emma does. We see his jealous glances and stares as Emma talks of Frank Churchill and his seething anger when she openly flirts with Frank. In the novel we can understand Knightley's motivation in criticizing Frank before he ever makes an appearance because we understand his subconscious feelings for Emma, feelings he discovers only when he is threatened with losing her. The film visualizes these undercurrents of jealous love through glances and fits of temper. The charismatic spark between Emma and Knightley is evident in this performance, with a flirtatious interaction that foreshadows their eventual engagement.

Mr. Elton, portrayed by Dominic Rowan, is definitive. Handsome and smug, yet foolish, especially in the "*cara sposa*" segments, he makes us understand how Augusta Hawkins can be both his prize and his punishment in life. Lucy Robinson's Mrs. Elton is appropriately rigged out in pearls and lace, and her contemptuous self-importance is never over the top.

Jane Fairfax in this adaptation has a strong presence. Olivia Williams is not a striking beauty, but her performance has the "elegance" that Austen gives Jane to set her apart from the community and the fate life has handed her. In this adaptation she is characterized as strong and forthright yet shyly radiant when around Frank. Raymond Coulthard's Frank Churchill is a curly-headed dandy, with enough deviousness to cover his dual roles as suitor to both Emma and Jane. This version makes it obvious where his heart is engaged, and Emma herself does not seem much involved with his time or attentions.

The role of Mr. Woodhouse is excellently performed by Bernard Hepton.

The childish valetudinarian is one of the annoyances of the novel (along with Miss Bates), and it becomes a challenge to portray him without driving viewers away. This film gets it right: Hepton's Woodhouse is childishly simple and self-centered but not overdone. His scenes are comic, and we realize Emma's kindness in caring for him at Hartfield.

Changes from Novel to Film
(Significant Deletions, Additions, and Revisions)

The Meridian film, more than any other of the *Emma* adaptations, makes visible the enormous household staff that supports the lavish and comfortable lifestyle of the upper classes. It's almost the *Gosford Park* of the Austen films. Servants are present in nearly every scene. One glaring example is the strawberry picking at Donwell Abbey, where liveried servants move silk pillows for the guests to kneel on as they pick the berries. Ironically, Mrs. Elton proclaims strawberry picking to be "so simple and natural." At the next day's excursion to Box Hill, the servants toil up the incline with huge baskets of food, umbrellas, tables, and pillows for the elaborate picnic lunch set with china and crystal. Carol Dole points out that "transitions between scenes characteristically turn on the movement of servants" (70). We see this when Mr. Woodhouse offers Harriet Smith a "small slice" of apple tart. Mr. Elton offers to get it but is handed the plate immediately by a servant. This adaptation almost foregrounds the servants in scenes, and while the film acknowledges the "truth" of how class was maintained in Austen's era, this visibility of the underclass was never central to Austen's subject. Phillips and Heal point out the film's characterization of Robert Martin and Jane Fairfax (farmer and governess, respectively) as part of a rising class in the nineteenth century who are "neither servants nor people of property." While the other *Emma* films diminish Jane's presence, in this one she is featured prominently and not just for her elegance and musical proficiency. Instead, she is forthright, speaks openly, and becomes more than a shadowy mystery. Robert Martin, too, is a confident and self-possessed young man, strong, attractive, and not unwilling to look directly into the face of Emma Woodhouse. While this visual representation of the underclasses may be "violating the spirit of *Emma* . . . the film raises questions about the lives of characters who rarely . . . appear in the pages of Austen" (Phillips and Heal).

Another addition occurs in the Christmas scene with the children of John and Isabella Knightley. As in the other three Austen film transpositions, Emma appears in a Madonna-like pose with little Emma. As we share

Knightley's observation of the scene, we can imagine his fantasy of Emma as mother to his own child. In this version, Knightley departs from Austen's text and tells Emma he held her in his arms much like this child in hers, accentuating their sixteen-year age difference but also suggesting again their near brother-sister relationship.

The harvest banquet that closes the film has prompted some controversy for its "democratization" of the characters. Mrs. Elton protests this event as a sitting down "with hobbledehoys," but because her credibility in the community has already been undercut and because she attends and partakes of the food and entertainment, we can assume that others view with acceptance the intermingling of classes in a social setting. Emma openly seeks an introduction to Mr. Martin, even though he is obviously not of the gentleman class. The gradations of class are retained, however, and visually displayed though the dance that ends the film, for a hierarchical pattern emerges. Emma and Knightley are centered, with Frank and Jane and then Harriet and Robert Martin branching outward in one line, while behind them Isabella and John Knightley are centered, with the Westons and then the Eltons forming a second branch. We can read the symbology of the pattern as the Knightleys and Woodhouses form a center with the Westons/Churchills as next in importance, and radiating outward, the Eltons and the Martins. Holding hands suggests the interconnection that is the basis of the community. Furthermore, Mr. Knightley speaks, in a patrician way, of stability and the continuation of his protectorate role, even though he will now be living at Hartfield. As Carol Dole says, "the harvest supper presents a fantasy of genial class intermingling that has no precedent in Austen's novel" (71–2). The harvest supper is a departure from the book's ending in which Emma's "union" with Mr. Knightley in marriage is witnessed by only "a small band of true friends" (*E* 484).

Cinematic Technique: Reading the Visual Elements of the Film

The most unique cinematic innovation in this adaptation is the use of dream sequences to reveal Emma's subconscious fears and fantasies. In one sequence Emma daydreams of Mr. Elton marrying Harriet Smith and of the gratitude and adulation Harriet will bestow on her. Another daydream has Frank Churchill "walking" out of his portrait at Randalls and gallantly kissing Emma's hand. In a visual irony, shortly thereafter, Mr. Elton in reality kisses Emma's hand in his inebriated proposal. Later, in what is a real nightmare for Emma, she dreams of Mr. Knightley and Jane Fairfax at the altar about to speak their vows of matrimony, but she, with Little Henry's best interests at heart, attempts to stop the ceremony, looking, as one critic says "more like a spurned single mother than a concerned aunt" (Ferriss 128). Ironically, as Lisa Hopkins notes, Emma "is, suggestively, as much breaker as maker of marriages," at least in this sequence. In a more romantic dream, Emma envisions the rescue of Harriet Smith from the gypsies by Frank Churchill. The gypsies have metamorphosed into flower children waving the hero and maiden on to castles in the sky. "What Davies shows us is the force of the inner drives which impel her. . . . Psychological drives of all kinds are at least hinted at" (Hopkins). Hopkins also sees in this film the "strangeness of the kick she derives from" matchmaking, not unlike the perverse food fetishes of Mr. Woodhouse. Suzanne Ferriss writes that "Davies's adaptation exploits cinematic innovations to probe Emma's psyche in typical twentieth-century psychoanalytic style, and Lawrence's direction employs contemporary cinematic techniques to stress the heroine's inner states and longing." She concludes, "Emma's imaginist tendencies are presented more as unconscious processes than as willed creations" (Ferriss 128).

Another interesting cinematic device is the use of light and dark. The McGrath film is set predominantly outdoors with summery sunshine highlighting the warm pastel tones of costume and settings. The Davies film, on the other hand, is set primarily indoors, and the coloration is darker and more subdued. Autumnal tones of brown, beige, rust, and black predominate. Candles, softening the tones and increasing the shadows, light the interior scenes. This could be read as recognition of the "dark side" of life in the great homes of the Regency period, the one lived by the servants and working classes. Occasionally, light is used to represent "insight," as when a sunbeam singles out Harriet Smith among the congregation and Emma gets the idea of Harriet as the future mate of Mr. Elton.

1996 Miramax Film

This adaptation is the prettiest of the *Emma* films and arguably the most cinematically beautiful of all the Austen film adaptations. Much of the film is set outdoors with scenes in parks displaying the well-manicured lawns and gardens attached to the English country house. The verdure of the English countryside is a pleasing backdrop to the scenes of picnics, archery, painting, and needleworking. Interior scenes are equally attractive, providing an elegant, classical setting for Gwyneth Paltrow as Emma. Costumes are youthful and set off Paltrow's figure and glamour. However, as many critics have commented, the film lacks conceptual integrity with Austen's *Emma*. One review says it "eviscerates the novel," reduces characterization to one dimension, eliminates elements of mystery, and violates the spirit of Austen's work (Phillips and Heal). Others criticize it for over-romanticizing the plot by making it a love story between two young people. Phillips and Heal call it "an enjoyable movie but not an adaptation that asks the viewer to engage Austen at all seriously." Its emphasis on romantic comedy is such that the novel is reduced to a comedy of errors with one-dimensional performers, shallow emotions, and a failure to understand or address the serious issues that underlie Austen's comic novel. Having Knightley appear as Emma's love interest so early in the story makes the rest of the film meaningless. If she knows her heart at the outset, we do not anticipate a discovery.

Casting and Characterization

For many viewers Gwyneth Paltrow is the reason for the film's popularity. Paltrow plays Emma as a beautiful model, as a spoiled child, as a rebellious teen, as a Grecian statue, but Austen critics fault her performance for failing to behave like an intelligent adult woman. Her typical gestures are pouting, rolling her eyes, sighing in exasperation, and whining. One of the ways Emma is characterized in the Austen novel is through comparisons, with Mrs. Elton, for example, but more importantly with Jane Fairfax. Jane is the standard of true elegance and female accomplishment. Her education and her proficiency at the pianoforte are marks of her application, contrasting with Emma's mere competency in drawing, music, and literature. In the McGrath film Emma/Paltrow refers in a voice-over to "that *ninny*, Jane Fairfax." Although Austen's Emma is jealous of Jane, she never underestimates her abilities and value; having Emma call Jane a "ninny" devalues Emma. Another moment played for comic effect is having Emma replace Harriet's picture with that of a dog, an unkindness not in keeping with Austen's Emma.

Casting the very handsome Jeremy Northam as Mr. Knightley obviously enhances the romance of the story. Since Emma and Mr. Knightley think of each other as "old friends," "brother and sister," even mentor and student, the "romance" is not dominant in the plot until their relationship is threatened by Harriet's fancying herself in love with Knightley. Emma then fears his absence from her life: "Mr. Knightley to be no longer coming there for his evening comfort!—No longer walking in at all hours, as if ever willing to change his own home for their's!" (*E* 422). Mr. Knightley thinks romantically of Emma only when jealousy is engendered by her flirtation with Frank Churchill. A rival brings each to the realization of love. In this film adaptation, the casting of two attractive actors of almost equal age makes the relationship flirtatious and charismatic at the opening. As one critic writes, "Their union [Emma and Knightley] is so aesthetically pleasing that Emma's inability to see Knightley as anything other than a brother-in-law is called into question within the movie's first five minutes" (Nachumi 134). Even less convincing is the game of love with the foppish Frank Churchill. How Emma could think of him when Jeremy Northam/Mr. Knightley is at hand is unfathomable. However, Northam's Knightley smiles too much, even as Mr. Elton flirts with Emma at the Weston Christmas party and at Box Hill.

Other characters are cast with varying degrees of success. Toni Collette plays Harriet Smith with bovine simplicity. Her bad teeth and poor posture early in the film cry out for a makeover. In the final scene, where she exalts herself into thinking Frank Churchill too low for her, she has a bit more style and appears to merit Mr. Knightley's assessment of her great improvements. Mrs. Weston, whose role in this production is greater than in any of the others as confidante and friend of Emma, is played with poise, warmth, and elegance by Greta Scacchi. In fact, she stands out among the female cast as one of the most attractive.

Mrs. Elton's role, played beautifully by Juliet Stevenson, is reduced to a few choice scenes, especially the one in which she visits Hartfield and passes judgment on the community. Her sneering self-importance is established, and little dialogue is necessary to capture the humor of her presence at other scenes, such as the ball at the Crown and the strawberry picking. While critics praise "the delivery and timing of Juliet Stevenson in a brilliant performance as Mrs. Elton," the film fails to acknowledge the similarities between her and Emma, a great source of comedy and insight into Emma's flaws (Phillips and Heal). Alan Cumming's Reverend Elton is eager but lacks much else in terms of character. The scene of proposal is played for comic effect, but having Elton say he doesn't care if Miss Smith is alive or dead goes for an easy laugh, hardly consistent with Austen's decorum.

Other characters whose roles are diminished, thankfully, include Mr. Woodhouse, who is much healthier and less "old maidish" than in other productions, and Miss Bates, played by a youngish Sophie Thompson, whose annoying garrulity is supplanted by an annoying laugh. Ewan McGregor as Frank Churchill is a foppish coxcomb badly in need of a haircut who seems totally disinterested in disguising his courtship of Jane with a flirtation with Emma. Jane Fairfax is vaguely present at the strawberry picking/Box Hill picnic and is featured in only one lovely piano scene where she and Frank join voices. The John Knightleys are barely seen, the notable exception being the enchanting scene of Emma's "dancing" little Emma on her knee as she and Mr. Knightley spar over her degree of blame in breaking up Harriet and Robert Martin.

Changes from Novel to Film
(Significant Deletions, Additions, and Revisions)

As in the 1972 BBC dramatization, this adaptation conflates the Donwell Abbey strawberry picking and the Box Hill excursion, events which occur on successive days in the novel. On the first day Jane Fairfax walks home in frustration at Mrs. Elton's pressing her to take the governess position she has arranged, then quarrels with Frank. The next day at Box Hill the same party assembles, but the mood is decidedly different. The party is out of sorts, and Frank's flirtation with Emma is designed to hurt Jane, who strikes back with her remark about ending alliances when the principals no longer love one another. This prepares us for the ill-tempered remark Emma makes to Miss Bates. When Emma insults Miss Bates, the scene is witnessed by Jane Fairfax and by the Eltons, both of whom feel the sting of the wit and the comment on relationships formed at a watering place. By conflating the strawberry-picking scene and the Box Hill episodes to one day and eliminating much of the dispirited banter that precedes the "game" Frank proposes, there is little prequel to Emma's exercise of her wit. Conflating the two scenes into one is appropriate in the interests of economy, but the result is the lack of preparation for the flirtation, the disjunction of the party, and the insult to Miss Bates. In this production it comes off as an unmotivated piece of meanness that is inconsistent with the Emma seen throughout the film, and we are not so much shocked by the cruelty of the remark as surprised by its appearance.

Emma's visit to Miss Bates after the insult at the picnic is changed from the novel. Emma is ushered into Miss Bates's apartment just as she is telling Jane to say she is lying down, and both shut out Emma. Their refusal to see Emma castigates her more thoroughly than in the novel, for she is denied exoneration through a proffered apology or the penance of suffering through a visit. Denying her an opportunity for forgiveness intensifies our sense of the wrongness of her behavior.

The gypsy scene strangely includes Emma. While the object of the attack is Harriet and her purse, Emma is involved in the fracas as she attempts to pull the attackers back. It seems improbable that the gypsies would have dared a robbery with someone of Emma's stature there and more improbable that they would not have attempted to rob her as well. The Paltrow Emma is bolder and more athletic than we are accustomed to seeing in an Austen heroine, so her attempt to defend Harriet and fight off the attackers is consistent with this vision, but the scene is not very believable.

The proposal scene is more romantic than in the novel, as both characters become shy and seem to dance around each other. Knightley twice kisses Emma, rather passionately, a display of emotion not in keeping with the novel's restrained discovery of mutual love. Paltrow's Emma declares she will cease calling him "Mr. Knightley" and instead say, "*My* Mr. Knightley." The wedding is attended by Mrs. Elton as well as "the small band of true friends" (*E* 484). Her remark about the insufficient amounts of satin is addressed to the camera or audience. As Troost and Greenfield have noted, the wedding ceremony ending the film includes the Eltons, the Churchills, and the Martins, "images [that] reinforce a sense of expanded community as the clincher for the happy ending."

Conceptual Integrity (Themes, Ideas, Spirit of Austen's Novel)

The feminist implications of the Miramax film have been noted by critics: "The image of Emma engaging simultaneously in athletic and verbal competition with Knightley has a particular resonance for contemporary women, who are regularly exhorted to 'Just Do It' like their male counterparts. McGrath's version thus offers an active, competitive heroine, whose physical daring mirrors her outspokenness and verbal self-confidence"; her driving a gig is cited as an example of her daring and "the emerging feminism of the era" (Ferriss 127). However, it seems a highly unlikely activity for any young woman of the Regency era, much less the heiress of Hartfield who would have had servants to drive her wherever and whenever she chose to go. Having her drive alone is emblematic of her independence and freedom in a modern way, although one wonders how she manages to keep her lemon-yellow gown from being spattered with mud. Countering the feminist argument, Sue Parrill points out that while she may take the reins in hand, when she gets stuck in the mud, she is rescued by a man—Frank Churchill. Likewise, she may be a skilled archer, but when Mr. Knightley faults her for meddling with Harriet, her arrows, like her advice to Harriet, miss the mark. John Greenfield sees the message in the film as negative: "power and independence for women is ultimately undesirable and dangerous" (qtd. in Parrill). In the novel Emma's authority is signaled through her care for her father and the management of their home, engagements, and servants. These signs of her being mistress of Hartfield are nearly absent in this modern adaptation. They are replaced instead with Emma moving about freely as a modern woman would.

The McGrath Emma also speaks like a contemporary feminist when she accuses Knightley of thinking that a woman who refuses marriage is the most incomprehensible thing in the world to a man and that men only value beauty and good nature in a woman. Knightley's response, that men of sense do not want silly wives, reveals his superior grasp of Harriet's suitability for Robert Martin, which is proven correct in the end when they find their way back together. While the McGrath film spouts a feminist doctrine, it undermines a feminist philosophy by focusing on Paltrow/Emma's beauty and figure and dumbing down her character to one who plucks the petals of a daisy and visits a chapel to pray for Knightley to remain single. Even Emma's good deed, her visit to the sick, is undercut by her attempting to use the young child seeking broth for his sick mother as a decoy to delay interrupting what appears to be Mr. Elton's proposal to Harriet. Her obsession with matchmaking and marriage as woman's ultimate fate is hardly feminist.

The class issues of *Emma* are also obscured in the McGrath script. Carol Dole writes that the *Emma* films made in America tend to "pay tribute to our ideology of classlessness and reinforce the class structures on which we implicitly rely" (69). Instead of an examination of the subtleties of class and its hierarchies within the Highbury community, the film tends to play class issues as a joke. Positioning characters within a scene so neither dominates is a visual device to lessen distinctions. In one scene Harriet rests her head in Emma's lap, and in another, Emma bows her head into Harriet's lap, gestures that denote an equal social level. The ouster of Harriet from Emma's circle is also eliminated, and Knightley refers to Robert Martin as "my good friend" (Dole 69). The setting of most of the film is the beautiful park of Hartfield, where gardens and elaborate tents are displayed without any evidence of human intercession. The scenes in Highbury itself are more "earthy" with animals, dirt, and weather that suggest a working-class world, almost as if the gods shine on the resplendent grounds of Hartfield alone. One of the attractions of the film is the "seductive spectacularizing of upper-class luxuries" (Dole 70). However, the film fails to explain how such a lifestyle is maintained.

Cinematic Technique: Reading the Visual Elements of the Film

The use of segue to transition between scenes is an excellent device for economical conflation of scenes without elaborate preparations. As Lisa Hopkins notes, "Emma's private wish that something should *not* come to pass invariably segues into a scene in which it *has*." And Phillips and Heal commend "the technique of verbal and visual segues between key scenes [as a] notable use of cinematic compression."

Camera angles and lighting are used to set off Paltrow's Emma as a kind of Greek goddess in portrait or as a statue. Nora Nachumi notes how her dress (while consistent with the empire gown of the period) gives the appearance of a Greek goddess, while her poses "emphasize the neoclassical aesthetic" (136).

Narration and interior consciousness are handled in a variety of ways including voice-over, especially as Emma writes to "Dear Diary." Conversations with Mrs. Weston allow for Emma to explore her thoughts openly. Since Mrs. Weston's voice narrates the opening and closing of the film, she is understood to be the equivalent of the narrative voice in the novel. Thus, Emma's thoughts, which are rendered as interior consciousness or free indirect discourse in the novel, can be voiced by Emma and critiqued by Mrs. Weston, as they would be through the narration in the text. A good example is when Emma discovers she is in love with Mr. Knightley. In the novel this is rendered as a free indirect thought, presented by a narrator who exposes Emma's failures to know herself through the mode of discourse. The same critique is provided by a conversation with Mrs. Weston in the film as Emma verbalizes her newly discovered feelings and Mrs. Weston chides her for lack of insight.

Much of the action that is set as interior scenes in Austen's novel is moved out of doors in this film as in so many of the 1990s Austen adaptations. Emma sits under elaborate umbrellas and canopies as she and Harriet do needlework, when she writes in her diary, and as she and Mrs. Weston discuss with Knightley their conjectures about Jane Fairfax. Emma and other female characters, often without hats, move about athletically in free-flowing gowns that never hinder their actions or detract from their beauty. Even the painting of Harriet is done out of doors, much to the horror of Mr. Woodhouse, who in the novel complains of the fact that the artificial setting of the painting is out of doors, threatening the health of poor Miss Smith. Even more dangerous, at the picnic at Donwell Abbey, the guests lounge on the ground. This is decidedly not what Mr. Knightley preferred in Austen's novel. Responding to Mrs. Elton's suggestion that a table be spread in the shade out of doors, Mr. Knightley says, "My idea of the simple and the natural will be to have the table spread in the dining-room. The nature and the simplicity of gentlemen and ladies, with their servants and furniture, I think is best observed by meals within doors" (*E* 355). Apparently, the filmmakers saw more to admire in the pretty lawns and gardens of the estate than in the drawing room of a great home.

Clueless 1995

Clueless is "arguably the most commercially and critically popular 'version' of a Jane Austen novel," writes Elsa Solender of this 1995 Paramount motion picture (113). Although Amy Heckerling, the writer and director, does not credit Austen or *Emma*, the parallels are clear, and the film has long since become established as an adaptation, inviting viewers to discover connections. Although the setting of the film is 1990s Beverly Hills instead of a rural village in Regency England, the film is distinguished, according to Solender, for its "fidelity to her muse's purposes, and the delicate tone and effect of her satire" (114). Lisa Hopkins also praises its conceptual integrity, calling it "a sassy, witty adaptation," acknowledging it as "a genuine, and very suggestive, reflection on what Austen's *Emma* said about the class system and some of the things which have or haven't changed across two continents and nearly two centuries."

Casting and Characterization

Alicia Silverstone as Cher is the perfect representation of Austen's heroine: "handsome, clever, and rich, with a comfortable home and happy disposition" (*E* 5). Similarly, Cher experiences the "real evils" of Emma's situation: possessing the "power of having rather too much her own way, and a disposition to think a little too well of herself" (*E* 5). However, I agree with Elsa Solender in that we come to love Cher, Heckerling's "pretty monster," for the same reasons we come to love Austen's creation Emma. By looking at Cher's faults, we find their source in overindulgence and being "prematurely elevated to positions of power" (Solender 114). But both have "good hearts," and Emma's eventual recognition of her own heart, of the pain her interference can cause and of her responsibility to those less fortunate, makes us like her "in spite of her faults." A counterpart is Cher's "makeover of her soul," which is motivated by a desire to prove herself worthy of her Mr. Knightley, Josh. Cher, like Emma, lost her mother, but whereas Emma's mother is rarely mentioned, Cher's mother (in a portrait) provides a motivation to get good grades in school. Most important, Cher and Emma share a need for control over their own lives and others. Comically, Cher remarks that makeup gives one a sense of control in a chaotic world. Emma's need to control the social hierarchy of Highbury is designed to prevent social change that would lessen her privilege and prestige. Her "makeover" of Harriet is an example of that need to control, while her dislike of Miss Bates stems perhaps from the older woman's tolerance of all her friends and neighbors and a willingness to visit and be visited indiscriminately. For Cher and Emma, chaos is avoided when people are compartmentalized by behavior or appearance (in Cher's world) or by social class (in Emma's).

Josh is a stepbrother to Cher, as the son of one of her father's ex-wives. Like Mr. Knightley, who is Emma's brother-in-law and not a biological relative, Josh acts as "big brother" to guide Cher's moral education. One example of Josh's guidance is when Cher attempts to learn to drive. When she fails to get a driver's license, she must depend on Josh to drive her. She realizes her power has limitations as she laments, "I failed something I couldn't talk my way out of," suggesting symbolically the obstacles to real independence and freedom. Just as Emma relies on Knightley to guide her moral education, so Josh "drives" Cher to "a makeover of her soul" with his example of selflessness and tolerance. In another example, Josh notes Cher's insensitivity to housekeeper Lucy's country of origin, just as Emma was corrected by Knightley after her joke at Miss Bates's expense at Box Hill. Cher's attempts at "good deeds" consist of giving her cast-off Italian designer outfits to Lucy (whose age and size would suggest the inappropriateness of the gesture) and later aiding a relief organization by collecting skis and caviar for the destitute. Her ineffectualness in relieving suffering suggests her limited perception of a world beyond her privileged one just as Emma fails to see how wrong are her attempts to promote Harriet's case in the social world of Highbury. At the same time their attempts to help the disadvantaged signify a good heart. As Cher remarks when considering the project of making over Tai: one should use popularity for a good cause. Josh dislikes the intimacy Cher develops with Christian and warns her father about her immodest dress, just as Knightley revealed a jealous regard for Emma when he thought she was growing fond of Frank Churchill. And, as Knightley did for Harriet, Josh rescues Tai when no one will dance with her, prompting her to believe he is in love with her. Emma realizes "the blindness of her own head and heart" (*E* 412), while Cher, at this moment, admits her own "cluelessness": "a virgin who can't drive."

Cher's Daddy replaces Mr. Woodhouse. Daddy's obsession with work and his poor nutrition are mirror opposites of Mr. Woodhouse's inertia and obsession with good health. An ironic twist is that Cher is overly concerned about Daddy's health, whereas Mr. Woodhouse fusses about Emma's. Daddy is also gruff and tyrannical, frightening everyone but Cher, a reversal of the gallant chauvinism and warm regard of Mr. Woodhouse.

Travis Birkenstock is the equivalent of the working-class farmer Robert Martin. However, Travis is distinguished not so much by "his rank in society" as by his behavior and life choices. He is awkward, loud, poorly coifed, badly dressed, and "a loadie," a user of marijuana. Cher finds him unsuitable for Tai (Harriet), even though they share the same behavior and habits. Because Cher changes Tai's clothing and makeup to fit in with the popular crowd, she thinks she has changed her societal position just as Emma thought she had done with Harriet. Unfortunately, the makeover is only cosmetic, and Tai remains an outsider (as Harriet does) because she is sexually active—although "technically a virgin." Also, she uses drugs, and her manners and speech are not as cool as those of the in-crowd. Cher eventually sees the appropriateness of uniting Travis and Tai, but only after Tai threatens her relationship with Josh and after Travis's drug reformation. Other aspects of their behavior make them a suitable match, just as Harriet finds in Robert Martin "what satisfies" her (*E* 472). As Carol Dole points out, Heckerling "justifies their coupling by invoking one of the few widely accepted class dividers in America (one also important to Austen): intelligence/education" (74).

Changes from Novel to Film
(Significant Deletions, Additions, and Revisions)

No exact counterpart for Jane exists in *Clueless* because Christian/Frank is gay. But the situation of Frank and Jane in the novel, their secret engagement, is realized in Christian's lack of openness about being gay. As Emma felt with Frank, Cher thinks herself interested in Christian romantically and even attempts to seduce him, but she finds him, mysteriously, not interested. Just so, Emma comes to think Frank is not in love with her anymore than she with him even before she learns of his secret engagement to Jane. Phillips and Heal find a similarity to the secret relationship of Jane and Frank in the Dionne and Murray romance. Although Dionne is sexually experienced, she claims to be a virgin. Jane's secret engagement has a moral taint, even though she has "technically" not violated any moral law. While Murray and Dionne's relationship is open, unlike that of Frank and Jane, their often angry relationship is not the real one, as is revealed by Cher's remarks that they are "considerate of each other" when no one sees them. Other parallels are Dionne's remarks about Murray's hair and an accusation of "jeeping," or jealousy, that equates to Jane's feelings about Emma (Phillips and Heal). After discovering Christian's sexuality, Cher attaches herself to him as her favorite shopping partner, a gay stereotype but also symbolic of the continued friendship Emma offers Frank after learning of his secret. Christian also saves Tai from the attackers at the mall, the gypsies of the novel. Violence in the world is visible on television, and Cher herself is mugged when Elton drops her off in a strange neighborhood. Like Highbury with its gypsy muggers and poultry thieves, Cher's community is not wholly safe, and even a young woman in the twentieth century realizes there are limits to her independence and freedom in an unsafe world.

The film ends with a wedding, but this one is the Miss Taylor/Weston marriage counterpart that opened *Emma*, the purported result of Cher/Emma's matchmaking. The three friends—Dionne, Tai, and Cher—attend and plan their own weddings, but none actually marries in the film because they are, after all, only sixteen! However, they are seated as equal friends, without racial or class barriers to their relationships, unlike the novel's Emma who attended Harriet at her wedding of Robert Martin, essentially ending their friendship.

Conceptual Integrity (Themes, Ideas, Spirit of Austen's Novel)

Many critics have written about Mrs. Elton as a parody of Emma. In *Clueless* Mrs. Elton's counterpart, Amber, is a kind of rival to Emma for popularity, and like Mrs. Elton, she is faulted for being overdressed (during the debate) and a wearer of imitation designer perfume. The parody is suggested when Cher is seen wearing an outfit similar to Amber's and when she uses the same vocabulary of put-down terms as her rival. These similarities suggest Amber to be a parody of Cher as Mrs. Elton is of Emma herself (Phillips and Heal).

The class issues in *Emma* revolve around Emma's sense of her home, family, taste, and manners being superior to all but the Knightleys in Highbury. In *Clueless*, those who are not in the first circle of Cher and her friends have reasons other than family and fortune to relegate them to a lower "class." For example, Cher dislikes Travis because of his marijuana use; he's a "loadie." While Cher can change Tai's clothes and hairstyle, in essentials she, like Harriet, cannot be made over, i.e., she is sexually promiscuous and uses drugs. Cher is happy to embrace the Tai/Travis relationship after he goes into a drug rehab program. Cher even attends Travis's skateboarding competition and applauds his skills.

Racially the film is diverse. Cher's closest friend, Dionne, is African

American. The slight to Miss Bates becomes an ethnic confusion as to the housekeeper Lucy's country of origin. The message of *Clueless* is one of tolerance, never really a central theme in *Emma*, spoken by Cher in the debate as she argues for the Haitians in America, saying "tolerance is always a good lesson." As Phillips and Heal write, "In *Clueless*, behavioral propriety rather than class distinction is foremost." A social conscience is more prized than wealth, property, or finery, as Josh sets the standard of behavior by choosing environmental law, where perhaps he will make less money but serve a good cause.

Reading the Film
—Questions for Discussion and Writing

1. Analyze the casting of Emma. How closely does she suit your ideas of Austen's Emma? Is she characterized as more "handsome" or more "clever"? Is she snobbish? Is her kindness to her father and the poor realized? How is she made likable in spite of her faults? Do you like the character? Why or why not?

2. Analyze the casting of Mr. Knightley. Is the sixteen-year age difference between him and Emma apparent? Is he more a "gallant man" or a "humane" one? Is he characterized more as a lover to Emma or a mentor? Is there an obvious change in his role from the novel?

3. Mrs. Weston's role in the novel is slight. How is her character utilized, if at all, in the film?

4. How is Jane Fairfax characterized in the film? How is her "elegance" depicted? Is her role an important one in the film? How is she compared with Emma?

5. How is Harriet portrayed in the film? Which of her qualities (beauty, simplicity, deference) is most highlighted? Does she change or develop in the film as Knightley observed?

6. What is Frank Churchill's character in the film? How obvious is the game he plays with Jane and Emma? Does he seem convincingly to be courting Emma? What clues does the film provide that Frank is actually Jane's suitor?

7. Emma and Mrs. Elton, while different in manners and class, are surprisingly alike in their tastes and judgments. While we as readers are aware of these similarities, the characters are not, creating dramatic irony. Does the film adaptation make us see their similarities? What is lost or gained through the representation of their "mirror" characters?

8. Miss Bates has a small role in the novel, but her presence looms larger, especially in Emma's mind. What purpose does her character serve in the film? How

does she contribute to our understanding of Emma's character? How does her character become a measure of Emma's moral education? Is her "popularity" within the community obvious in the film?

9. How is Mr. Woodhouse characterized in the film? Is his tedious hypochondria tempered? How does he relate to Emma in the film? Is his role significant?

10. Analyze the major scenes from the film comparatively with the novel. What issues or ideas emerge from the scenes? Consider the Christmas Eve party at the Weston's, the strawberry picking at Donwell Abbey, the Box Hill excursion, Knightley's proposal, and the weddings that end the plot. Identify the changes made to the characters, dialogue, and events; analyze why these changes were made and the effect of the changes.

11. Analyze the costuming, makeup, and hairdressing of Emma and the other female characters. How is Emma costumed compared to the other female characters such as Jane Fairfax or Mrs. Elton? One critic describes Paltrow's Emma as costumed like a Greek statue. What details of dress, makeup, and hairdressing suggest a Greek goddess? What colors are predominant in the costuming of each film? What mood or tone is set through light and color?

12. Emma does not become aware of her feelings toward Mr. Knightley until she is threatened with losing him. Does the film version give us clues to her feelings earlier than this moment in the novel? Examine the relationship between Emma and Knightley in various adaptations and define their relationship.

13. How are Emma's faults established? Does the film depict Emma's education and reformation? Where is change most apparent?

14. How is music used in the film? Consider not only the music within scenes but the score as well.

15. How is class represented in the film? Is Emma's social hierarchy evident? Are the servants and their support of the upper class apparent in the film? Are servants a visible presence? What does the film say about classism?

16. *Emma* is Austen's most comic novel. How is the comedy played in the film? What characters, dialogue, or events suggest comedy? What is the overall tone of the film? What kinds of comedy—satire, slapstick, irony—are evident?

17. A trend in recent film adaptations is moving scenes out of the drawing room and onto the lawn. How does each film handle setting? What scenes transition well from indoors to out of doors? Which seem inappropriate set outside?

18. Emma is one of Austen's most independent and feminist of heroines. Does the film expand the characterization of a liberated heroine? How are her self-sufficiency and freedom realized on the screen?

Film Credits

Emma

1972 BBC miniseries, 257 minutes.
Screenplay by Denis Constanduros.
Directed by John Glenister.
Produced by Martin Lisemore.

Cast

Emma Woodhouse	Doran Godwin
Mr. Weston	Raymond Adamson
Harriet Smith	Debbie Bowen
Mr. Knightley	John Carson
Miss Bates	Constance Chapman
Mrs. Weston	Ellen Dryden
Frank Churchill	Robert East
Mr. Woodhouse	Donald Eccles
Jane Fairfax	Ania Marson
Mr. Elton	Timothy Peters
Mrs. Elton	Fiona Walker
Robert Martin	John Alkin
Mrs. Goddard	Mollie Sugden
Mrs. Cole	Hilda Fenemore
Isabella Knightley	Meg Gleed
John Knightley	John Kelland
Mrs. Ford	Lala Lloyd
Williams	Vivienne Moore

Emma

Based on Jane Austen's *Emma*.
1996 Miramax, 121 minutes.

Screenplay by Douglas McGrath.
Directed by Douglas McGrath.
Produced by Patrick Cassavetti, Steven Haft.

Cast

Emma Woodhouse	Gwyneth Paltrow
Mr. Weston	James Cosmo
Mrs. Weston	Greta Scacchi
Rev. Elton	Alan Cumming
Mr. Woodhouse	Denys Hawthorne
Miss Bates	Sophie Thompson
Mr. Knightley	Jeremy Northam
Harriet Smith	Toni Collette
Mrs. Goddard	Kathleen Byron
Mrs. Bates	Phyllida Law
Mr. Martin	Edward Woodall
Little Boy	Brett Miley
John Knightley	Brian Capron
Isabella	Karen Westwood
Footman	Paul Williamson
Jane Fairfax	Polly Walker
Miss Martin	Rebecca Craig
Frank Churchill	Ewan McGregor
Mrs. Cole	Angela Down
Mr. Cole	John Franklyn-Robbins
Mrs. Elton	Juliet Stevenson
Bates Maid	Ruth Jones

Jane Austen's Emma

1996 Meridian-ITV/A&E, 107 minutes.
Screenplay by Andrew Davies.

Directed by Diarmuid Lawrence.
Produced by Sue Birtwistle.

Cast

Emma Woodhouse	Kate Beckinsale
Mr. Woodhouse	Bernard Hepton
Mr. Knightley	Mark Strong
Mrs. Weston	Samantha Bond
Mr. Weston	James Hazeldine
Mr. Elton	Dominic Rowan
Harriet Smith	Samantha Morton
Miss Bates	Prunella Scales
Mrs. Bates	Sylvia Barter
John Knightley	Guy Henry
Isabella Knightley	Dido Miles
Frank Churchill	Raymond Coulthard
Jane Fairfax	Olivia Williams
Mrs. Elton	Lucy Robinson
Mr. Perry	Peter Howell
Mrs. Goddard	Judith Coke
Robert Martin	Alistair Petrie
Elizabeth Martin	Phoebe Welles-Cooper
Miss Otway	Tabby Harris
Thomas	Neville Phillips
Henry Knightley	Sunny Jim Dickinson

Clueless

1995 Paramount, 113 minutes.
Screenplay by Amy Heckerling.

Directed by Amy Heckerling.

Produced by Robert Lawrence and Scott Rudin.

Cast

Cher Horowitz	Alicia Silverstone
Dionne	Stacey Dash
Tai Fraiser	Brittany Murphy
Josh	Paul Rudd
Murray	Donald Faison
Amber	Elisa Donovan
Travis Birkenstock	Breckin Meyer
Elton	Jeremy Sisto
Mel Horowitz	Dan Hedaya
Lucy	Aida Linares
Mr. Hall	Wallace Shawn
Miss Geist	Twink Caplan
Christian Stovitz	Justin Walker
Paroudasm	Sabastian Rashidi
Principal	Herb Hall
Miss Stoeger	Julie Brown
Heather	Susan Mohun

Persuasion

Persuasion is Jane Austen's last completed novel. It was written between August 1815 and August 6, 1816. The last two original chapters of the novel survive in manuscript (the only manuscript copies of Austen's novels). These chapters eventually were revised into chapters ten, eleven, and twelve, the final chapters of the novel. Austen died on July 18, 1817. After her death, the two-volume *Persuasion* was published together with *Northanger Abbey* in 1818 and included "a Biographical Notice of the Author" identifying Austen as the author of the previous works and detailing her life (Chapman, "Introductory Note to *Northanger Abbey* and *Persuasion*" xi–xiii).

Jane Austen wrote *Persuasion* during the illness that would eventually take her life. At the same time she was working on the manuscript of *Sanditon*, which was never completed. It is not surprising that these last two works are filled with accidents, illnesses, death, and a sense of loss. While Austen's characteristic satire is as biting as in earlier novels, especially when directed at vanity, hypochondria, selfishness, arrogance, and stupidity, the tone is predominantly somber and reflective. The heroine, Anne Elliot, is older, at age twenty-seven seemingly without prospects for love or even a stable home. Her own family pays her little attention except when she can be of use to them. The romantic moment of her life occurred when she was nineteen, and now she watches as the heroic and wealthy Captain Wentworth courts another woman. Not only the heroine but others as well have experienced pain, separation, and loss. Captain Benwick's story mirrors Anne's own, for he delayed his marriage until his future was more certain, only to have his fiancée die while he was away at sea. Mrs. Croft speaks of loneliness when separated from her husband, the admiral of a fleet. The wounded Captain Harville lives with a growing family, confined in a small house near the sea, nursed by his wife. Anne's former school friend, who consoled Anne when her mother died, is a pauper confined to a wheelchair. A novel so filled with loss and pain ends happily with the reunion of Anne and Wentworth. However, while endurance, duty, and constancy are celebrated, Austen's intention seems to be that the rational and prudent approach to marriage at the expense of romance and feeling leads to suffering. The primacy of feeling is lauded in a manner new to Austen's fiction.

Viewing the Novel
—Approaches to Teaching *Persuasion*

I include here a general discussion of the main issues, themes, and ideas in *Persuasion*. My "Approaches to Teaching *Persuasion*" complement the analytical questions that follow this discussion.

Issues of Class and Aristocracy. Persuasion contains Austen's most scathing depiction of the faults of the aristocratic class. Austen portrays Sir Walter Elliot, baronet (the lowest rung of the hereditary aristocracy), as vain, self-absorbed, obsessed with rank, and unable to manage his estate. By refusing to adapt to changing conditions in English culture and economics, such families as his are doomed to removal and loss. By contrasting Sir Walter and his eldest daughter Elizabeth with the young men of the navy and their families, Austen dramatizes the changes in English class structure from aristocracy to a more practical middle class. Sir Walter's removal from the ancestral hall at Kellynch is brought on by extravagance and poor management, although the entail on the property guarantees that his heir will benefit from the system that privileges ancestry over self-made wealth. Anne Elliot, middle daughter of the aristocratic line of Elliots, rejects marriage to the heir of Kellynch in favor of an attachment to Captain Wentworth of the British Navy, wealthy but beneath her in rank. The newly wealthy navy men have the capital to buy and rent the great homes increasingly abandoned by the aristocrats. However, it is the values of the "useful," active men of the navy that attract the heroine. As Claudia Johnson asserts, "if in *Persuasion* the landed classes have not lost their power, they have lost their prestige and their moral authority for the heroine" (145). While the irony at work in all of Austen's novels invites a critique of the class structure in England, Austen's representation of the upper classes in *Persuasion* as vain, indolent, and ineffectual is particularly negative. Carol Dole notes that Austen's view of class is markedly changed in *Persuasion* "from the early vision of a harmonious traditional world represented by Darcy's estate Pemberley, to the implication in *Persuasion* that the old social order had lost its usefulness as a guide to proper behavior" (59). In this novel, the characters who evoke admiration for their practicality, energy, and loyalty are drawn from the middle classes.

Austen's review of the changes in class structure also includes characters drawn from the lower or working classes. Mrs. Smith, widowed and infirm, was defrauded of her fortune, but she finds occupation in marketing handiwork to the wealthy vacationers at Bath. Her nurse is useful to her both in her infirmity and in her enterprise. Mrs. Harvillle, too, is a nurse who cares for her injured husband. Two other characters whose class reflects changing times are Mrs. Croft, wife of an admiral who travels with him at sea, and Mrs. Clay, the daughter of a solicitor. The changing class system is evidenced in the good fortunes of Mrs. Clay, the divorced daughter of Sir Walter's legal agent, as she manages to catch the eye of the wealthy Sir Walter and later elopes with his rich heir, William Elliot. Eventually, she may become mistress of Kellynch Hall.

Austen is concerned in all of her novels with the issue of judgment: how to know good character and worth in a society where manners are formalized and may disguise wickedness. In this novel a clear opposition between the highest levels of aristocracy (Dalrymples, Lady Russell, and Elliots) and the middle classes (Musgroves, Wentworths, Hayters, Crofts, and Hargroves) shows the balance tipped in favor of those with ease of manners, who value friendship and loyalty over extravagance, ostentation, and selfishness. As example, Lady Russell, the voice of aristocracy and guardian in her mother's stead, offered Anne the advice that results in eight years of loneliness and unhappiness. As a moral guide Lady Russell represents not just cautionary prudence but class snobbery, for Captain Wentworth, even with his fortune, is less attractive to her than William Elliot, who will inherit title, estate, and fortune. Lady Russell supports an outworn system of rank and property while deriding the self-made man with values of thrift, usefulness, and unaffected manners. Above all, the new society is open and inclusive, willing to change and adapt to changing times.

The Navy. Jane Austen's two youngest brothers, Francis and Charles, were sailors; both received high promotion, Francis as Admiral of the Fleet and Charles as Rear Admiral. Austen much admired her sailor brothers and followed with great interest the activities of the navy. According to Brian Southam, *Persuasion* was for Austen a kind of morale-boosting work, paying tribute to the trials and hardships her brothers had endured and an expression of her admiration for their heroism. They, like Admiral Croft and Captains Wentworth, Harville, and Benwick, were turned back onto land, with half-pay, in the summer of 1814 (Southam 265). *Persuasion* is set in the period following the Napoleonic Wars, after the victory at Trafalgar and the exile of Napoleon to Elba. During the peace that continued until Napoleon's escape from Elba and the Battle of Waterloo in summer 1815, the sailors, many wealthy with prize money, were integrating into the English social and cultural scene. *Persuasion* celebrates the attributes of this class whose prosperity is based on merit rather than birth. Anne Elliot, although the daughter of a baronet, praises her new friends among the navy: "She prized the frank, the open-hearted, the eager character beyond all others. Warmth and enthusiasm did captivate her still" (*P* 161). *Persuasion* is cited as the novel least respectful of class traditions (Dole 61), and Austen's plot ends with the union of Anne, of a fading aristocracy, with the heroic Wentworth, who represents hope and change, strength and activity.

Austen's celebration of the men of the navy is matched with her tribute to the naval wife, exemplified in Mrs. Croft. She is not admired for beauty or drawing-room accomplishments, but for her solidity, strength, and business sense, for it is she who handles the financial details of the Kellynch lease (Southam 274). She speaks up to defend the presence of women on ships, even though, according to Southam, rules forbade carrying women on board without special orders from the Admiralty (276). Southam explains that in spite of Mrs. Croft's arguments to the contrary, the comfort and safety of women would have been uncertain at best. A woman on ship might witness the violence of battles, the sometimes brutal disciplining of a ship's crew, and the injuries and sicknesses that befell the sailors, although a wife's role would not have extended to nursing her husband (276–78). Mrs. Croft defies these arguments and, with an "unladylike toughness," rebukes Wentworth for refusing to take women on board his ship. Austen never suggests that Anne, also known for fortitude, would be expected to take to the sea in her married life (Southam 284).

The Romantic vs. the Prudent. Austen's earlier novels privileged the rational, prudent path to marriage, where the "business" of marrying meant couples were often more concerned with money to live on than with affection and compatibility. In *Persuasion*, the prudent course for Anne was following Lady Russell's "persuasion" to reject the proposal of marriage of a young naval officer "who had nothing but himself to recommend him" (P 26), without fortune and a secure future. Seen from the angle of hindsight, it was the wrong decision, for Captain Wentworth makes his fortune and comes back in glory to celebrate his success—and to find a wife. Of Anne Elliot it is said, "She had been forced into prudence in her youth, she learned romance as she grew older—the natural sequel of an unnatural beginning" (P 30). This passage conveys the sense of loss and missed opportunity that characterizes her life. Anne eventually forgives Lady Russell, the family friend and mother figure who advised her to reject Wentworth. But Lady Russell's "prejudices on the side of ancestry" (P 11) closed the door on Anne's "wishes on the side of early warm attachment, and a cheerful confidence in futurity" (P 30), a failure to seize the moment and capture love when it made its rare appearance.

In *Persuasion* Austen gives emphasis to the primacy of feeling. The long engagement of Fanny Hargrove and Captain Benwick resulted in the tragedy of his losing her before their love could be consummated in marriage. His romantic attachment to Louisa Musgrove follows a short courtship and engagement. Speaking out of the pain of her own sad history, Anne lauds the Musgroves, who "seem so totally free from all those ambitious feelings which had led to so much misconduct and misery" (P 218). The Musgroves willingly pay dowries for two daughters without complaint although wishing "the gentlemen were richer." Anne praises them as "such excellent parents," who "do every thing to confer happiness" (P 218). Her eight years of separation are not easily dismissed.

In no other Austen novel is the impassioned proposal of the hero so touching as Captain Wentworth's letter to Anne. "You pierce my soul," he writes. "I am half agony, half hope" (P 237). His declaration to her is intensely feeling: "I offer myself to you again with a heart even more your own, than when you almost broke it eight years and a half ago" (P 237). Not plotted to move young lovers to the discovery of mutual respect and esteem, *Persuasion* instead is about the return to love kindled in a distant past. The union of Anne and Wentworth proceeds not from understanding, appreciation of "lively minds," or "cleverness" but from knowing one's own and another's heart. Anne expresses this sentiment in her reflection, "if there be constant attachment on each side, our hearts must understand each other ere long" (*P* 221). *Persuasion* revisits the prudent and rational road to marriage and celebrates instead feeling and romance.

Changing Image of the Heroine. Austen's heroine in *Persuasion* is older, more mature, and at twenty-seven, seemingly destined to a life of spinsterhood. In Austen's canon Anne is the first "independent" or "autonomous" heroine in that she owes little to her family. She is without a mother or caring sisters or involved father. "The duty of filial piety . . . is nowhere dignified with the status of being at issue" (Johnson 146). Her fate and fortunes rest with her alone, and as an autonomous heroine, she makes judgments about duty and obligations separate from paternal authority (Johnson 146). Her future looks bleak, however, and Anne's temperament is almost depressed, with an air of melancholy, lost youth, and reflection about her. The "autumnal" tone of the novel suggests a closing of hope and opportunity rather than the youthful promise of the earlier novels. While the heroine recovers some of her "lost bloom," the sense of lost time, of what "once" was, pervades the novel.

Anne Elliot is also a changed Austen heroine in her "usefulness" to those around her. Rather than the "ornamental" role of earlier heroines with their drawing-room accomplishments, she makes herself useful nursing, counseling, organizing, and ordering the lives of others. In the process she rekindles in Captain Wentworth the love she had thought extinguished by her rejection of his earlier marriage proposal. In addition to Anne, the novel has other examples of intelligent and useful women. Mrs. Croft boldly travels on board ship with her husband and defends women as rational creatures, not shrinking violets: "as if women were all fine ladies, instead of rational creatures" (*P* 70). She and Admiral Croft provide one of the few examples in Austen's canon of a married couple who live on equal footing, who are companionable and take pleasure in each other's company. The novel also depicts women with occupations and characters of a lower, working class. The infirm Mrs. Smith, Nurse Rooke, and Mrs. Harville, who nurses her husband, are resourceful, intelligent, and energetic women, precursors of heroines like Jane Eyre later in the century, who can if necessary make their way alone in the world. These practical and useful women contrast the indolence and wasteful lives of the old aristocracy, most evident in Elizabeth and Sir Walter Elliot.

"Persuasion." All of Austen's heroines eventually learn about the exercise of power and the limits of authority. As heroines struggle with autonomy and adult independence, they are challenged to learn whose authority or judgment

is trustworthy, whose is dangerous or destructive, and whose is merely interfering. Nearly all of the heroines are relatively young, making their first forays into the adult world of decision-making, especially choices about marriage, money, and love. As heroines grapple with the choices of freedom and duty, they define their characters. The conflicts test character issues of strength of mind and constancy, and their options often threaten individualism and independence. In *Persuasion*, Anne Elliot at nineteen was dutifully persuaded away from the romance of her young life because Wentworth's future was unsure. In hindsight she regrets the loss of happiness but does not fault the adult who gave her the advice nor her dutiful acceptance of it. Lady Russell serves to transition Anne from filial obligation and respect to full adult independence and autonomy. Anne's character at twenty-seven reveals the constancy, independence, and newfound individualism earned from eight years of separation.

But Austen's novel also distinguishes between the easily persuaded and the headstrong. Anne Elliot's intelligent and judicial choices contrast with the willfulness, obstinacy, and stubborn independence of the incautious Louisa Musgrove, who nearly dies for being too headstrong (pun not intended). Captain Wentworth admits that, at Lyme, "he had learnt to distinguish between the steadiness of principle and the obstinacy of self-will, between the darings of heedlessness and the resolution of a collected mind" (*P* 242). Good judgment involves, among other things, heeding authority and knowing the limits of your own knowledge. While Anne Elliot, at nineteen, dutifully accepts the advice of Lady Russell, she always trusts the authority of her own heart. She is never dissuaded from her early attachment to Wentworth and is never seduced by the charms and polite manners of William Elliot. She is also sensitive to the authority of literature and its power to influence moods and beliefs. Anne counsels Captain Benwick against reading the Romantic poets, whose emotional self-indulgence may be a harmful influence on him in his grieving state. Likewise, she faults Captain Harville for his reliance on books for his understanding of female constancy. Thus, the authority of books and of history is called into question as well as the advice of friends and family.

Viewing the Novel
—Questions for Analysis and Discussion

The questions below address the larger issues of each volume and are designed to promote analytical thinking as the basis for discussion. These questions ask students to "see" into the text and complement the central issues of "reading the film" that follow.

Volume I

1. Describe the family of Sir Walter Elliot as they are introduced in the earliest chapters. What scenes, descriptions, and details are most revealing of the characters of Sir Walter, Elizabeth, and Anne?
2. What values of Sir Walter and Elizabeth contrast with Anne's?
3. How does Lady Russell compare with the Elliots? How is she like and unlike Sir Walter? What scenes and dialogue show her character?
4. What is Anne's role in her own household and in the extended Musgrove family?
5. Is Captain Wentworth's resentment of Anne justified, in your opinion?
6. How does Mrs. Croft contrast with Lady Russell and Elizabeth Elliot?
7. Describe the Musgrove family, including Charles and Mary's relationship. What scenes, descriptions, and details are most revealing of their characters, especially of Louisa Musgrove and Mary Musgrove?
8. What does Captain Wentworth learn about Anne from Louisa Musgrove during the excursion to the Hayter farm? What does he also learn about Louisa? What does Anne learn about Wentworth?
9. How do the men of the navy, including Admiral Croft, and Captains Harville, Benwick, and Wentworth, distinguish themselves from the aristocratic and rural gentry? What scenes and details at Lyme reveal their character and personalities?
10. How does the visit to Lyme advance the reunion of Wentworth and Anne? Which scenes are most revealing of their feelings for each other?

Volume II

1. What obstacles, both obvious and underlying, prevent the reunion of Captain Wentworth and Anne Elliot? How are these obstacles eliminated?
2. How does William Elliot's admiration for Anne at Lyme affect Captain Wentworth? Does Elliot's appearance at Bath hasten or hinder Wentworth's progress toward Anne?
3. How is Captain Benwick's story similar to Anne and Wentworth's? How is it different?

4. Why is Anne mistrustful of William Elliot? If Wentworth had married Louisa Musgrove, would Anne have been more receptive to his attentions? Why or why not? Can you identify scenes, dialogue, or gestures that suggest Elliot's true feelings for Anne? Are his attentions to Anne convincing? What evidence of dishonesty is present?

5. What role does Mrs. Smith play in the novel? Why does she not disclose to Anne earlier what she knows about William Elliot's history? How are Lady Russell and Mrs. Smith alike in their relationship to Anne Elliot? How are they different?

6. How would you evaluate Lady Russell's role in Anne Elliot's life? Would you have been as forgiving and understanding as Anne in her judgment of Lady Russell? How is "duty" celebrated in this novel? Consider the men of the navy as well as filial obligation.

7. What concept of the "new woman" is nascent in *Persuasion?* Consider Nurse Rooke and Mrs. Smith, Sophia Croft, Mrs. Clay, and Anne Elliot as examples. Refer to specific passages and events that suggest a feminist viewpoint.

8. What middle- and working-class values are celebrated in this novel? How does "occupation" contrast with "ornamentation"? List characters and qualities that stand in opposition to aristocracy. Is there a positive model among the aristocratic or moneyed class?

9. What does *Persuasion* say about the romance/prudence opposition? How do "persuasion," "duty," and "strength of will" complement or conflict with "romance"?

10. Describe the overall tone of the novel. What is Anne's state of mind at the outset? Does it change? What descriptions of the setting and the natural world are relevant to tone?

Reading the Film
—Approaches to Teaching the Film

Using Film in the Classroom

Nick Dear's screenplay of *Persuasion* resists the romanticized nostalgia that so popularized the Emma Thompson *Sense and Sensibility*. As such, the film does not "harlequinize" or romanticize the characters (see Kaplan: "Mass Marketing Jane Austen"). According to one critic, "*Sense and Sensibility* ... is shrouded in the rose-colored sheen of nostalgia.... *Persuasion*, by contrast, is unstinting in its depiction of both the beautiful and the bleak aspects of life in the nineteenth century" (Collins 85). Some will see this as a fault in the film and a failure on Dear's part to make the characters attractive to contemporary viewers. Others of us see this film as more faithful to Austen's world as characters are played with less glamour and more realism than other Austen film productions. Elsa Solender praises "its gritty authenticity" and borrows Robert Giddings' term "synthetic historical realism": "a filmmaker's presentation of an authentic 'look,' doctored to suit contemporary tastes, prejudices, and expectations" (Solender 104). Her examples include Captain Wentworth's bold kiss of Anne in the streets of Bath and Anne's venturing out of doors without a hat (Solender 104). Overall, the film was a critical success. My film analysis is restricted to the 1995 BBC *Persuasion*, screenplay by Nick Dear.

Casting and Characterization

Amanda Root plays the lead role of Anne Elliot. Although Root plays Anne Elliot as having a mature, more composed and dignified manner than her sisters and others around her, she fails to appear as elegant as the daughter of a baronet would be expected to be. Austen describes Anne as having "an elegance of mind and sweetness of character" (*P* 5), but Root's temperament borders on bitterness. She is faithful to Austen's description of Anne, "her bloom had vanished early" (*P* 6), and her appearance is not helped by her unkempt hair and drab costumes. Her wide-open eyes register surprise, even shock, when she experiences some new and intense feeling. Cosmetically, she is made to appear softer and rosier after the experience at Lyme, when we learn Anne's bloom has been restored, and she is more feminine and pretty in the scenes in Bath when she feels the possibility of renewed friendship with Wentworth. One reviewer faults Root's performance for failing to hold our attention, primarily because Austen's novel plays out the time between rejected romance and a final romantic renewal. "She has pleasant eyes but a grim mouth—a countenance that doesn't invite speculation, a sensibility and technique that are just barely up to average" (Kauffmann).

Ciaran Hinds as Captain Wentworth is admirably cast. He is tall, handsome, and strong, with a military bearing that suggests authority and consequence. His costuming in navel dress blues, with gold trim, heightens the heroic aspect of his character. To a lesser degree he is a romantic hero, registering his admiration and renewed feelings for Anne. His confusion over his conflicted feelings is also rendered effectively. His elegance and posture contrast well with the buffoonish figure of Charles Musgrove, who also proposed marriage to Anne. Charles is excellently played by Simon Russell Beale as a country bumpkin, who talks with food in his mouth and ignores his household responsibilities in favor of hunting and visiting.

Contributing characters are also well cast and generally well performed. Stanley Kauffmann admires the performances of Corin Redgrave as Sir Walter Elliot and Richard McCabe as Captain Benwick. I agree that Redgrave's performance as Sir Walter hits the mark in many scenes, but a tendency to "chew the scenery" distracts from other scenes, especially in the Camden Place apartments at Bath. Sophie Thompson's whining, hypochondriacal Mary Musgrove is both comically and ironically true to Austen's character. When she laments at Lyme that *she* should stay to nurse her sister-in-law Louisa because she is related, not Anne, we are reminded of her using the reverse of relational intimacy as a reason *not* to stay and nurse her own child: "you, Anne, are by far the properest person to sit with the boy, for you haven't a mother's feelings" (Dear 26). Samuel West, as William Elliot, looks the part of the dandy, soft and refined, and contrasts nicely with the more ruggedly handsome Wentworth. However, I can't imagine Amanda Root's Anne ever giving a moment's consideration to him as a possible spouse; her intelligence and "experience" make her unlikely to see much to admire here.

The characterization of Elizabeth Elliot, as performed by Phoebe Nicholls, is a major flaw in the Nick Dear script. In the novel Elizabeth is said to have "well-bred, elegant manners" (*P* 140). Although her character, with her selfishness and disregard for Anne's feelings, is one of the most unlikable in the novel, this adaptation instead exaggerates her coarseness (Dickson 45). Nicholls snorts, slumps and slouches, and talks with food in her mouth. Dickson cites examples where Elizabeth is portrayed as "loud," "shrill," "indolent," and "unbalanced emotionally" (46). A woman of her class and breeding would know the price of such rebellion from established norms. She would face social ostracism and even disgrace according to Dickson (48). To suggest that Elizabeth Elliot is a nonconformist rebel who speaks her mind and acts as she pleases is a complete misreading of her character. According to Dickson, it also undermines the more subtle and intelligent feminist voices of Sophia Croft and Anne Elliot. Both conform to established norms of good breeding and manners yet live their lives making choices that break with repressive rules and expectations that limit and confine women. The portrayal of Elizabeth Elliot's coarseness in upper-class society suggests that the freedom to act and say what you please was allowable and tolerated when in fact it was not. Instead, the pro-feminist voice of Austen speaks quietly but effectively through the characters of Mrs. Croft and Anne, both of whom conform to established etiquette of the time (Dickson 49). As with Lydia Bennet and Mrs. Bennet in the Andrew Wright *Pride and Prejudice*, it seems filmmakers feel the only way to depict bad manners is to make the character coarse and crude by contemporary standards. In the novel Elizabeth's aloof, cold, haughty bearing (while conforming to the accepted manners of the time) reveals to readers her character as selfish, unfeeling, and unworthy of respect without reducing her to a comic exaggeration of loutishness.

Changes from Novel to Film
(Significant Deletions, Additions, and Revisions)

Invented Scenes. Austen's novel is set entirely on terra firma, but the opening scenes of the film show a naval vessel and crew on the sea as the war ends. The film closes with Anne Wentworth aboard ship with her new husband, Captain Wentworth, as war is again in progress. It is announced at the Elliots' card party that Bonaparte has escaped from Elba and that war will resume. This time Anne joins her new husband on board his ship as he returns to the sea, apparently having revised his thinking about women aboard ships. By framing the film with scenes of life aboard naval vessels, Dear visually pays tribute to the navy. Austen praised the men of the navy and especially their active, useful, practical natures in her novel. In this adaptation, it is out of the drawing room and onto the sea.

The film also includes scenes that show more characters of lower and middle working classes: Nurse Rooke and Mr. Shepherd, agent to Sir Walter, and his daughter Mrs. Clay, divorced from her husband, are from a working, professional class not often seen in an Austen novel. The Nick Dear script deglamorizes life of the time by showing the workers behind the scenes who would have supported and made possible the comfortable life of the aristocracy: lamplighters, hostellers, coachmen, fishermen, and farmers begging to be paid are some examples. These scenes are unobtrusive background to the action in the forefront, giving a fuller spectrum of life in the period.

Another invented scene that has stirred criticism is the one near the end of the film when Captain Wentworth bends to kiss Anne Elliot, on the mouth and on a public street in Bath. Such a public display of affection would be highly irregular for a lady and gentleman of the period, much less in a Jane Austen novel. Incidentally, the cover picture on the video box shows the kiss, but the costuming and setting are not from the novel or the film. The background of the scene is a mansion in the country, not the busy streets of Bath. The cover photo and the film's "kiss" promote the romance of the story.

Also added to the film is the love interest of Elizabeth Elliot in Captain Wentworth. In the film Sir Walter and Elizabeth greet the return of Captain Wentworth with little interest until his wealth and mien make him desirable in their circle. The handsome Ciaran Hinds in his gold-trimmed uniform becomes suddenly the object of Elizabeth's romantic interest. In the film, unlike the novel, she seems rather easily to have conceded Mr. Elliot to her sister, not realizing that she will lose out to both Anne and to her dear friend, Mrs. Clay, in the mating game. Ironically, in the film Elizabeth requests of Anne that she not monopolize Captain Wentworth at the card party moments before his entrance, when he boldly announces to the assembled party his engagement to Sir Walter's daughter Anne. We might read this scene as Wentworth's "rescue" of Anne from the enclosed confines of the drawing-room card party, where she, not a card player, has no role and is being pressured by Lady Russell and William Elliot to bind herself in marriage to this very world. As Wentworth bursts upon the scene to claim her as his prize, he turns the novel's quiet evening of conversation between the lovers into a scene of triumph, a bold and forthright expression of his claims, although it comes off as a rather boorish celebration of victory.

The most radical "invented scene" is the inclusion of Captain Wentworth's proposal at the apartments of Admiral Croft after relaying to Anne the news that the admiral will vacate Kellynch Hall should she and William Elliot wish to live there after their marriage. This scene is not truly invented but borrowed from the canceled chapters that Austen revised into the present chapters ten and eleven of *Persuasion*. (For a full discussion of these additions and changes, see "Viewing the Novel/Reading the Film— Comparative Screen Analysis.")

Additions to Characters. The film heightens Lady Russell's continued attempts to influence Anne to give up the past and accept the overtures of William Elliot. While this is suggested in the novel, the scenes created near the end of the film show her *arguing* for an engagement with Elliot. At the Elliots' card party, moments before Captain Wentworth arrives to announce his engagement, she presses Anne: "When you make a decision, Anne, you must stick with it. There is no going back. At your age I found out what *I* wanted, and I made a decision to marry, and I am married till I die. I hope, one day, to see you do the same" (Dear 90). There is a bit of irony here, for Lady

Russell argues for the strength of mind, the commitment to a decision that Captain Wentworth believes Anne lacked when she was "persuaded" by Lady Russell not to marry him. Anne's response, "I hope so too" (Dear 90), is also ironic, since she has made a decision to marry Captain Wentworth and indeed plans to "stick with it." In an earlier invented scene between Anne Elliot and Lady Russell, Anne expresses regret over her decision to break her engagement. This scene sets the melancholy tone of the film as Anne shows a deep sadness and sense of loss that Lady Russell cannot argue her out of. It is unlikely that Anne would listen to Lady Russell's "persuasion" to marry or not marry a second time.

Another addition to Lady Russell's characterization is in the invented scene in which Captain Wentworth confronts her face-to-face after he has presented Anne with the admiral's offer to vacate Kellynch. Their exchange is heated and the mutual dislike is consistent with the novel, in which Wentworth retains his resentment toward Lady Russell even after his marriage. The openness of the exchange, however, is uncharacteristic of Austen's novels, where a display of feeling is considered bad manners. The scene in the film highlights the issue of influence and authority, for each accuses the other of having "an extraordinary ability to influence" Anne (Dear 81). This scene appears moments before Anne speaks up to assert her own "authority," negating rumors of her impending marriage to William Elliot. She soon after argues against Captain Harville's "authority" derived from reading, which claims women are more inconstant than men. The scenes seem designed to establish Anne's independence and individual authority.

Conceptual Integrity (Themes, Ideas, Spirit of Austen's Novel)

Working Classes. Several reviewers agree that Nick Dear's *Persuasion* has greater fidelity to the spirit of Austen's novels than other recent adaptations. Carol Dole says that it is the only film version that draws attention to class issues and is more thoroughly British than the other Austen adaptations (60). Dole notes, "Even its wealthy characters are shown to have bad teeth and unkempt hair, and to live in poorly lit houses" (60). It is a rare look into the working classes that support the indolent lifestyles of the rich. The film additions visually display these "behind-the-scenes" activities of the working class: the servants gathered as Sir Walter departs Kellynch, the farmers and cart that convey Anne to Uppercross, the menservants arrayed for service at Bath, the fishcutters at Lyme, and the beaters who stir up the game for the hunters at Uppercross.

Tone. The "autumnal" tone of the novel is captured well in the scenes of autumn that begin the film. The blowing winds suggest change, although the direction is not clear. The heroine is despondent, unloved and unwanted, dislocated, and feeling "ill used." Rarely do we see the characters without heavy cloaks trudging through the autumn countryside, facing the near-wintry winds. Even the comic country scenes at Uppercross with the hypochondriacal Mary are more bitter and ironic than funny. The closeness and darkness of the houses suggest confinement and smothering. At Lyme, too, where the sea and the sun would normally suggest a renewal of hope and happiness, the persistent winds instead affirm danger. The happy excursion turns to illness and suffering as Benwick details his loss and his refusal to be comforted. Finally, the injury to Louisa threatens not only her life but also the future of Captain Wentworth and Anne.

Cinematic Technique: Reading the Visual Elements of the Film

Metaphoric Use of Landscape. Like the other recent Austen film adaptations, much of the action is set out of doors. The various landscapes can be read symbolically. For example, the vacated house at Kellynch with its shroud-like coverings on the furniture suggests the death of aristocracy or at least the extravagant lifestyle of the class. The Camden Place apartments at Bath taken by the Elliots suggest a new and modern world. At the same time the "modern" Empire furnishings and chaises longues and the elaborate ice sculptures, ices, and fruit are extravagances that threaten the financial stability of a family in retrenchment. Sir Walter, Elizabeth, and Mrs. Clay are seen eating or lounging, poses suggesting idleness and a lack of useful occupation to enrich their lives.

At Uppercross the homes of the senior Musgroves and of Mary and Charles appear cramped and cluttered, dark and noisy. The Charles Musgrove home has small rooms and low ceilings, almost like a cave. Not much in Mary's "cottage" suggests marriage to the eldest son of a country squire. Her failure to make her life useful or to improve her situation contributes to her existence as a confined, dreary, and unhappy woman who imagines herself ill, especially when it proves convenient. Anne's visit to Uppercross sets off another series of ironies, because, before he proposed to Mary, Charles approached Anne, who declined his proposal. She chose to remain constant to her first love rather than commit to a life with a man she could not love. However, it is she who is asked to set things right among the Musgrove family while her own happiness is never of interest or concern.

Mary's temperament is unlike that of Sophie Croft, a woman who delights in the adventurous companionship of her husband, and only fancies herself ill when separated from him. While Mary's husband is always near, she finds little solace or joy in his company.

The scenes at Lyme, near the water, where Anne's bloom is restored, represent a kind of symbolic rebirth for Anne and Wentworth. The "killing off" of her rival Louisa and the renewal of Wentworth's awareness of Anne's attentive and strong-minded character mark a turning point in their relationship.

Reading the Film —Questions for Discussion and Writing

1. Before students have read the first chapters of the novel, screen the opening sequence of the film, about the first half-hour. Ask them to write what direction they think this novel will take. Who will be the central character? What will happen to her? How is this film different from the previous films? Then, after students have read the first several chapters, ask them to compare and comment on their "reading" of the film's opening sequence. Later, after reading the novel and viewing the film in its entirety, ask students to comment on what in the film they correctly read and what misdirection they have predicted.

2. Examine how the spatial elements in the novel and the visual depiction of space in the film are used symbolically. Consider the spatial aspects of the homes of the Elliots, at Kellynch Hall and at Bath, Mary and Charles Musgrove's cottage at Uppercross, and Captain Harville's house at Lyme near the sea. How do these spaces come to represent freedom or enclosure?

3. Consider how the dialectic of passion and reason plays out in this novel. Who is represented as expressive? Who is restrained and reasonable? What cinematic techniques does the film use to depict intense emotions or passion? How are reason and control displayed? Consider facial close-ups and camera movements.

4. Consider the contrasts between the terms "headstrong" and "strong minded"; "steadiness of principle" and "obstinacy"; "elasticity of mind" and "persuasion" as they are represented by various characters in the novel. How does the film depict these nuances of behavior in various characters? Is dialogue the primary means? What cinematic techniques are most effective?

5. Does the film present a feminist viewpoint? Examine scenes that support or contradict the feminist elements of the novel. In the novel Mrs. Croft speaks openly about women as "rational creatures." How is her feminist "rationality"

depicted in the film? Anne speaks of women's constancy in love. How is this portrayed?

6. How is the contrast of "occupation" versus "ornamentation" represented visually in the film? What various professions and occupations are represented? Which characters are "occupied" in activities? What scenes show characters being useful and busy? What ornamental roles do various characters play out? What gestures, costumes, and individual scenes best represent these opposing characteristics?

7. How is Amanda Root changed cosmetically to depict the return of "bloom" at Lyme? Describe her appearance in the early scenes at Kellynch Hall and at Uppercross, and compare her costumes and makeup with the later appearances at Bath.

8. How is the confusion of the accident at Lyme rendered cinematically? Examine especially the behavior of Louisa Musgrove, Captain Wentworth's words and actions, Mary and Charles Musgrove's responses, and Anne Elliot's. What camera angles, movements, and sounds render the crisis more frightening?

9. What examples of the working and lower classes are depicted in the film? Are they integral to the action or as backdrop to the central characters? What effect do they have on the climate of the film?

10. Read the canceled chapters that Jane Austen discarded in favor of the final two published ones. How are elements of the canceled chapters incorporated into the film? Evaluate their effectiveness.

11. Captain Wentworth is one of the most gallant and courageous of Austen's male protagonists. How does the film heighten the sense of his heroism, both as a naval officer and as a romantic figure? Consider costuming, makeup, gesture, and mien. How does he compare to other male figures as they are depicted in the film, especially Charles Musgrove, a former rival; William Elliot, his current rival; and officers Benwick and Harville?

12. Louisa Musgrove is set up as a competitor with Anne Elliot for Captain Wentworth's affections and hand in marriage. How is she depicted in the film as a rival to Anne? Consider her appearance, costuming, and gestures as well as her intelligence and beauty. How does the presence of her sister Henrietta further her appeal or diminish her attractiveness? How do Anne and Louisa interact in the novel? Is the same degree of interaction present in the film?

13. Lady Russell is presented in the novel as a mother figure and friend to Anne Elliot. Which scenes in the film depict her in the role of mother? Of friend? Does the film's characterization of Lady Russell clarify her powerful involvement in

Anne's life? Compare her with the film's depiction of Sophie Croft. Is Mrs. Croft a person of importance to Anne in the novel? How do she and Anne interact in the film?

Viewing the Novel/Reading the Film —An Exercise in Film Adaptation

This assignment asks students to take on the role of a screenwriter. For this exercise, we will pretend no existing script or movie exists. The first stage is to "view the novel" through the eyes of the screenwriter and create an "outline for a film adaptation" of *Persuasion*. The adaptation will be a "transposition," using Geoffrey Wagner's terminology: the original is transferred to the screen with minimal interference. The second stage is to "read the film" and determine how well the expectations for adapting the novel in the outline have been met. Students will then analyze, discuss, evaluate, and write about the Nick Dear screenplay and film relative to the outline prepared.

STAGE ONE—Viewing the Novel. This is the beginning creative stage, and the task is to focus on important elements of character and action in Volume I of *Persuasion*. Working in small groups, students should prepare an outline that addresses the following questions:

- What genre will the film fall into? (comedy, historical epic, romance, satire, etc.) Consider Austen's original intention.
- Describe the central characters as they will be portrayed in the film, taking into account the historical context, the social context, Austen's intention, and contemporary audience tastes. Make a list for both Anne and Wentworth:
  1. How would each look?
  2. What demeanor or manner would you expect the actors to project?
  3. What are the central character traits that have to be portrayed?
  4. What activities or daily actions would they be involved in?
  5. Identify any special requirements for costuming or makeup that might help to accent character.
- Consider who among contemporary actors you would have play the roles. List why you think the actors would be appropriate for these character roles.
- Identify three key scenes from Volume I that you feel *must* be included, and for each identify the following:
  1. What character traits dominate each scene?

2. What is central about character interaction in the scene?
3. What does the scene attempt to reveal about character relationships? What does this scene contribute that *must* be presented before the audience?
4. What are the important elements of setting for each scene?

- Identify where the film should open, and what should be the first scene.

Working again in small groups, select three scenes from the entire novel that you think *must* be a part of any film adaptation. Again, determine the following:

1. What character traits dominate the scene?
2. What is central about character interaction in the scene?
3. What does the scene reveal about character relationships? What does this scene contribute that *must* be presented before the audience?
4. What are the important elements of setting for each scene?
5. What should be the final scene in the film?

STAGE TWO—Reading the Film. As you are viewing the film, be prepared to "read the film" and evaluate it using the following criteria:

- To what extent did the filmmakers select the same scenes chosen by your group?
- To what extent do differences exist?
- If significant differences exist, has anything been lost in leaving out the scene(s) you felt to be central?
- What, if anything, is lost in the adaptation? (Consider character traits, satirical intention, and thematic concerns.)
- Have any changes been made that you can trace to the fact that we are a twenty-first century audience trying to engage a nineteenth-century text?
- Does setting conform to your imagined sense of space?
- Does the casting of the Anne and Wentworth characters seem appropriate to you?
- Why or why not?
- Do costuming and makeup conform to your preconceptions?
- Did the film open where you expected it to open?
- Is the final scene consistent with your expectations?

After screening the film, a variety of activities can complete the assignment, including collaborative projects, class discussions and debates, and writing.

Viewing the Novel/Reading the Film —Comparative Screen Analysis

Austen's original plan for the concluding two chapters of *Persuasion* was changed so that two new chapters, ten and eleven, replaced the original chapter ten. Chapter eleven of the original became almost exactly the new chapter twelve. These two original chapters, referred to as the "canceled chapters," survive and show a different means for Captain Wentworth to learn that Anne's feelings for him have not changed. (See Chapman, "The Original Version of the Concluding Chapters of *Persuasion*" 253–73.)

Essentially, canceled chapter ten has Captain Wentworth commissioned by Admiral Croft to inform Anne that rumors of her impending marriage to Mr. Elliot may prompt Admiral Croft's removal from Kellynch Hall. The admiral wishes Anne to know that he and Mrs. Croft would defer to Anne and Mr. Elliot's living there upon their marriage, since Mr Elliot is the eventual heir to Kellynch Hall. Captain Wentworth's mission, to inform the woman he loves that nothing will impede her marriage to another, is much like the one Elinor Dashwood is given by Colonel Brandon in *Sense and Sensibility*. She, too, is asked to inform the man she loves, Edward Ferrars, that a living will be made available so that he is free to marry Lucy Steele. As with Elinor, Captain Wentworth is much embarrassed, discussing with Anne a marriage to a rival at a time when his own feelings for her have returned. It is a scene that recalls, too, the overheard conversation between Captain Wentworth and Louisa Musgrove that let Anne know that Captain Wentworth's strong feelings were reserved for a woman who was not easily persuaded.

In the new chapter eleven of the novel, Austen has Captain Wentworth overhear a conversation with Captain Harville about love and constancy. Anne defends her sex as "loving longest, when existence or when hope is gone" (*P* 235), a reference to her own life over the eight-year span since she broke her engagement to Captain Wentworth. His letter to her is a passionate avowal of his enduring love: "You pierce my soul. . . . I have loved none but you" (*P* 237), a much stronger expression of love than what appears in the earlier draft chapter.

In the canceled chapter, he asks only that she say the words "he may," permitting Admiral Croft to write to Sir Walter, conceding Kellynch to Anne and Mr. Elliot. Anne's response is rendered in a series of negatives: "No Sir," "no message," he is "misinformed," "mistaken," "no truth" (Chapman, "Original" 263). Wentworth, in this canceled scene, says to Anne, "A very few words however will put an end to the awkwardness & distress we may *both* be feeling" (Chapman, "Original" 263). These lines are somewhat preserved in Wentworth's letter in the revised chapter as he writes, "A word, a look will be enough to decide whether I enter your father's house this evening, or never" (*P* 238). What follows in both versions is similar. In the canceled chapters Captain Wentworth and Anne stay with the Crofts through the evening and revisit the past years, especially the business at Lyme. In the revision she meets him outside, and as they wander the streets of Bath, they discuss the past. Later, they renew their discussions at her father's apartments in Camden Place. In chapter twelve the narration is an indirect recounting of the departure of Mrs. Clay with William Elliot and the responses of those around them to the marriage of Anne and Wentworth.

In the film, screenwriter Nick Dear inserts this canceled scene from the novel but retains the revised scene as well so that essentially he has it both ways. In the film, Wentworth's mission from Admiral Croft is shortened considerably as he asks only that she "give me a yes or a no, and we are both released" (Dear 81). There is an ironic double meaning here, for the literal meaning is that her reply will release him of his duty and the admiral from his lease. The second meaning is that a "yes" would mean she and Captain Wentworth are released from any further involvement. Dear subtly invents irony in keeping with the spirit of the Austen text.

In the film, though, Dear has Anne walk away from Wentworth in confusion and anger over the rumors that she is to marry William Elliot. Thus, Dear also makes necessary the scene in which Wentworth writes his impassioned letter to Anne as he overhears her conversation with Captain Harville. Two transitions quickly follow as Wentworth runs into Lady Russell and Anne visits Mrs. Smith. Both scenes are filmed very rapidly, and each relates to the issue of "persuasion." Both Captain Wentworth and Lady Russell accuse the other of "influence" over Anne, while Mrs. Smith and Nurse Rooke share their news about Mr. Elliot's real intentions. The film is a bit unclear here as to how Elliot was to secure his inheritance through marriage to Anne. The important point is that they have "facts" (albeit learned through gossip) that refute Lady Russell's authority that the "facts" argue in favor of Mr. Elliot. Thus, Anne is exposed to a variety of influences that test her "steadiness of principle" and strength of mind. She emerges as a strongly independent character through the assertions of selfhood that are evidenced in these scenes.

The Dear screenplay returns to the Austen revision as Anne arrives at the Musgroves' rooms at the White Hart, where Captains Wentworth and Harville are preparing the letter to accompany Captain Benwick's portrait for Louisa. The conversation overheard by Wentworth is essentially as in the novel, and his letter to Anne is then "read" with voice-overs by both Wentworth and Anne, a conjoining of their voices symbolic of the union of their hearts and minds. The film then follows Anne into the street where she and Captain Wentworth touch hands and embrace, a decidedly un-Austen-like moment, for a gentleman and lady would never kiss in such a public place. Dear accompanies the reunion of the couple with a parading circus troupe, which provides a cathartic "laughing and cheering" to celebrate the joyful end to this long and difficult separation. Neither seems to notice the celebration, though, for they are centered on their own happy world.

One final addition in the Dear screenplay is Captain Wentworth's announcement at the Elliots' card party that evening: "My proposal of marriage has been accepted by your daughter Anne, and I respectfully request permission to fix the date" (91). This "business" swiftly ends the conflict (only a glance of recognition between Mrs. Clay and Mr. Elliot foretells their future involvement). However, his boldness in this highly conventionalized social gathering seems out of keeping with his character. Captain Wentworth has proven himself to have, if not "fine" manners, certainly the manners of a gentleman. This bold assertion of his claims on Anne is rude and spiteful, hardly the manners we've come to associate with Captain Wentworth. The filmmakers may have intended it to be a gesture to suggest Captain Wentworth's "victory" over the Elliots and Lady Russell as he intrudes upon their card party to claim his prize. It may also be read as an heroic rescue of sorts as Anne is saved from the tedium of a card party where she doesn't play, a social event that is confined to a stuffy room with guests lacking in "good conversation," emblematic of her life among the aristocratic class. More important, she is rescued from loneliness and despair to become the wife of the man she has been constant to in her heart for eight long years.

Film Credits

Persuasion

1996, Methuen Film/BBC production in association with WGBH/Boston and Millesime/France 2.

Screenplay by Nick Dear.
Directed by Roger Michell.
Produced by Fiona Finlay.

Cast

Anne Elliot	Amanda Root
Captain Wentworth	Ciaran Hinds
Lady Russell	Susan Fleetwood
Sir Walter Elliot	Corin Redgrave
Mrs. Croft	Fiona Shaw
Admiral Croft	John Woodvine
Elizabeth Elliot	Phoebe Nicholls
Mr. Elliot	Samuel West
Mary Musgrove	Sophie Thompson
Mrs. Musgrove	Judy Cornwell
Charles Musgrove	Simon Russell Beale
Mrs. Clay	Felicity Dean
Mr. Musgrove	Roger Hammond
Louisa Musgrove	Emma Roberts
Henrietta Musgrove	Victoria Hamilton
Captain Harville	Robert Glenister
Captain Benwick	Richard McCabe
Mrs. Smith	Helen Schlesinger
Nurse Rooke	Jane Wood
Mr. Shepherd	David Collings
Lady Dalrymple	Darlene Johnson
Miss Carteret	Cinnamon Faye
Henry Hayter	Isaac Maxwell-Hunt
Sir Henry Willoughby	Roger Llewellyn
Mrs. Harville	Sally George
Naval Officers	David Acton, Justin Avoth

Jemima	Lonnie James
Landlord	Roger Watkins
Apothecary	David Plummer
Coachman	Richard Bremmer
Tradesmen	Bill McGuirk, Niall Refoy
Lady Dalrymple's Butler	Ken Shorter
Footman	Dermot Kerrigan
Little Charles	Tom Rigby
Little Walter	Alex Wilman
Concert Opera Singer	Rosa Mannion

Works Cited

Chapter 1: Introduction

Bluestone, George. *Novels into Film*. 1957. Berkeley: U of California P, 1971.

Gillie, Christopher. *A Preface to Jane Austen*. London: Longman, 1974.

McFarlane, Brian. *Novel to Film: An Introduction to the Theory of Adaptation*. Oxford: Clarendon Press, 1996.

The Oxford English Dictionary. Compact Edition. 1971. Cited as OED.

Solender, Elsa. "Recreating Jane Austen's World on Film." *Persuasions*. 24 (2002): 102–20.

Tave, Stuart M. *Some Words of Jane Austen*. Chicago: U of Chicago P, 1973.

Troost, Linda, and Sayre Greenfield. "Watching Ourselves Watching." Introduction. *Jane Austen in Hollywood*. Eds. Troost and Greenfield. 2nd ed. Lexington: UP of Kentucky, 2001. 3–12.

Whelehan, Imelda. "Adaptations: The Contemporary Dilemmas." *Adaptations: From Text to Screen, Screen to Text*. Eds. Deborah Cartmell and Imelda Whelehan. London: Routledge, 1999. 3–20.

Chapter 2: *Northanger Abbey*

Austen, Jane. *Northanger Abbey*. Ed. R. W. Chapman. 3rd ed. Oxford: Oxford UP, 1933. Cited as *NA*.

Chapman, R. W. "Introductory Note." *Northanger Abbey* and *Persuasion*. By Jane Austen. Ed. Chapman. 3rd ed. Oxford: Oxford UP, 1933. xi–xiii.

McGuire, Karen. "Gothicism." *Encyclopedia of Romanticism: Culture in Britain, 1780s–1830s.* Ed. Laura Dabundo. New York: Garland Publishing, 1992. 239–43.

Northanger Abbey. Dir. Giles Foster. Screenwriter Maggie Wadey. BBC, 1987.

Roberts, Marilyn. "Adapting Jane Austen's *Northanger Abbey:* Catherine Morland as Gothic Heroine." *Nineteenth Century Women at the Movies: Adapting Classic Women's Fiction to Film*. Ed. Barbara Tepa Lupack. Bowling Green, OH: Bowling Green State U Popular Press, 1999. 129–39.

Solender, Elsa. "Recreating Jane Austen's World on Film." *Persuasions* 24 (2002): 102–20.

Stovel, Bruce. "*Northanger Abbey* at the Movies." *Persuasions* 20 (1998): 236–47.

Chapter 3: *Sense and Sensibility*

Alleva, Richard. "Emma Can Read, Too." Review of Sense and Sensibility. *Commonweal*. 8 March 1996: 15-18.

Austen, Jane. *Sense and Sensibility*. Ed. R. W. Chapman. 3rd ed. Oxford: Oxford UP, 1933. Cited as *SS*.

Chapman, R. W. "Introductory Note." *Sense and Sensibility*. By Jane Austen. Ed. Chapman. 3rd ed. Oxford: Oxford UP, 1933. xiii–xiv.

Dickson, Rebecca. "Misrepresenting Jane Austen's Ladies: Revising Texts (and History) to Sell Films. Troost and Greenfield 44–57.

Goldstein, Norma B. "Sentimentalism." *Encyclopedia of Romanticism: Culture in Britain, 1780s–1830s*. Ed. Laura Dabundo. New York: Garland Publishing, 1992. 519–21.

Jeffrey, David. K. "Sense and Sensibility." *National Forum*. 76.2 (Spring 1996): 43 (3).

Kaplan, Deborah. "Mass Marketing Jane Austen: Men, Women and Courtship in Two Film Adaptations." Troost and Greenfield 175–87.

Libin, Kathryn L. Shanks. "'—a very elegant looking instrument—': Musical Symbols and Substance in Films of Jane Austen's Novels." *Persuasions*. 19 (16 December 1997): 187–94.

Nixon, Cheryl L. "Balancing the Courtship Hero: Masculine Emotional Display in Film Adaptations of Austen's Novels." Troost and Greenfield 22–43.

Parrill, Sue. "What Meets the Eye: Landscape in the Films *Pride and Prejudice* and *Sense and Sensibility*." *Persuasions* 21 (1999): 32–43.

Samuelian, Kristin Flieger. "'Piracy Is Our Only Option': Postfeminist Intervention in *Sense and Sensibility*." Troost and Greenfield 148–58.

Sense and Sensibility. Dir. Ang Lee. Screenwriter Emma Thompson. Columbia Pictures, 1995.

Solender, Elsa. "Recreating Jane Austen's World on Film." *Persuasions*. 24 (2002): 102–20.

Thompson, Emma. *The Sense and Sensibility Screenplay and Diaries: Bringing Jane Austen's Novel to Film*. New York: Newmarket Press, 1995.

Troost, Linda, and Sayre Greenfield, eds. *Jane Austen in Hollywood*. 2nd ed. Lexington: UP of Kentucky, 2001.

Chapter 4: *Pride and Prejudice*

Alleva, Richard. "Emma Can Read, Too." Review of Sense and Sensibility. *Commonweal*. 8 March 1996: 15-18.

Austen, Jane. *Persuasion*. Ed. R. W. Chapman. 3rd ed. Oxford: Oxford UP, 1933. Cited as *P*.

———. *Pride and Prejudice*. Ed. R. W. Chapman. 3rd ed. Oxford: Oxford UP, 1933. Cited as *P&P*.

Birtwistle, Sue, and Susie Conklin. *The Making of Pride and Prejudice*. London, Penguin Books, 1995.

Bluestone, George. *"Pride and Prejudice." Novels into Film*. 1957. Berkeley: U of California Press, 1971.

Chapman, R. W. "Introductory Note." *Pride and Prejudice*. By Jane Austen. Ed. Chapman. 3rd ed. Oxford: Oxford UP, 1982. xi–xiii.

Ellington, H. Elisabeth. "'A Correct Taste in Landscape': Pemberley as Fetish and Commodity." Troost and Greenfield 90–110.

Flavin, Louise. "Free Indirect Discourse and the Clever Heroine of *Emma*." *Persuasions*. 13 (16 December 1991): 50–57.

Hopkins, Lisa. "Mr. Darcy's Body: Privileging the Female Gaze." Troost and Greenfield 111–21.

Lascelles, Mary. *Jane Austen and Her Art*. Oxford: Clarendon Press, 1939.

Libin, Kathryn L. Shanks. "'—a very elegant looking instrument—': Musical Symbols and Substance in Films of Jane Austen's Novels." *Persuasions*. 19 (16 December 1997): 187–194.

Nixon, Cheryl L. "Balancing the Courtship Hero: Masculine Emotional Display in Film Adaptations of Austen's Novels. Troost and Greenfield 22–43.

Pride and Prejudice. Dir. Robert Z. Leonard. Screenwriters Aldous Huxley and Jane Murfin. MGM, 1940.

Pride and Prejudice. Dir. Cyril Coke. Screenwriter Fay Weldon. BBC, 1980.

Pride and Prejudice. Dir. Simon Langton. Screenwriter Andrew Davies. BBC/A&E, 1995.

Solender, Elsa. "Recreating Jane Austen's World on Film." *Persuasions*. 24 (2002): 102-20.

Troost, Linda, and Sayre Greenfield, eds. *Jane Austen in Hollywood*. 2nd ed. Lexington: UP of Kentucky, 2001.

Van Ghent, Dorothy. *The English Novel: Form and Function*. New York: Harper, 1953.

Chapter 5: *Mansfield Park*

Austen, Jane. *Emma*. Ed. R. W. Chapman. 3rd ed. Oxford: Oxford UP, 1933. Cited as *E*.

——. *Mansfield Park*. Ed. R. W. Chapman. 3rd ed. Oxford: Oxford UP, 1933. Cited as *MP*.

——. *Northanger Abbey*. Ed. R. W. Chapman. 3rd ed. Oxford: Oxford UP, 1933. Cited as *NA*.

Chapman, R. W. "Improvements." *The Novels of Jane Austen*. Ed. Chapman. Vol. 3. 3rd ed. Oxford: Oxford UP, 1933. 557–60.

——. "Introductory Note." *Mansfield Park*. By Jane Austen. Ed. Chapman. 3rd ed. Oxford: Oxford UP, 1933. xi–xiii.

Duckworth, Alistair. "Film Review: *Mansfield Park*." *Eighteenth-Century Fiction*. 12.4 (July 2000): 565–71.

——. *The Improvement of the Estate: A Study of Jane Austen's Novels*. Baltimore: Johns Hopkins University Press, 1971.

Flavin, Louise. "*Mansfield Park:* Free Indirect Discourse and the Psychological Novel." *Studies in the Novel*. 19.2 (Summer 1987): 137–59.

Johnson, Claudia L. "Run Mad, But Do Not Faint: The Authentic Audacity of Rozema's *Mansfield Park*." *Times (London) Literary Supplement* 31 December 1999. Patriciarozema.com. 27 January 2003. http://www.patriciarozema.com/mad.html.

Lovers' Vows: A Play in Five Acts. *The Novels of Jane Austen*. Ed. R. W. Chapman. Vol. 3. 3rd ed. Oxford: Oxford UP, 1933. 475–539.

Mansfield Park. Dir. and Screenwriter Patricia Rozema. BBC/Miramax, 1999.

Solender, Elsa. "Recreating Jane Austen's World on Film." *Persuasions*. 24 (2002): 102-20.

Troost, Linda, and Sayre Greenfield. "The Mouse That Roared: Patricia Rozema's *Mansfield Park*." *Jane Austen in Hollywood*. Eds. Troost and Greenfield. 2nd ed. Lexington: UP of Kentucky, 2001. 188–204.

Chapter 6: *Emma*

Austen, Jane. *Emma*. Ed. R. W. Chapman. 3rd ed. Oxford: Oxford UP, 1933. Cited as *E*.

Chapman, R. W. "Introductory Note." *Emma*. By Jane Austen. Ed. Chapman. 3rd ed. Oxford: Oxford UP, 1933. xi–xiii.

Clueless. Dir. and Screenwriter Amy Heckerling. Perf. Alicia Silverstone and Paul Rudd. Paramount, 1995.

Dole, Carol M. "Austen, Class, and the American Market." Troost and Greenfield 58-78.

Emma. Dir. John Glenister. Screenwriter Denis Constanduros. With Doran Godwin and John Carson. BBC, 1972.

Emma. Dir. and Screenwriter Douglas McGrath. With Gwyneth Paltrow and Jeremy Northam. Miramax, 1996.

Emma. Dir. Diarmuid Lawrence. Screenwriter Andrew Davies. With Kate Beckinsale and Mark Strong. Meridian-ITV/A&E. 1996.

Ferriss, Suzanne. "Emma Becomes Clueless." Troost and Greenfield 122-29.

Flavin, Louise. "Free Indirect Discourse and the Clever Heroine of *Emma.*" *Persuasions.* 13 (16 December 1991): 50-7.

———. "*Mansfield Park:* Free Indirect Discourse and the Psychological Novel." *Studies in the Novel.* 19.2 (Summer 1987): 137-59.

Hopkins, Lisa. "*Emma* and the Servants." *Persuasions On-Line.* Occasional Papers. 3 (Fall 1999). 22 October 2002. http://www.jasna.org/PolOP1/toc.html.

Johnson, Claudia. *Women, Politics, and the Novel.* Chicago: U of Chicago Press, 1988.

Nachumi, Nora. "'As If!': Translating Austen's Ironic Narrator to Film." Troost and Greenfield 130-39.

Parrill, Sue. "Metaphors of Control: Physicality in *Emma* and *Clueless.*" *Persuasions On-Line.* 20.1. 27 January 2003. http://www.jasna.org/P0101/parrill.html.

Phillips, William, and Louise Heal. "Extensive Grounds and Classic Columns: *Emma* on Film." *Persuasions On-Line.* Occasional Papers. 3 (Fall 1999). 22 October 2002. http://www.jasna.org/PolOP1/toc.html.

Solender, Elsa. "Recreating Jane Austen's World on Film." *Persuasions.* 24 (2002): 102-20.

Thomlin, Claire. *Jane Austen: A Life.* New York: Knopf, 1997.

Troost, Linda, and Sayre Greenfield. "Filming Highbury: Reducing the Community in *Emma* to the Screen." *Persuasions On-Line.* Occasional Papers. 3 (Fall 1999). 22 October 2002. http://www.jasna.org/PolOP1/toc.html.

Troost, Linda, and Sayre Greenfield, eds. *Jane Austen in Hollywood.* 2nd ed. Lexington: UP of Kentucky, 2001.

Chapter 7: *Persuasion*

Austen, Jane. *Persuasion.* Ed. R. W. Chapman. 3rd ed. Oxford: Oxford UP, 1933. Cited as P.

Chapman, R. W. "The Original Version of the Concluding Chapters of *Persuasion.*" *The Novels of Jane Austen.* Ed. Chapman. Vol. 3. 3rd ed. Oxford: Oxford UP, 1933. 253-73.

———. "Introductory Note." *Persuasion*. By Jane Austen. Ed. Chapman. 3rd ed. Oxford: Oxford UP, 1933. xi–xiii.

Collins, Amanda. "Jane Austen, Film, and the Pitfalls of Postmodern Nostalgia." Troost and Greenfield 79–89.

Dear, Nick. *Persuasion by Jane Austen: A Screenplay*. London: Methuen Film, 1996.

Dickson, Rebecca. "Misrepresenting Jane Austen's Ladies: Revising Texts (and History) to Sell Films. Troost and Greenfield 44–57.

Dole, Carol M. "Austen, Class, and the American Market." Troost and Greenfield 58–78.

Johnson, Claudia. *Women, Politics, and the Novel*. Chicago: U of Chicago Press, 1988.

Kaplan, Deborah. "Mass Marketing Jane Austen." Troost and Greenfield 44–57.

Kauffmann, Stanley. *"Persuasion "* (movie reviews). *The New Republic*. 9 October 1995. 20 November 2002 http://web3infotrac.galegroup.com/itw/informark/340/761/ 54681824w3/ purl+rcl_EAIm_O_.

Persuasion. Dir. Robert Michell. Screenwriter Nick Dear. BBC, 1996.

Solender, Elsa. "Recreating Jane Austen's World on Film." *Persuasions*. 24 (2002): 102–20.

Southam, Brian. *Jane Austen and the Navy*. London: Hambledon and London, 2000.

Troost, Linda, and Sayre Greenfield, eds. *Jane Austen in Hollywood*. 2nd ed. Lexington: UP of Kentucky, 2001.

Index

-A-
Alleva, R., 67
Austen, Jane
   at Chawton, 123
   "Brontification" of, 116
   death of, 157
   film adaptations of novels, 2, 4
      approaches to, 4-7
      cultural values and, 6
   popularity of, 3-4
   teaching the novels of, 2
      difficulties for students, 11-12
      vocabulary list for, 11-12
Austen, H., 117

-B-
Bamber, D., 73,
Beale, S. R., 167
Beckinsale, K., 131, 132, 135, 136
Birtwistle, S., 67, 75, 79, 82, 94, 154
Bluestone, G., 4, 6, 57, 65, 66, 68, 69
Bonham-Carter, C., 73

-C-
Carroll, D. R., 102
Carson, J., 133, 136
Cassavetti, P., 153
Castle of Otranto (Walpole), 18
Catherine. See Northanger Abbey
Chapman, R. W., 55, 105, 123, 177
Clueless, 13, 131, 132, 146-150
   casting and characterization, 146-48
   changes from novel to film, 148-49
   conceptual integrity, 149-50
   racial issues in, 149-50
Coke, C., 93
Collette, T., 141
Collins, A., 166
commentary, 13
Conklin, S., 75, 79
Conrad, J., 4
Constanduros, D., 152
Coulthard, R., 136
Cumming, A., 141, 153
Curtis, S., 121

-D-
Davidtz, E., 112, 113
Davies, A., 23, 72, 79, 80, 85, 88, 94, 135, 139, 153

Dear, N., 165, 166, 167, 168, 169, 170, 174, 177, 178, 179
Diaries (Thompson), 37
Dickson, R., 43, 167, 168
Dole, C., 137, 138, 144, 148, 159, 160
Doran, L., 53
Duckworth, A., 102, 103, 104, 105, 109, 114
Duncan, L., 113

-E-
East, R., 133
Ehle, J., 67, 72, 75, 76, 89, 91
Elinor and Marianne. See Sense and Sensibility
Emma, 13, 83, 87, 123
  approaches to teaching the film, 131-50
    1972 BBC miniseries, 132-35
      casting and characterization, 133-34
      changes from novel to film, 134-35
    1996 Meridian-ITV film, 135-39
      casting and characterization, 135-37
      changes from novel to film, 137-38
      visual elements of the film, 138-39
    1996 Miramax film, 131, 139-46
      casting and characterization, 140-42
      changes from novel to film, 142-43
      conceptual integrity in, 143-44
      visual elements of the film, 144-46
    choosing a film adaptation, 131
    using film in the classroom, 131-32
  approaches to teaching the novel, 124-28
    classism and feminism in, 126-28, 143, 144, 149
    education of the heroine in, 124-26
    narration and irony in, 128
  film credits, 152-55
  questions for analysis and discussion (novel), 129-31
  questions for discussion and writing (film), 150-51
Encyclopedia of Romanticism, 18, 36
Epstein, J., 6, 65

-F-
Ferriss, S., 139, 143
film adaptations. *See* Austen, Jane
film
  as an art form, 5
  use in the classroom, 7-8
Finlay, F., 179
First Impressions, 35, 55
Firth, C., 67, 68, 72, 87, 88, 91
Firth, P., 24, 31
Flavin, L., 87
Foster, G., 31, 32
Francois, E., 44
Franklyn, S., 70

-G-
Garson, G., 68
Garvie, E., 66
Gidding, R., 166
Glenister, J., 152
Godwin, D., 133
Goldstein, N. B., 36
Gothic novels, 17, 18, 20, 23, 27
Grant, H., 43, 46, 50, 51
Greenfield, J., 143
Greenfield, S., 7, 8, 13, 110, 111, 112, 114, 115, 143
Griffith, D. W., 5
Gwenn, E., 68

-H-
Haft, S., 153
Hardy, R., 25, 31
Harker, S., 73
Heal, L., 133, 135, 137, 140, 141, 144, 148, 150
Heckerling, A., 131, 146, 148, 154, 155
Hepton, B., 136, 137
Hinds, C., 166, 169
Hopkins, L., 74, 77, 135, 139, 144, 146
Huxley, A., 92

-I-
intertextuality, 6, 7

Index

-J-
Jane Austen in Hollywood, 7, 13
Jane Austen's Emma, 131, 135
Jane Austen Society of North America Conference, 131
Jeffrey, D. K., 47
Johnson, C., 109, 111, 112, 116, 118, 119, 126, 158
Jones, G., 43
Juvenilia, 36

-K-
Kaplan, D., 42, 165
Kauffmann, S., 166, 167

-L-
Lacey, I., 25
Langton, S., 94
Lascelles, M., 59
Lawrence, D., 154
Lawrence, R., 155
Lee, A., 47, 49, 53
Leonard, R. Z., 92
Libin, K. L. S., 78
Lisemore, M., 152

-M-
Mansfield Park, 13, 14, 83, 97-98
   approaches to teaching the film, 108-19
      casting and characterization, 110-13
      changes from novel to film, 113-16
      choosing a film adaptation, 108-109
      conceptual integrity in, 116-17
      explicit sexuality in, 114-16
      modeling Austen in, 110, 115
      themes of freedom and confinement in, 119
      using film in the classroom, 109
      visual elements of the film, 118-19
   approaches to teaching the novel, 98-106
      heroine rivalry in, 98-100
      landscape improvements in, 103-05
      ordination in, 100-01
      slavery issues in, 105-106, 113-14
      theatricals in, 101-03

film credits, 121-22
questions for analysis and discussion (novel), 106-108
questions for discussion and writing (film), 120-21
Marks, L., 32
Marson, A., 133
McCabe, R., 167
McFarlane, B., 4, 5, 6, 7, 13
McGrath, D., 135, 139, 140, 143, 144
McGregor, E., 141
McGuire, K., 18
Memoir, 35
Menand, L., 74
Metropolitan, 13
Michell, R., 179
Miller, J. L., 113
Morgan, P., 70
Murfin, J., 92
Murray, J., 123
Mysteries of Udolpho (Radcliffe), 18, 23, 24, 26, 29, 31

-N-
Nachumi, N., 141, 145
New York Review of Books, 74
Nichols, P., 167
Nivola, A., 113
Nixon, C. L., 43, 45, 47, 73, 74, 75
Northanger Abbey, 14, 83, 118
   approaches to teaching the film, 23-30
      casting and characterization, 24-26
      changes from novel to film, 26-28
      conceptual integrity in, 28-30
      using film in the classroom, 23-24
      visual elements of the film, 30
   approaches to teaching the novel, 18-21
      education in, 19-20
      gothic and sentimental fiction in, 18-19
      narration in, 20-21
   film credits, 32-33
   questions for analysis and discussion (novel), 21-23
   questions for discussion and writing (film), 30-32
Northam, J., 136, 140, 141

-O-
O'Connor, F., 110, 111, 113, 120
Olivier, L., 68
O'Sullivan, M., 68

-P-
Paltrow, G., 131, 135, 139, 140, 142, 144, 145
Parfitt, J., 71
Parrill, S., 48, 49, 143
Persuasion, 14, 17, 86, 157-58
   an exercise in film adaptation of, 174-76
   approaches to teaching the film, 165-72
      1995 BBC film
         casting and characterization, 166-68
         changes from novel to film, 168-70
         conceptual integrity, 170-71
         reading visual elements in film, 171-72
      using film in the classroom, 165-66
   approaches to teaching the novel, 158-63
      changing image of the heroine in, 162
      issues of class and aristocracy in, 158-59
      issues of power in, 162-63
      the navy in, 160
   canceled chapters in, 176-78
   comparative screen analysis, 176-78
   film credits, 178-180
   questions for analysis and discussion (novel), 163-65
   questions for discussion and writing (film), 172-74
Phillips, W., 133, 135, 137, 140, 141, 144, 148, 150
Pinter, H., 110, 111, 112, 120
Powell, J., 93
Pride and Prejudice, 4, 6, 15, 55-56, 97, 119, 123, 168
   approaches to teaching the film, 65-79
      1940 feature film, 65-66, 68-70, 92
         casting and characterization, 68
         changes from novel to film, 69
      1979 BBC mini-series, 66, 70-71
         casting and characterization, 70-71

      1995 BBC mini-series, 66-67, 72-79, 94
         casting and characterization, 72-74
         changes from novel to film, 74
         conceptual integrity, 75-76
         reading visual elements in film, 76-79
   choosing a film adaptation, 65-67
   approaches to teaching the novel, 56-62
      courtship and marriage in, 56-58
      feminism and education in, 59-60
      issues of "pride" and "prejudice" in, 58-59
      manners and morals in, 60-62
   comparative analysis of films
      film adaptations, 85-91
      marriage proposals, 83-85
   film credits, 92-95
   questions for analysis and discussion (novel), 62-65
   questions for discussion and writing (film), 80-82

-R-
Radcliffe, A., 18, 23, 24
"reading" film, 5
   questions for analysis and discussion, 8-11
Redgrave, C., 167
Rennie, M., 70
Rickman, A., 43, 46, 47, 50
Rintoul, D., 66, 68, 88, 89, 91
Roberts, M., 24, 26, 27
Robinson, L., 136
Root, A., 166
Rowan, D., 136
Rozema, P., 108, 109, 110, 111, 113, 114, 115, 116, 117, 118, 119, 120, 121
Rudin, S., 155

-S-
Sanditon, 157
Scacchi, G., 141
Schlesinger, K., 24, 30
Scott, W., 123
sense, 36, 44, 46

Sense and Sensibility, 15, 75, 83, 97, 119, 165, 176
   approaches to teaching the film, 42-50
      casting and characterization in, 42-44
      changes from novel to film, 44-45
      conceptual integrity, 46
      using film in the classroom, 42
      visual elements of the film, 47-50
   approaches to teaching the novel, 36-39
      class and society in, 38-39
      judgment, authority, and manners in, 39
      marriage and money in, 37-38
      sense, sensibility, and sentiment in, 36-37
   film credits, 53-54
   questions for analysis and discussion (novel), 39-42
   questions for discussion and writing (film), 50-53
sensibility, 36, 40, 43, 44, 46, 75
Sentimental Journey (Sterne), 119
sentimental novels, 36
Silverstone, A., 146
Smith, H., 133
Solender, E., 23, 42, 65, 66, 109, 131, 135, 146
Southam, B., 160
Sterne, L., 119
Stevenson, J., 141
Stillman, W., 13
Stovel, B., 29
Stromberg, H., 92
Strong, M., 136
Stuart, C., 25
Stubbs, I., 44, 52
Susan. See Northanger Abbey
synthetic historical realism, 166

-T-
Tan, M., 78
Thomlin, C., 123
Thompson, E., 37, 42, 47, 49, 50, 51, 52, 53, 165
Thompson, S., 141
transposition, 13, 174

Troost, L., 7, 8, 13, 110, 111, 112, 114, 115, 143

-V-
Van Ghent, D., 58
"viewing" text, 5
   questions for analysis and discussion, 8-11

-W-
Wadey, M., 23, 24, 26, 32
Wagner, G., 6, 13, 174
Walker, F., 134
Walpole, H., 18
Watson, M., 70
Weldon, F., 66, 89, 93
West, S., 167
Whelehan, I., 6
Whitrow, B., 73
Williams, O., 136
Winslet, K., 42, 50
Wise, G., 44
Wright, A., 168